MW00509380

LESSONS LEARNED FROM MY CHILDREN

MOSAICA PRESS

מכל מלמדי השכלתי

LESSONS LEARNED
FROM MY CHILDREN

insights and inspiration
from everyday life

RABBI BORUCH OPPEN

Copyright © 2021 by Mosaica Press

ISBN: 978-1-952370-47-2

All rights reserved. No part of this book may be used or reproduced or transmitted in any form or by any means, electronic or mechanical, including photocopying, recording, or by any information storage and retrieval system, without written permission from the publisher.

Published by Mosaica Press, Inc.
www.mosaicapress.com
info@mosaicapress.com

This *sefer* is dedicated
with much love and gratitude
to my dear beloved *eishes chayil*

Chaya Freyda

and our wonderful children

Daniel, Ayelet, Eliana, and Talia

In loving memory of

חנה מלכה ע״ה בת הרב גדליה אפרים

הרב אברהם דוד בן הרב שלמה זצוק״ל

הרב ישעיהו בן הרב שבח מרדכי זצוק״ל

ת.נ.צ.ב.ה.

Congregation Eitz Chaim
530 Central Ave • Cedarhurst, NY 11516

CONGREGATION
EITZ CHAIM

Rabbi Gedaliah Oppen
Rav

לכבוד בני בכורי היקר, מחנך ילדי ישראל במסירות ובנאמנות, עוסק בתורה ובמצוות, הרב ר׳ ברוך זלמן שליט״א ברגשות גיל וברוב שמחה ונחת, אעלה על הכתב את ברכתי לספרך "מכל מלמדי השכלתי".

בן זומא אומר: "איזהו חכם? הלומד מכל אדם, שנאמר: מכל מלמדי השכלתי כי עדותיך שיחה לי" (אבות פרק ד׳ משנה א׳). התנא הקדוש, שהיה במדרגה גדולה כל כך, שכאשר ראה את רבבות עולי הרגל לירושלים אמר "ברוך שברא כל אלו לשמשני", מלמד אותנו יסוד. "הלומד מכל אדם". מכל אחד, מכל אדם, גדול וקטן, חכם ושאיננו חכם, צעיר ומבוגר, אפשר וצריך ללמוד. והפסוק שהוא מביא הוא: "מכל מלמדי השכלתי, כי עדותך שיחה לי". כלומר, דוד המלך ע״ה מעיד על עצמו, שרק בגלל ש"עדותיך שיחה לי", בגלל האהבה הגדולה לתורה ולדברי תורה, רק מסיבה זו "מכל מלמדי השכלתי", קניתי חכמה מכולם. פעמים רבות מובאים מעשים בגמרא ובמדרשים, שתנאים ואנשים חשובים שאלו תינוקות של בית רבן "פסוק לי פסוקך", או למדו מוסר השכל מדברי ילדים.

וממך בני היקר, למדתי פירוש נוסף ל"מכל מלמדי השכלתי, כי עדותך שיחה לי". למדתי לראות, שבכל דבר ובכל מעשה, בין של גדולים ובין של קטנים, ניתן לראות שאין בהם חידוש, אלא הכל עדותך. ליכא מידי דלא רמיזי באורייתא. אין כל חדש תחת השמש.

הספר החשוב שחיברת מבוסס על יסוד זה. דברים חשובים ויסודיים למדת ממעשי ילדיך – נכדי – ותלמידיך היקרים, נשמות טהורות ויקרות. הרכבת משקפי תורה וראית שהכל בתורה. הכל רמוז בתורה ובדברי חז״ל.

ויהי רצון מלפני אבינו שבשמים, שיתן לך אורך ימים ושנות חיים, יחד עם רעייתך החשובה מרת חיה פריידא שתחי׳ העומדת לימינך בהרבצת התורה ובגידול ילדיכם נ"י. שתזכו להרבות כבוד שמים בעולם, להגדיל תורה ולהאדירה, בבריאות גופא ונהורא מעליא, ויתקיים בכם "כי לא תמוש התורה מפינו ומפי זרעינו וזרע זרעינו עד עולם.

באהבה רבה,
אבא

אהרן יצחק קאופמן

Ahron Kaufman

November 2020

Rabbi Boruch Zalman Oppen possesses a remarkable talent for simply and clearly transmitting ideals of great depth. His sefer, "Lessons Learned From My Children," is a brilliant all-encompassing educational guide in which teachers, parents and children will find much needed insight. Each chapter of his sefer contains clever comparisons in a parable form.

Unfortunately, the effects of coercion and manipulation often used in motivating our children do not last, and sometimes they even have an adverse outcome. Rabbi Oppen's methods of motivation have enjoyable, positive long-lasting favorable effects. He understands children and understands what motivates them to achieve.

It is a privilege for Yeshiva Ateres Shmuel of Waterbury, and for me personally, to claim Rabbi Oppen as a very beloved talmid, whose relationship I have cherished for over a decade.

I know that you and your children will enjoy reading this sefer, and I hope that you too will learn from these "Lessons Learned From My Children."

והננו בזה לברכו שיזכה להמשיך עבודתו הקודש ללמוד וללמד, ולהשפיע נעימות,חן, אור ושמחה ולהעמיד תלמידים מלאים תורה ויראת שמים כל הימים. ושיזכה בהרבה ברכה ונחת מכל משפחתו.

Ahron Kaufman

אגודת ישראל בית בנימין
Agudath Israel Bais Binyomin
2913-15 AVENUE L • BROOKLYN, N.Y. 11210

משה טובי-ה ליף
מרא דאתרא
HaRav Moshe Tuvia Lieff שליט"א

בס"ד

יום ה' לסדר וירא אליו וגו' תשע"ג

לכבוד ידידי בן ידיד המחנך הדגול מופלג במדות טובות
יניק וחכים מופלג בתורה ויר"ש הר"ר ברוך זלמן שליט"א
בן הרה"ג הרב גדלי' שליט"א מיסד דבית יעקב [illegible]
ומנהל רוחני ד[illegible] חיים הגדולה והקדושה.

השלום והברכה!

„חוט המשולש לא במהרה ינתק" פירוש הדבר כחוט משולש (3 PLY CORD)
ממשיך ביותר ושמירה ובכלל לא יבול. כ"א דבן אדם הוי יצירה מבאה ובמה
השפעות ומכנן לא במהרה ינתק דכל מהשפעות ות"ב מיוסד מבמה ובמה אנשים
חשובים. הסבא זצ"ל הרה"ג ר' דוב אויגן ה' ראש ישיבה בטלז שיקגו ואח"כ
השפיע על רבבות בנות ישראל והדריכן ברוח ישראל סבא במכון לתורה וחוק
מוסדות התורה. אביך שליט"א ידידי והחביבי הג' ר' גדלי' הקים שם בעולם
התורה בכלל ובעולם החינוך בפרט במוסר התורה ומחנך במסד עליון.
ידידי אני מכיר אותך משחר טל ילדותך - מתוקים מדבש דעת חיים ונורא.
ושמחת החיים. ועכשיו כשאתה מוציא העבודה הגדולה והגדולה שלך
ניכר לכל שורה ובכל מילה שאתה בח"ח ויראי ה' באומן ולא רק באומן
ובמסד עליון אתה הולך בדרך אבותיך להגדיל תורה ולהאדירה.

יהי רצון שחפץ ה' יצליח בידיך
ותעלה מעלה מעלה בשלמות התורה והיראה לנחת משפחתך והוריך
החשובים והגדולים ביראתן ובכוח אשר בעזה"י במחנך החשוב.
יהי רצון שנזכה להשלום קרובה - ספרים על שולחן מלכים מאן מלכי רבנן!

הברכה ואומץ בידידות עוז ובאהבה עמוקה
ידידך ידיד משפחתך הנאמן
משה טוביה

קהק כנסת ישראל

CONGREGATION KNESETH ISRAEL

בס"ד

728 Empire Avenue
Far Rockaway, NY 11691

Phone: 718.327.0500
Fax: 718.327.7415

www.whiteshul.com
office@whiteshul.com

Rabbi
Rabbi Eytan Feiner

Associate Rabbi
Rabbi Motti Neuburger

Rabbi Emeritus
Rabbi Ralph Pelcovitz זצ"ל

President
Daniel Liss

Senior Vice-Presidents
Domenico Antonelli
Mottie Schwartz

Vice-Presidents
Adam Kay
Ely Pasternak
Barry Solamon
Aryeh Satt

Treasurer
Shimmy Berger

Co-Chairmen of the Board
Nesanel Feller
Tuvia Silverstein

**Vice-Chairman of
the Board**
Matisyahu Hedvat

ערב שבת קודש, פרשת בא, תשפ"א

Our daily lives are replete with lessons to be learned, messages to be gleaned, words of wisdom to imbibe – and oftentimes the most insightful and enlightening of them all escape the precious mouths of our dear children. So pure, pristine, and innocent in their thoughts and words, they convey teachings that leave an indelible impression and impact on our hearts, minds, and souls.

In the wonderful – and truly enjoyable – sefer before you, Rabbi Boruch Oppen has succeeded immensely in sharing with us illuminating lessons he learned from his children. Sprinkled with amusing anecdotes and humorous vignettes, Rabbi Oppen's sefer invites us warmly into his delightful home, and motivates us to ponder the myriad tidbits of wisdom emerging from everyday life in the Oppen mishpacha. Sit back and enjoy an exciting journey together with this fantastic family...

Perusing the sefer's timeless teachings, the reader will be moved, inspired, and uplifted, and will depart from this valuable work yearning to becoming a bigger and better Eved Hashem each and every day.

יהי רצון שיזכה להמשיך לחגדיל תורה ולהאדירה מתוך שמחה ורב נחת
מכל יוצאי חלציו, עד ביאת גואל צדק בב"יא.

בברכת כל טוב תמיד מעומקא דליבא,
ובידידות רבה ונאמנה,

Rabbi Eytan Feiner,
Congregation Kneseth Israel / The White Shul

I am very moved by Rav Boruch's sefer, Lessons Learned from My Children. Beyond the incredible insight and lessons he shares, the entire premise of the sefer has so much to teach us. One of the keys to chinuch ha'banim is to truly respect our children, appreciating their perspective and looking to understand them. Who is the wise man? The one who learns from everyone (Avos 4:1). Undoubtedly, our children are included in this teaching. They have so much to teach us, and they will gain so much from our ability to listen to what they have to say.

Moreover, every experience in our life is there to teach us something. It takes an astute and growing person to notice what is going on and glean its lessons. Rav Boruch teaches us to open our eyes and learn not only from our children, but from every person and every experience.

There are many valuable teachings in this sefer, both in areas between man and G-d, and between man and his friend. We should merit to apply these lessons, as well as learn our own, as we travel the beautiful journey of life. May Rav Boruch only have continued nachas from his children and students.

With much respect,

Rabbi Moshe Don Kestenbaum
Mashgiach, Heichal Hatorah and Mesivta Sha'arei Pruzdor
Mechaber, Olam Hamiddos, Olam Ha'avodah

Table of Contents

Part I

LESSONS FROM HOME

Section Two

LESSONS AT THE PARK

Section Three

LESSONS FROM SCHOOL

Chapter Four

LESSONS FROM CAMP

Section Five

LESSONS FROM THE GRANDPARENTS' HOME

Foreword

By Rabbi Moshe Hubner

The story is told of a great sage who awakes on a cold winter morning and begins to wonder if he should get out of bed and face the freezing weather to head out to shul. The *yetzer hara* pipes up to tell him that of course he shouldn't go at all, but if he feels he must go on such a cold day, he should at least try to grab an extra few minutes of sleep, which will enable him to better serve Hashem throughout the day. After all, everyone else is going to be late too, so what's the point of getting up so early for nothing? The wise man responds to the *yetzer hara*, "But everyone else is not late; you, too, *yetzer hara*, have gotten up early on this cold, bitter day to come to my house and persuade me to delay, all in the name of following your command from Hashem to entice man to sin. Why should I not follow you and do the same? I know Hashem wants me to rise early and leave for shul to daven on time…"

The Torah teaches us that we are to serve Hashem with "all our heart, all our soul, and all our money." This is part of the *Shema* prayer we say every day. The word for "heart" is written as *levavecha*, with an additional *beis*—rather than *libcha*—which the Gemara tells us is to indicate that we are to serve Hashem with both inclinations, the *yetzer tov* and the *yetzer hara*, good and evil inclinations.

On Yom Kippur, in one of the stanzas of "*Al Cheit*," we ask Hashem for forgiveness, for "we have sinned before You with our evil inclination."

The *mefarshim* question this for an obvious reason: Isn't every sin done with the evil inclination? Is there any sin that is done with the backing of the *yetzer tov*? One answer is that we are supposed to serve with subduing our *yetzer hara*, or in spite of him, and instead we have sinned with him, as if in partnership.

We are obligated to use the tools given us by Hashem in order to succeed in all areas of life. The *yetzer hara* is a tool that should be used for personal improvement and spiritual growth. The great ones use him as an advantage instead of an obstacle.

This principle applies to *chinuch* as well. We must do our utmost to recognize what we are up against, and from there figure out the best way to outsmart the *yetzer hara* and raise *Torahdik* children in the proper *derech*.

That's easier said than done. How can we learn from the *yetzer hara* if we don't know what he looks or sounds like? It is, after all, virtually impossible to outsmart an "invisible man" (just ask any comic book fan). And further, if every act we do is a combination of good and evil, how are we to know if what we want to do is coming from the good side or the evil one? Am I praying with sincerity because I want to become closer to Hashem or because I want to look good in the eyes of others and thereby feel good about myself?

How is one to discern the ways of the *yetzer hara* if he is intertwined with the *yetzer tov*?

The answer can be found within the mitzvah of *chinuch* itself.

Chazal teach us that a child has a *yetzer hara* from the day he is born but does not welcome his *yetzer tov* until he becomes of age to be obligated in mitzvos—thirteen for a boy, twelve for a girl. We should take advantage of this by watching the behavior of young children closely; in that way, we can pick up some of the evil inclination's "tricks of the trade," and thus know how to recognize him as he ages. It's a revolutionary approach to "nipping things in the bud."

Through *chinuch*, we not only get to properly raise good *Yiddishe* children, but, if done with some common sense and our eyes open, we can also learn some tricks from our children on how to improve ourselves, which will have a rebound affect, since everything we do affects our children.

Children love to play hide and seek. A child will call out to his parents to come and find him, and 99 percent of the time, the hiding place is a fairly obvious one. If we observe the way young children—who have only the *yetzer hara*, and not yet the *yetzer tov*—play this game, we can learn a lot.

A really young child won't even hide, but will merely cover his eyes or crawl under a blanket and think he's hidden. The child may be laughing and giggling, but he still believes it when he hears his parent proclaim, "Where's Mendy? I can't find him." As long as the parent plays along, the child will continue to think he's invisible. At some point, Mendy will open his eyes or lift the blanket and delightedly screech, "Here I am!" The excited look on his parent's face will convince him he had found the perfect hiding place, and he'll immediately repeat the entire action again.

What can we, as adults, learn from this?

One of the main lessons to be learned from "hide and seek" is that we should recognize that we, too, think we're invisible when we're not. Every giggle, every laugh, and every word we utter is being heard and recorded—not only by Hashem, but by our children! (As you can see, the lessons of *chinuch* and *teshuvah* go hand-in-hand.) A parent might mumble certain remarks under his breath and then wonder in astonishment where his child learned to speak in such an un-*Torahdik* way. If a parent asks his child where he learned to speak in such a derogatory manner, assuming the response will be "a boy from school" or "a neighbor down the block," the revealing answer—"From you!"—should be a real eye-opener. The way a parent speaks both to and about others—not just the words, but the tone as well—will create a long-term effect on how their children react to others as well.

Our impressionable young children are at the mercy of the *yetzer hara*, and it is our *tafkid* to help them out. If we think ourselves invisible, that's when the problems begin. By figuring out who the *yetzer hara* is and how he behaves, we can begin to recognize our own motives and actions.

Chinuch is for parents as much as it is for children, and it is a give-and-take situation.

The Mishnah in *Avos* states, "I learned more from my friends than my *rebbeim*, and more from my students than everyone." Every child is a potential student, and therefore a potential teacher to his or her parents. A parent can see different personalities in each child, and if he observes them carefully enough, he should be able to discern the *yetzer hara*'s many different approaches. By simply watching the games of young children, we can become familiar with the wily ways of the *yetzer hara* on an intimate level, and thus have an edge when it comes to outsmarting him. The *yetzer hara* has been around a long time, and he constantly changes his tactics, so we have to take an all-encompassing interest in our children—both for their sake, and for ours.

When reviewing *Lessons Learned from My Children*, I was left with the feeling of having a secret weapon, so-to-speak—some extra protection in traversing the challenging roads of parenting; roads paved with both absolute bliss as well as the sometimes-sour taste of *tzaar gidul banim*. Presented by Rabbi Boruch Oppen, a former colleague of mine and the son of my close *chaver* Rabbi Gedaliah Oppen, this book is a true gem for anyone involved in the field of *chinuch* or immersed in the worry-laden stage of child-raising—in short, for anyone who has something to teach, be it to students or to his own offspring.

I wish *hatzlachah rabbah* to Rabbi Oppen and look forward to utilizing the many treasures to be found within the coming pages.

Acknowledgments

akaras ha'tov—recognizing the good is something one cannot live without. From a very young age, we are taught to say "thank you" to those who help and are there for us. The first thing we say when waking in the morning is *Modeh Ani*. Every time we daven, we express our recognition to Hashem for giving us everything we have.

The Gemara tells us:

וֹאָמַר רבי יוחנן משום רבי שמעון בן יוחai: מיום שברא הקדוש ברוך הוא את עולמו לא היה אדם שהודה להקדוש ברוך הוא, עד שבאתה לאה והודתו, שנאמר: "הפעם אודה את ה'."[1]

Rabbi Yochanan said in the name of Rabbi Shimon Ben Yochai, "The first person who expressed thanks since the world was created was Leah Imeinu when she gave birth to Yehudah. The pasuk says, "Ha'pam odeh es Hashem—this time I will 'thank' Hashem."[2]

The word "*odeh*—thanks" comes from the word "*modeh*—to admit." The way to be truly thankful toward someone else is by admitting and recognizing that something was done for you. I express my *hakaras ha'tov* to those without whom I would never be where I am today.

---

1   *Berachos* 7b.
2   *Bereishis* 29:35.

We find throughout the Torah that whenever the Jewish People moved to a new place, they immediately set up yeshivos.

וְאֶת יְהוּדָה שָׁלַח לְפָנָיו אֶל יוֹסֵף לְהוֹרֹת לְפָנָיו גֹּשְׁנָה וַיָּבֹאוּ אַרְצָה גֹּשֶׁן:[3]

And Yehudah was sent ahead of him to Yosef, to guide the way before him to Goshen. And they came to the land of Goshen.

Yehudah was the one who set up yeshivos when he was sent to Goshen.

קָדְמָה דֶּרֶךְ אֶרֶץ אֶת הַתּוֹרָה.[4]

Proper mannerisms precede Torah.

"*Derech eretz kadmah laTorah*" is in our roots. The way we act and speak will guide our children how to carry out their lives in the future. Yehudah, whose essence of his name is recognizing the good, is the one who initiated setting up yeshivos for the future of B'nei Yisrael when we were headed to *galus*. Without building for the future, there is no way we would survive.

I will now admit thanks and recognition to those who have helped me along the way of writing this book and helped me become who I am today.

Throughout each day, we admit that Hashem is the Master of the entire universe as well as in every minute detail one can imagine.

אי לאו דאמרינהו משה רבנו באורייתא, ואתו אנשי כנסת הגדולה ותקנינהו בתפלה—לא הוינן יכולין למימר להו.[5]

Had Moshe Rabbeinu not said them in the Torah, and the Anshei Knesses HaGedolah not incorporated them in our davening, we would not be allowed to say them.

Chazal teach that one cannot add more praises than what was composed by the *Anshei Knesses HaGedolah* since no words can truly describe

---

3   Ibid. 46:28.

4   *Vayikra Rabbah* 9:3.

5   *Berachos* 33b.

or illustrate the greatness of Hashem. I will not deviate from what Chazal teach us, but simply reiterate what we say multiple times a day by admitting much appreciation and gratitude to Hakadosh Baruch Hu, Who has given me the wisdom and strength to publish this *sefer* and for giving us our beautiful children, whom we constantly learn so many life lessons from.

To my dear parents, Abba and Mommy, thank you for always setting the proper example of how to live a life as a Torah Jew. Teaching us to be T.C. in a world that focuses on the P.C. Thank you for constantly going above and beyond when it comes to helping and guiding us. Without your instruction and assistance, this *sefer* would not be possible. Words cannot explain how fortunate we are to have Abba and Mommy as parents; two people who have been involved in *chinuch* for many years. To be able to witness the change you've made in the lives of others is inspiring. Your selflessness and *emunas chachamim* is next level. Learning and working together with Abba are moments I'll always cherish. Mommy, if there is anyone who goes out of their way to make others feel like a billion dollars, it is you. May you have endless *berachah* and *siyata d'Shmaya* in all that you do and continue to have *Yiddishe nachas* from your children and grandchildren.

To my dear in-laws, Abba and Ema Feierman, thank you for always being there for us and assisting in guiding our children on the path of Hashem. Your *chessed* and generosity know no bounds. You are pillars of your community and role models to all. May you continue to be a source of inspiration and continue to get *Yiddishe nachas* from your children and grandchildren.

The Mishnah teaches,

אֲבָל כָּל שֶׁמַּעֲשָׂיו מְרֻבִּין מֵחָכְמָתוֹ, לְמָה הוּא דוֹמֶה, לְאִילָן שֶׁעֲנָפָיו מְעָטִין וְשָׁרָשָׁיו מְרֻבִּין, שֶׁאֲפִלּוּ כָל הָרוּחוֹת שֶׁבָּעוֹלָם בָּאוֹת וְנוֹשְׁבוֹת בּוֹ אֵין מְזִיזִין אוֹתוֹ מִמְּקוֹמוֹ, שֶׁנֶּאֱמַר וְהָיָה כְּעֵץ שָׁתוּל עַל מַיִם וְעַל יוּבַל יְשַׁלַּח שָׁרָשָׁיו וְלֹא יִרְאֶה כִּי יָבֹא חֹם, וְהָיָה עָלֵהוּ רַעֲנָן, וּבִשְׁנַת בַּצֹּרֶת לֹא יִדְאָג, וְלֹא יָמִישׁ מֵעֲשׂוֹת פֶּרִי:[6]

One whose deeds exceeds his wisdom, what is he compared to?
A tree with few branches and many roots so that even if all of
the winds in the world come and blow it, they will not move it
from its place. As it says, He shall be like a tree planted near
water whose roots extend toward the stream. It does not notice
the heat coming, its leaves are fresh, and in a year of a drought,
it does not stop producing fruit.

To our grandparents, Bubby and Zaidy Muller, Bubby Oppen and Zaidy, *zt"l*, and Bobby, *a"h*, and Zaidy Klein, *zt"l*, thank you for enrooting within us proper morals and values, and watering us in the ways of the Torah so that we can withstand the strong winds of the world. Thank you for raising and guiding us to be true *b'nei Torah*, as well as helping us nurture our children to be true *b'nei Torah*. Thank you for all that you have done for us throughout the years. May you be like a tree planted by the waters and that spreads its roots by the river; it shall not see when the heat comes, but its leaf shall be green; and it shall not be anxious in the year of drought and should never discontinue from having fruit.

I owe a great debt of gratitude to my dear *eishes chayil*, Chaya Freyda. The Mishnah teaches, "*Beiso zu ishto*—A man's home is his wife,'" which means that without you, I'd be homeless.[7] The *pasuk* says, "*Chochmas nashim bansah beisah*—The wisdom of the woman builds the home."[8] You are my rock, support, my *bayis*, and because of your self-sacrifice, I am able to dedicate much time to learning, teaching, and writing. Thank you for your continuous support and for all that you do for us! May Hashem continue to grant us much health, happiness, and *Yiddishe nachas* with *arichas yamim*.

יְהוֹשֻׁעַ בֶּן פְּרַחְיָה אוֹמֵר, עֲשֵׂה לְךָ רַב...[9]

Yehoshua ben Perachya says, appoint for yourself a teacher.

---

7   *Yoma* 1:1.

8   *Mishlei* 14:1.

9   *Avos* 1:6.

The Mishnah instructs us to make a mentor for ourselves. A mentor isn't just one who teaches Torah from a *sefer* in class; rather, a mentor is one who teaches life through action. Rabbi Yochanan ben Zakkai explains that the proper path one should connect with is a *lev tov*, since a good heart includes all other proper *middos*.[10]

אמר ר' שמעון בן אבשלום...מה תמר זה אין לו אלא לב אחד אף ישראל
שבאותו הדור לא היה להם אלא לב אחד לאביהן שבשמים.[11]

*Rabbi Shimon ben Avshalom says…just as a palm tree only has
one heart, so too, Yisrael in that generation had only one heart
toward their Father in Heaven.*

The Gemara points out that just as a palm tree has one heart, so too, B'nei Yisrael in the generation of Devorah were unified with one heart. This must be the reason why *tzaddikim* are compared to palm trees, as the *pasuk* says, *"Tzaddik katamar yifrach k'erez ba'levanon yisgeh*—The righteous bloom like a palm tree; they flourish like a cedar in Lebanon."[12] When our *rebbeim* and *moros* demonstrate their love, care, and concern, it unites individuals and brings students closer to the Torah.

We count forty-nine days of Sefiras Ha'omer, beginning from the lowest level. Each day, we work to improve our *middos* in order to connect with the Torah. At the end, we reach the greatest level of accepting the Torah with a *lev tov*. The *gematria* of *"lev tov"* is forty-nine.

Thank you to all of my *rebbeim* and *moros* for your time and effort in guiding, teaching, and preparing me for all of life's great adventures, and most importantly for helping me refine my *lev tov*. So much thanks and gratitude go to all of the *moros*, *rebbeim*, and educators that have given it their all to help guide our dear children to grow into true *b'nei* and *b'nos Torah*. May you continue to produce beautiful, sweet fruit and have the ability to enjoy the fruit of your labors.

---

10   Ibid. 2:6.
11   *Megillah* 14a.
12   *Tehillim* 92:13.

My Rosh Yeshiva, Harav Ahron Kaufman, once told me that the word *mishpachah*, family, has in it the words "*sameach po*—happiness here."[13] As the saying goes, "Family isn't an important thing, it is everything." To all of our wonderful family, aunts, uncles, and cousins, thank you for your positive influence that you are constantly role-modeling to our children.

To my dear brother-in-law and sister-in-law, Mo and Dani Feierman, thank you for your support with this *sefer* and all of your generosity and *chessed* that you do for your family, community, and all of Klal Yisrael. May you continue to be an inspiration for others and continue to have the ability to give for all of your days.

To my dear brother-in-law and sister-in-law, Shmuli and Shoshana Friedman, thank you for your time, insights, and dedication in helping me with this *sefer* and always being there for us. May this be a *zechus* that all of your *tefillos* be answered *l'tovah, b'karov mamash!*

I also extend much thanks to my brother-in-law and sister, Itche and Shira Steigman, and to my brother-in-law and sister-in-law Chaim and Esther Feierman for their support of this *sefer*. May you see much *berachah* in all of your endeavors.

Congregation Eitz Chaim of Cedarhurst is not just a shul but a family. Without the following families, this *sefer* would not have come to fruition. A heartful thank you goes to the Assor, Deutsch, England, Grinspan, Gutlove, Isaacs, Landau, Lerner, Miller, Newman, Novak, Samuels, and Schechter families. May you continue to see much *berachah* and *hatzlachah* in all that you do.

First-time things can be nerve-racking and confusing, especially when it comes to publishing a *sefer*. Rabbi Doron Kornbluth gave me the advice and guidance on what was best for me, taking a mere manuscript and transforming it into this beautiful *sefer*.

Working with Rabbi Yaacov Haber, Mrs. Sherie Gross, Mrs. Rayzel Broyde, and the entire team at Mosaica Press was a very pleasant experience. The balance of professionalism while making it all about the

---

13   משפחה has the same letters as שמח פה.

author is truly incredible. Thank you for your time, effort, guidance, and patience in helping take my vision and making it into a reality. I look forward to building our relationship with the publishing of future *sefarim, iy"H.*

To my Rosh Yeshiva, Harav Ahron Kaufman, *shlita*, thank you for your *haskamah, divrei berachah,* and all that Rebbe does. I am very fortunate to have learned *b'chavrusa* with Rebbe and would not be who I am today without Rebbe's Torah, advice, and guidance. May you continue to be a bright light in a world of darkness and continue to see the fruits of your labor blossom.

To my *rebbi*, Rabbi Moshe Don Kestenbaum, *shlita*, I've learned so much from your *shiurim* and *sefarim.* I feel such excitement when I am able to build a *kesher* with my students through learning Rebbi's *sefarim* (*Olam HaMiddos*). Thank you for your *haskamah* and *divrei berachah.* May you continue to be an inspiration for your *talmidim* and all of Klal Yisrael.

To the Mara D'Asra of Agudas Yisrael Bais Binyomin of Brooklyn, NY, Harav Moshe Tuvia Lieff, *shlita*, thank you so much for your *haskamah* and *divrei berachah.* It is a special *zechus* that our families have a special connection dating back to the days in Minnesota. May you continue to be *marbitz Torah*, and may you and your wonderful *mishpachah* have much *berachah* and *simchah.*

To the Mara D'Asra of Kehilas Knesses Yisrael of Far Rockaway, NY, Harav Eitan Feiner, *shlita*, thank you so much for your *haskamah* and *divrei berachah.* I always enjoy listening to your inspiring words of Torah, which are constantly shared by my wonderful in-laws with our *mishpachah.* May you continue to instill a love of Hashem in the hearts of Klal Yisrael through your words of Torah and inspiration.

Thank you to my esteemed colleague Rabbi Moshe Hubner, *shlita*, for writing the foreword of this *sefer* and for your *divrei chizuk.* Through your *harbatzas haTorah*—whether it be your lectures or *sefarim*—many are inspired and strengthen their bond to Yiddishkeit. May you continue to have the strength and enthusiasm to enlighten the *neshamos* of Klal Yisrael.

"Rabbi Chanina said: I have learned much from my teachers and even more from my peers, but from my students I have learned more than from all of them."[14] Thank you to my dear students from whom I have learned so much.

And of course, to our dear children, *shetichyu*, Daniel (7), Ayelet (5), Eliana (3), and Talia (1), thank you so much for all of these wonderful lessons you've taught us. May you continue to give us much *Yiddishe nachas* and continue to strengthen your connection with Hashem, *ad me'ah v'esrim shanah*. We love you so much!

ויהי רצון מלפני אבינו שבשמים, שיתן לך בנים ובנות, צדיקים וצדקניות,
עוסקים בתורה ובמצות כל ימיהם.

And may it be the will of our Father in Heaven that He grant you righteous sons and daughters, that are occupied with Torah and mitzvos all of their days.

Boruch Oppen
Rosh Chodesh Shevat 5781

---

14   *Taanis* 7a.

Introduction

The Baal Shem Tov used to teach his students that every event and occurrence in this world is meant for us to learn from. There are many stories from the Baal Shem Tov that stress this teaching. One example is of the son of the Baal Shem Tov; as he was leaving his house, a man was yelling, "If anyone needs furniture fixed, I can fix it! I can fix anything!" When the son of the Baal Shem Tov heard this and said to himself, "What an amazing lesson. We all need to work on ourselves and fix something within us," this caused him to do a *cheshbon ha'nefesh*—calculation of the soul.

Another example is brought from the *Gemara*.

לא הוו ידעי רבנן מאי (תהלים נה, כג) השלך על ה' יהבך, אמר רבה בר
בר חנה זימנא חדא הוה אזילנא בהדי ההוא טייעא וקא דרינא טונא ואמר
לי שקול יהביך ושדי אגמלאי.[1]

The Rabbanan didn't understand the pasuk, "Cast upon Hashem your yehav." Rabbah bar bar Chanah said, "Once I was traveling with an Arab and I was carrying a load and he said to me, 'Take your yehav and throw it on my camel.'" The pasuk means, "Cast upon Hashem your burden and He will support you."

---

1   *Megillah* 18a.

בֶּן זוֹמָא אוֹמֵר, אֵיזֶהוּ חָכָם, הַלּוֹמֵד מִכָּל אָדָם, שֶׁנֶּאֱמַר (תהלים קיט) מִכָּל
מְלַמְּדַי הִשְׂכַּלְתִּי כִּי עֵדְוֹתֶיךָ שִׂיחָה לִי.[2]

The Mishnah in *Avos* teaches us that a wise person doesn't only learn from one's teachers, rather he considers everyone a teacher, thus learning from everyone.

The Gemara relates an incident between Rabbi Yochanan ben Berokah and Rabbi Elazar ben Chasma, who went to visit their *rebbi*, Rabbi Yehoshua, in Peki'in:

ת״ר מעשה ברבי יוחנן בן ברוקה ורבי אלעזר בן חסמא שהלכו להקביל
פני ר' יהושע בפקיעין אמר להם מה חידוש היה בבית המדרש היום אמרו
לו תלמידיך אנו ומימיך אנו שותין אמר להם אף על פי כן אי אפשר
לבית המדרש בלא חידוש שבת של מי היתה שבת של ר' אלעזר בן
עזריה היתה ובמה היתה הגדה היום אמרו לו בפרשת הקהל ומה דרש בה
(דברים לא, יב) הקהל את העם האנשים והנשים והטף אם אנשים באים
ללמוד נשים באות לשמוע טף למה באין כדי ליתן שכר למביאיהן אמר
להם מרגלית טובה היתה בידכם ובקשתם לאבדה ממני?[3]

The Rabbanan taught: there was a story with Rabbi Yochanan ben Beroka and Rabbi Elazar ben Chasma when they went to greet Rabbi Yehoshua in Peki'in. Rabbi Yehoshua said to them, "What new idea was taught in the beis ha'midrash today?" They replied, "We are your disciples, we drink your waters."[4] Rabbi Yehoshua answered, "Even so, it's impossible that something new wasn't taught in the beis ha'midrash." He asked them, "Whose week was it [to give the lecture]?" They answered, "It was the week of Rabbi Elazar ben Azarya." He then asked, "What did he speak about today?" Rabbi Yochanan and Rabbi Elazar responded, "He spoke about the portion of bringing the children to Hakhel." Rabbi Yehoshua asked, "And what did he expound on this? 'Gather the people, the men, and the women,

---

2   *Avos* 4:1.

3   *Chagigah* 3a.

4   Water represents Torah. The students were telling their *rebbi* that "we learn from you" and not the other way around.

*and the children' (Devarim 31:12). If the men come to learn,
and the women come to hear, for what reason do the children
come? They come in order to give reward to those who bring
them." Rabbi Yehoshua then asked, "You had a precious gem in
your hand, and you wanted to keep it from me!?"*

The *Gemara* questions:

אמר רב נחמן בר יצחק למה נמשלו דברי תורה כעץ שנאמר (משלי ג, יח)
עץ חיים היא למחזיקים בה לומר לך מה עץ קטן מדליק את הגדול אף
תלמידי חכמים קטנים מחדדים את הגדולים והיינו דאמר ר' חנינא הרבה
למדתי מרבותי ומחבירי יותר מרבותי ומתלמידי יותר מכולן.[5]

*Rav Nachman, the son of Yitzchak, said, "Why are matters of
Torah compared to a tree, as it is stated, '[The Torah is] a tree
of life for those who grab on to it'"?[6] The Gemara answers,
"Just as a small piece of wood can ignite a large piece of wood,
so too, simple talmidei chachamim can sharpen great talmidei
chachamim. And this is what Rabbi Chanina said, 'I have
learned a lot from my teachers and even more from my friends,
but from my students I have learned the most.'"*

Lessons Learned from My Children is based on stories and moments
from which I have learned valuable life lessons. These lessons didn't
come from a rabbi or someone of high authority. These lessons were
taught to me by my very own children, who have no idea of the effect
they have on others. You may have shared similar experiences with your
own children, and they may seem like simple and enjoyable stories;
however, they pack powerful life lessons that we can all learn from.
Lessons Learned from My Children was written over several years, and
during this time I noticed that there are many similarities in the behaviors of children.

The goal of *Lessons Learned from My Children* is not to elaborate on
any *chiddushim* or hidden secrets of life. I am simply conveying some of

---

5   *Taanis* 7a.
6   *Mishlei* 3:18.

the personal lessons and precious gems that I have learned and received from my own children. I believe that a person could have a whole new perspective on life if one understood that lessons can be learned from anyone and anything, and that each individual may very well be someone else's role model.

When there is a new player on the team, we give him a learning curve because it takes time to figure things out. There are twists and turns in every direction. So too, when it comes to our children. Children don't want to annoy their parents. They aren't looking to cause harm. Rather, children are experimenting and figuring things out as they go. They are new to the team and deserve a learning curve as well. By observing their behaviors and growth, one can learn so many lessons and apply them to their own life. Understanding this will help bring peace of mind, body, and soul, as well as peace at home.

Lessons Learned from My Children is also meant to show that everything is connected to and sourced from the Torah. Sometimes we go through life as mechanical beings, day after day. We must recognize that everything that we do, especially as a Jew, has a much deeper meaning and lasting effect. The Yevanim wanted to take the *kedushah* of Torah away and make it into "just another subject"—something for intellectual stimulation. When we acknowledge that everything is deeper than just face value, we show that we won the war. Chanukah comes from the word *chanoch*—educate. When we educate our children, students, or others in anything, we have to educate them through a Torah vision and perspective.

There are pages at the end of this book to take notes. I encourage you to take notes on how you could apply these lessons to your personal life and add your own ideas, events, or lessons to make the stories more applicable. Also, you could share lessons you've learned from your children or life in general by emailing them to me at fromallmyteachers@gmail.com.

Part I

LESSONS
FROM HOME

Follow the Leader

Each and every one of us has a much greater effect on others than we may think. Yes, we may be our own *olam katan*,[1] and yet, we are all gears in a machine that is larger than life. When one gear turns, all of the gears turn. It doesn't matter where in the machine that gear is located; it has an effect on every other gear and the machine as a whole. The problem is that we too easily forget this. This world is full of pleasures and instant gratifications that cause us to forget to think about the greater consequences that stem from our actions.

This lesson was taught to me by my wonderful children. My son, Daniel, and my daughter, Ayelet, were playing together one morning, and I noticed that whatever Daniel did, Ayelet imitated.

- Daniel clapped his hands, so Ayelet clapped her hands.
- Daniel climbed up the steps, so Ayelet climbed up the steps.
- Daniel cleaned the toys, so Ayelet cleaned the toys.

It was very cute. Later that day, I was with Ayelet, playing with some toys. As we were finishing up, Ayelet began putting the toys back into the bucket! I was so impressed! Then I remembered that earlier in the morning, Daniel had shown her how to put the toys away.

Daniel refers to himself as a grownup for his sisters. He recognizes that his sisters learn from his actions and copy what he does—both positively

---

1   Rabbeinu Bachya, *Vayikra* 24:10.

7

and negatively. When Daniel needs motivation to do something, we remind him that he is a grownup for his sisters and that they learn from what he does. Daniel recognizes this and does not want Ayelet or Eliana to learn to do the wrong things.

It occurred to me that if my son had that effect on his younger sister, how much more so is the effect I have on my children and others.

בילגה לעולם חולקת בדרום: ת״ר מעשה במרים בת בילגה שהמירה דתה
והלכה ונשאת לסרדיוט אחד ממלכי יוונים כשנכנסו יוונים להיכל היתה
מבעטת בסנדלה על גבי המזבח ואמרה לוקוס לוקוס עד מתי אתה מכלה
ממונן של ישראל ואי אתה עומד עליהם בשעת הדחק וכששמעו חכמים
בדבר קבעו את טבעתה וסתמו את חלונה...אלא למ״ד מרים בת בילגה
שהמירה דתה משום ברתיה קנסינן ליה לדידיה אמר אביי אין כדאמרי
אינשי שותא דינוקא בשוקא או דאבוה או דאימיה.[2]

Bilga always divides in the south: The Rabbanim taught an incident involving Miriam, the daughter of a member of the Bilga watch, who rebelled and went and married a soldier of the Greek kings. When the Greeks entered the Sanctuary, she entered with them and was kicking with her sandal on the Mizbei'ach and said: "Wolf, wolf, until when will you consume the property of the Jewish People, and yet you do not stand with them when they face threatening circumstances?" And when the chachamim heard about this matter and how she denigrated the Mizbei'ach, they established the ring of the Bilga watch in place [rendering it nonfunctional], and fixed its cupboard...However, according to the one who said it is due to Miriam, daughter of Bilga, who rebelled, [do we penalize the entire watch of Bilga] because of his daughter? Abaye said: "Yes, as people say, 'The speech of a child in the marketplace is learned either from that of his father or from that of his mother.'"

2   *Sukkah* 56b.

Miriam would never have said such things had she not heard talk of that kind in her parents' home. Education begins at home; children notice the smallest of details in everything.

וְהַעֲמִידוּ תַלְמִידִים הַרְבֵּה[3]...וְלֹא הַקַּפְּדָן מְלַמֵּד.[4]

Establish many students...and one who is impatient cannot teach.

The Mishnah teaches us to have many students. The Mishnah isn't telling everyone to become a teacher, as it mentions later that an impatient person should not teach. However, the Mishnah is teaching us that we must recognize that we are role models and many people look up to us and learn from our actions.

חֲנֹךְ לַנַּעַר עַל פִּי דַרְכּוֹ גַּם כִּי יַזְקִין לֹא יָסוּר מִמֶּנָּה.[5]

Educate a lad according to his way, so that he does not deviate in old age.

We may not all be teachers, but we are all educators. Who sets the path for the child other than the parents? Home is generally the "safe zone" for people, especially children. When a child learns a lesson at school and comes home to actions that conflict with his learning, the child will be confused.

An example of this is Elifaz, the son of Eisav and grandson of Yitzchak Avinu. When Yaakov left Be'er Sheva and headed toward Charan, he was robbed by his nephew. Why? Eisav told his son to attack Yaakov and kill him. However, when Elifaz met Yaakov, Yaakov pleaded with him to take all of his belongings instead of taking his life, which would also be considered as if he killed him. As the Gemara states:

ארבעה חשובין כמת עני ומצורע וסומא ומי שאין לו בנים.[6]

---

3   *Avos* 1:1.
4   Ibid. 2:5.
5   *Mishlei* 22:6.
6   *Nedarim* 64b.

Four types of people are considered dead: a pauper, one with leprosy, a blind person, and one who doesn't have children.

The question is, why did Elifaz heed Yaakov's suggestion? *Rashi* tells us the answer:

ולפי שגדל אליפז בחיקו של יצחק משך ידיו.[7]

And because Elifaz was raised on the lap of Yitzchak, he withdrew.

Elifaz was raised by Yitzchak Avinu. That means he knew Torah and mitzvos. Elifaz had a dilemma:

- On the one hand, the Torah tells us to honor our parents.
- On the other hand, the Torah also tells us not to kill or steal.

אתה ואביך חיבים בכבודי לפיכך לא תשמע לו לבטל את דברי.[8]

You and your father are obligated to honor Me! Do not therefore obey him if it results in canceling My words.

Rashi teaches us that if a person is in a dilemma between listening to their parents and listening to Hashem, remember that your parents are also obligated to listen to Hashem, and that will resolve your dilemma.

We are taught that Amalek was the son of Elifaz. Amalek is all about creating doubt; even the numerical value of *Amalek* is *safek*—doubt.[9] Elifaz was a confused person since he learned Torah and mitzvos at the house of Yitzchak, but he also learned negative traits from his father Eisav.

ואמרו כל מה שאירע לאבות סימן לבנים.[10]

And they said, "Everything that happened to our forefathers is a sign for the children."

---

7   *Bereishis* 29:11; *Rashi, s.v. Va'yeivk.*

8   *Vayikra* 19:3, *s.v. Ani Hashem Elokeichem.*

9   ספק = 240 = עמלק.

10   *Ramban, Bereishis* 12:6.

Maaseh avos siman l'banim—the actions of the fathers are signs for the children.

ברתיה דר״ע עבדא ליה לבן עזאי הכי והיינו דאמרי אינשי רחילא בתר
רחילא אזלא כעובדי אמה כך עובדי ברתא.[11]

*Rabbi Akiva's daughter did the same thing for Ben Azzai. This
explains the saying that people say: "The ewe follows the ewe;
the daughter's actions are the same as her mother's."*

As the Gemara says, "Like the mother does, so too does the daughter."
The way parents act and speak at home will have a much greater and
lasting impression on children than what they learn in school. The best
way to lead is by example.

To Summarize

It doesn't matter how old we are and what status we hold; we are a role
model to others. We have to make sure that the way we act reflects what
we believe and want to portray to others.

Points to Ponder

- What are some ways I can set a better example for others?
- If I were a child, would I view myself as a positive role model?
- How can I be the best that I can be?

---

11 *Kesubos* 63a.

Bump! Bump! Bump!

My daughter Ayelet was a one-year-old when she began to stand up on her own. It is very exciting for us as parents to watch our children reach new levels, however, it may be difficult for the child to reach these new levels. My daughter taught me a great lesson, and I'm sure she will reinforce the lesson as she continues to get older and progresses from learning how to walk to riding a bike, etc.

The lesson I learned is what Shlomo HaMelech teaches us in *Mishlei*:

כי שבע יפול צדיק וקם.[1]

A tzaddik falls seven times and he gets back up.

Goals are made up of many steps. It doesn't matter how many times one may fall as long as they get back up. If one learns how to use their fall to help them stand, they will achieve greatness. Consider a few examples:

- Thomas Edison was labeled unintelligent by his teachers. As an inventor, he was unsuccessful a thousand times when attempting to invent the lightbulb. When asked about how he felt about his thousand failed attempts, Edison replied, "I didn't fail a thousand times. The lightbulb was an invention with a thousand steps."

---

1   *Mishlei* 24:16.

- Another great example is Babe Ruth. Although he is known for his record of the most home runs, for many years Babe Ruth held the name "King of Strikeouts." Ruth said, "Every strikeout brings me closer to the next homerun."
- Michael Jordan once said, "I've missed more than nine thousand shots in my career. I've lost almost three hundred games. Twenty-six times I've been trusted to take the game winning shot…and missed. I've failed over and over and over again in my life. That is why I succeed."

These are just some of the many people who went through many struggles to get to their pinnacle success. Others include Abraham Lincoln, Albert Einstein, and Steve Jobs, to name a few, and the list goes on.

Baruch Hashem, Ayelet is able to stand up all by herself now. It came with a few bumps and plops, yet that didn't stop her from continuing to work on achieving her goal.

Part of growing up and learning about life is making mistakes. Part of making mistakes is learning to take responsibility for them and to grow from them. Many times, parents feel that it is their duty to clean up their child's mess. Parents should definitely be there to guide their children, but they should also let them learn how to grow from mistakes and become responsible people. If children know that they can rely on their parents to dig them out of a hole they create, why would they learn from their mistakes? Part of learning from one's mistakes is learning how to cope and/or move past them.

In her book *Mindset*, Carol Dweck discusses the difference between how those with a "fixed" mindset and those with a "growth" mindset view failure. "Even in the growth mindset, failure can be a painful experience. But it doesn't define you. It's a problem to be faced, dealt with, and learned from…In the fixed mindset, however, the loss of one's self to failure can be a permanent, haunting trauma."[2]

---

2   C.S. Dweck, *Mindset* (London: Robinson, an imprint of Constable & Robinson, 2017), p. 33.

The Gemara offers us an example of someone with a fixed mindset.

אחר קיצץ בנטיעות עליו הכתוב אומר (קהלת ה, ה) אל תתן את פיך
לחטיא את בשרך מאי היא חזא מיטטרו-ן דאתיהבא ליה רשותא
למיתב למיכתב זכוותא דישראל אמר גמירא דלמעלה לא הוי לא ישיבה
ולא תחרות ולא עורף ולא עיפוי שמא חס ושלום ב' רשויות הן אפקוהו
למיטטרו-ן ומחיוהו שיתין פולסי דנורא א"ל מ"ט כי חזיתיה לא קמת
מקמיה איתיהיבא ליה רשותא למימחק זכוותא דאחר יצתה בת קול
ואמרה (ירמיהו ג, יד) שובו בנים שובבים חוץ מאחר אמר הואיל ואיטריד
ההוא גברא מההוא עלמא ליפוק ליתהני בהאי עלמא נפק אחר לתרבות
רעה נפק אשכח זונה תבעה אמרה ליה ולאו אלישע בן אבויה את עקר
פוגלא ממישרא בשבת ויהב לה אמרה אחר הוא...א"ל לינוקא פסוק לי
פסוקך אמר לו (ישעיהו מח, כב) אין שלום אמר ה' לרשעים עייליה לבי
כנישתא אחריתי א"ל לינוקא פסוק לי פסוקך אמר לו (ירמיהו ב, כב) כי
אם תכבסי בנתר ותרבי לך בורית נכתם עונך עייליה לבי כנישתא
אחריתי א"ל לינוקא פסוק לי פסוקך א"ל (ירמיהו ה, ל) ואת שדוד מה
תעשי כי תלבשי שני כי תעדי עדי זהב כי תקרעי בפוך עיניך לשוא תתיפי
וגו' עייליה לבי כנישתא אחריתי עד דעייליה לתליסר בי כנישתא כולהו
פסקן ליה כי האי גוונא לבתרא א"ל פסוק לי פסוקך א"ל (תהלים נ, טז)
ולרשע אמר אלקים מה לך לספר חקי וגו' ההוא ינוקא הוה מגמגם בלישניה
אשתמע כמה דאמר ליה ולאלישע אמר אלקים איכא דאמרי סכינא הוה
בהדיה וקרעיה ושדריה לתליסר בי כנישתי ואיכא דאמרי אמר אי הואי
בידי סכינא הוה קרענא ליה.[3]

*Acher chopped down the saplings [becoming a heretic]. About
him, the pasuk states: "Do not let your mouth bring your flesh
into guilt" (Koheles 5:5). What was it that led him to heresy?
He saw the angel Mitatro-n, who was granted permission to sit
and write the merits of Yisrael. He said: "There is a tradition
that in the world above there is no sitting, no competition, no
turning one's back before Him, and no disinterest." Seeing that
someone other than God was seated above, he said: "Perhaps,
Heaven forbid, there are two authorities [and there is another
source of power in control of the world in addition to God."*

3   *Chagigah* 14b–15b.

Such thoughts led Acher to heresy]. They removed Mitatro-n [from his place in heaven] and smote him with sixty rods of fire so that others would not make the mistake that Acher made. They said to the angel: "What is the reason that when you saw Elisha ben Avuya you did not stand before him?" Despite this conduct, since Mitatro-n was personally involved, he was granted permission to erase the merits of Acher and cause him to stumble in any manner. A Divine voice went forth saying: "Return, rebellious children" (Yirmiyahu 3:22), apart from Acher. Upon hearing this, Elisha ben Avuya said: "Since that man, meaning himself, has been banished from that world, let him go out and enjoy this world." Acher went astray. He went and found a prostitute and solicited her for relations. She said to him: "And are you not Elisha ben Avuya?" He uprooted a radish from a patch on Shabbos and gave it to her [to demonstrate that he no longer observed the Torah]. She said: "He is other than he was. He is not the same Elisha ben Avuya, he is Acher, other"...Acher said to a child: "Recite your pasuk to me." He recited to him: "And you, spoiled one, what are you doing, that you clothe yourself with scarlet, that you adorn yourself with ornaments of gold, that you broaden your eyes with paint? In vain you make yourself fair" (ibid. 4:30). He brought him to another shul, until he had brought him into thirteen synagogues, where all the children recited to him sim- ilar pesukim that speak of the hopeless situation of the wicked. At the last one, he said to a child: "Recite your pasuk to me." He recited to him: "And to the wicked [v'la'rasha], God says, 'What is it for you to declare My statutes?" (Tehillim 50:16). That child had a stutter, so it sounded as though he were say- ing to him: "V'l'Elisha [and to Elisha], God says..." This made Elisha think the child was deliberately insulting him. Some say Acher had a knife, and he tore the child apart and sent him to the thirteen synagogues. And others say that Acher said: "Had I a knife, I would have torn him apart."

When a heavenly voice called out, "Return to Me, My children, except for Acher," Acher mistakenly understood this to mean that he was banished from *Olam Haba* without any chance of repentance, and immediately set out to sin. As the Gemara continues, it relates a series of episodes where Rabbi Meir brought Acher to different shuls and asked children to repeat *pesukim* they were learning in yeshiva. With his fixed mindset, Acher interpreted each *pasuk* as something negative against himself. At the last shul, the child said the *pasuk*, "And to the wicked (*v'la'rasha*) Hashem says, 'What is it for you to declare My statutes...'" This child had a speech impediment, and Acher thought the child said "*v'l'Elisha*." Acher thought this child was insulting him, and some say that he killed the child. Acher was a *talmid chacham*. He knew the *pasuk*, but he was so caught up in his negative frame of mind that he heard what he wanted to hear. Instead of understanding and accepting these *pesukim* as rebuke, he understood them in a negative way.

An example of a growth mindset we can learn from is the *rasha* who is mentioned in the Passover Haggadah. He is rebuked and told that "אלו היה שם, לא היה נגאל—had he been there, he wouldn't have been redeemed." Had he been with us in *Mitzrayim*, he would have been part of the four-fifths of Jews who died during *Makas Choshech*. How are these words supposed to encourage him to change his ways?

We are telling him that had he been there (past tense), there would be no hope for his survival. However, let's focus on the present. We are not in *Mitzrayim*, and it is not too late to change in time for the next *geulah*. Yes, you may be a *rasha* this year, but it's not too late to change. The Ropshitzer Rebbe asked, why is it that every year so many new Haggados are published? He answered that the *rasha* accepted the *mussar* and became a *tzaddik*.

We are all human and make mistakes; that's part of living. We need to realize that if we stay down in the mud, we can never become clean. We have to get back up and dust ourselves off in order to be successful. If we recognize our potential and don't label ourselves as failures, not only will we learn to walk, we will learn to run.

To Summarize

One who is unsuccessful yet continues to work toward his goal is not considered a failure. Failure only comes when one gives up. Our mind is very powerful; don't let it become swayed by those who want to see us fail.

Points to Ponder

- How can I learn and move on from my mistakes instead of dwelling on them?
- How can I teach others from my mistakes?
- How can I separate my mistakes from who I truly am?

Like a Lion

יתגבר כארי לעמוד בבוקר לעבודת בוראו.[1]

*One should strengthen himself like a lion to get up in the morn-
ing to serve his Creator.*

The first halachah in *Shulchan Aruch* teaches, "We should wake
up in the morning like a lion to serve our Creator..." It doesn't
matter what time we go to sleep or when we awake; we must
be cognitive that every action we do is to serve our Creator, Hakadosh
Baruch Hu.

My son Daniel sleeps on the top bed of a bunk bed. Every morning, we
know when he is awake, as we hear a thud from down the hall. Daniel is
a perfect example of what the *Mechaber* teaches us—to wake up full of
energy to serve Hashem. As soon as he wakes up, Daniel jumps down
from his bed and runs into our room, full of energy, to let us know that
it is time to wake up and say *Modeh Ani*. He has taught me an incredible
lesson: It doesn't matter what time he went to sleep the previous night,
because he wakes up full of energy, just like a lion.

---

1   *Shulchan Aruch, Orach Chaim* 1:1.

יְהוּדָה בֶן תֵּימָא אוֹמֵר...וְגִבּוֹר כָּאֲרִי, לַעֲשׂוֹת רְצוֹן אָבִיךָ שֶׁבַּשָּׁמָיִם.[2]

Yehudah ben Teima says, one should be mighty like a lion to fulfill the will of Hashem.

Rabbeinu Yonah comments on this Mishnah, saying:

להתגבר על המצות. כלומר שכל מחשבתו ופעולות איבריו אל מעשה ה'.

To be mighty with the mitzvos. To say that all of one's thoughts and the actions of one's body should be to serve Hashem.

When the morning comes, some may turn over and close their eyes for "just five more minutes," but what about using those five minutes to get ready in order to be on time for davening or performing other mitzvos?

וכי תימא זריזין מקדימין למצות נבדוק מצפרא דכתיב וביום השמיני ימול בשר ערלתו ותניא כל היום כולו כשר למילה אלא שזריזין מקדימים למצות שנאמר וישכם אברהם בבקר.[3]

And in case you say the vigilant are early in the performance of mitzvos, let us search in the morning. As it is written: "And on the eighth day, the flesh of his foreskin shall be circumcised" (Vayikra 12:3). And it was taught in a Beraisa: The entire day is suitable for the mitzvah of a bris milah; however, the vigilant are early in the performance of mitzvos, and circumcise in the morning. As it is stated, "And Avraham arose early in the morning."

The Gemara mentions that although the mitzvah to perform *bris milah* is the entire eighth day, we do it in the morning because of the concept of *zerizin makdimin l'mitzvos*—the vigilant perform mitzvos as early as possible, just like Avraham who arose early with eagerness to perform Hashem's commandment.

---

2   *Avos* 5:23.

3   *Pesachim* 4a.

The Gemara quotes a source for performing a mitzvah with vigilance: The *pasuk* from the morning of the *Akeidah*, which says, *"Va'yashkeim Avraham ba'boker*—And Avraham arose early [the next] morning."

Rashi comments, *"Nizdarez la'mitzvah*—Avraham got up early to perform the commandment of Hashem."[4]

There are other examples of this concept:

- Another example of *zerizin makdimin l'mitzvos* that we learn from Avraham is in the previous *perek*, when Avraham sent Hagar and Yishmael away. The *pasuk* also says there, *"Va'yashkeim Avraham ba'boker*—And Avraham arose early the next morning."[5]

  The Malbim explains that the *pasuk* is telling us how righteous Avraham was:

  מספר צדקת אברהם: שהשכים בבקר לקיים מצות ה'.

  Avraham woke up early in the morning to fulfill the commandments of Hashem.

- Another role model we can learn from is Dovid HaMelech, who says in *Tehillim*:

  חַשְׁתִּי וְלֹא הִתְמַהְמָהְתִּי לִשְׁמֹר מִצְוֹתֶיךָ.[6]

  I have hurried and not delayed to keep your mitzvos.

  The *Ibn Ezra* comments that Dovid HaMelech performed *zerizin makdimin l'mitzvos*. Although he went through a life full of tragedy and stress, when it came to Torah and mitzvos, Dovid says:

  טוֹב לִי תוֹרַת פִּיךָ מֵאַלְפֵי זָהָב וָכָסֶף.[7]

  Better for me is the teachings of Your mouth than thousands of gold and silver.

---

4   *Bereishis* 22:3, *Rashi* s.v. *Vayashkem*.
5   *Bereishis* 21:14.
6   *Tehillim* 119:60.
7   Ibid., v. 72.

How do we reach this level of *zerizin makdimin l'mitzvos*? One must be honest with oneself; consider if the situation were different and the opportunity that was sitting in front of you was a chance to meet a celebrity, an athlete, a *gadol ha'dor* (*l'havdil*), or anything one may have a passion for. When considering this, think of using that energy toward performing mitzvos for our Father, our King!

When I was young, my family went to Virginia one Sukkos, and our accommodations were a couple of miles from the shul. It was Erev Yom Tov, and we were about to head out to shul when we saw what the meteorologist called a tropical rain storm. It was the hardest I have ever seen rain fall; it was coming down in buckets. My father and I looked at each other and contemplated whether we should attempt to walk to shul or wait the storm out. We asked each other, "If this were a Minnesota Vikings game, would we hesitate from going and getting drenched? There was no need to deliberate any further—we walked to shul with joy. We recognized that this was an opportunity to show what we valued and prioritized. I'd venture to say that at the pace we ran, we were definitely *zerizin makdimin l'mitzvos*!

Every moment of one's life can be used to fulfill the commandments of Hashem. Every moment is an opportunity. Let's be like lions and pounce at the opportunities that come our way.

To Summarize

When we want something, we figure out how to get it done. When performing mitzvos, we must act with eagerness and excitement as we would when performing a task for ourselves.

Points to Ponder

- Do I run to do the will of Hashem like I would for my own desires?
- How can I make my desires align with Hashem's?
- Am I using the most of my time and abilities to serve Hashem?

Mitzvos Are Here for Us

There was a time period while Daniel was in the process of becoming toilet-trained when he refused to wash his hands after going to the bathroom. However, he loved washing *negel vasser*. So instead of washing his hands after the bathroom, he would wash *negel vasser* (with soap, of course).

The lesson here is that sometimes one may feel that the mitzvos are a burden, but if one just thinks about it, and maybe does a little research, one will find they have so many benefits. One example is washing one's hands when waking in the morning and before one eats bread. Jews were often blamed for the Black Plague due to the fact that they had the least amount of people affected by it. How were we significantly less affected by a plague that killed millions? The answer is that Jews had mitzvos, such as *netilas yadayim*, to keep them clean and hygienic.

In a recent article, researchers found that wearing tefillin on a daily basis offers benefits for one's heart. "We found people who wear tefillin in either the short or long term recorded a measurable positive effect on their blood flow. That has been associated with better outcomes in heart disease."[1]

---

1   See https://bit.ly/3eL7Ji1.

The Gemara teaches:

אמר רב חייא בר אשי: מפני מה אמרו מים אחרונים חובה? מפני שמלח
סדומית יש, שמסמא את העינים.[2]

*Rav Chiya the son of Rav Ashi says, "For what reason did [the
chachamim] say mayim acharonim [after a meal] is an obligation? Due to the salt from Sodom that even a small amount of
can blind one's eyes."*

There is a well-known *mashal* of a businessman who arrived at his stop
and departed the train. The man found a porter to pick up and deliver his
luggage to the inn he was staying at. After giving the porter the details of
his luggage, the man headed to his inn. About three hours later, there was
a loud knock on the man's door. When he opened the door, the man was
shocked to see the bellboy dripping in sweat and leaning on the wall trying to catch his breath. The man asked the bellboy, "Why are you sweating so much?" The bellboy responded that he had *schlepped* the package
all the way from the train station and up the steps to the man's room.
The man told him that he was truly sorry, but it was the wrong package.
The bellboy let out a gasp and asked, "How do you know? I brought the
luggage that you described!" The man answered, "My luggage contained
a few precious diamonds. It wouldn't have been so heavy!"

The mitzvos were given to us for our benefit. If we look at mitzvos
as a burden, it will be extremely difficult to carry them around with us.
However, when looking at mitzvos as precious diamonds and treasures,
it doesn't matter how heavy the package may be; one won't see it as
a burden because of its value.

The *pasuk* in *Tehillim* says:

טוֹב לִי תוֹרַת פִּיךָ מֵאַלְפֵי זָהָב וָכָסֶף.[3]

*Better for me is the teachings of Your mouth than thousands of
gold and silver.*

---

2   *Eruvin* 17b.
3   *Tehillim* 119:72.

ר׳ חנניא בן עקשיא אומר רצה הקב״ה לזכות את ישראל לפיכך הרבה
להם תורה ומצות שנאמר (ישעיהו מב, כא) ה׳ חפץ למען צדקו יגדיל תורה
ויאדיר.[4]

*Rabbi Chananya ben Akashya says: Hakadosh Baruch Hu
wanted B'nei Yisrael to have many merits, therefore, He increased for them Torah and mitzvos. as it says in the pasuk,
"Hashem wished for the sake of increasing B'nei Yisrael's
righteousness to make the Torah great and glorious."[5]*

The *Rambam* comments:

מעקרי האמונה בתורה כי כשיקיים אדם מצוה מתרי״ג מצות כראוי וכהוגן
ולא ישתף עמה כוונה מכוונת העולם בשום פנים אלא שיעשה אותה לשמה
מאהבה כמו שבארתי לך הנה זכה בה לחיי העולם הבא ועל זה אמר רבי
חנניא כי המצות בהיותם הרבה אי אפשר שלא יעשה אדם בחייו אחת
מהם על מתכונתה ושלמותה ובעשותו אותה המצוה תחיה נפשו באותו
מעשה.[6]

*It is among the roots of faith in the Torah that when a person
upholds one of the 613 mitzvos [properly] and does not in
any way combine it with any intent for gain in the world, but
rather does it lishmah, out of love, as I have explained to you
[elsewhere], see how he merits through it life in the World
to Come. This is what Rabbi Chananya was communicating;
because there are many mitzvos, it is impossible that a person
will not in his lifetime do one of them properly and completely.
In performing this mitzvah, his soul will come alive through
this deed.*

ואמר רבי יהושע בן לוי בשעה שעלה משה למרום אמרו מלאכי השרת
לפני הקדוש ברוך הוא רבונו של עולם מה לילוד אשה בינינו אמר להן
לקבל תורה בא אמרו לפניו חמדה גנוזה שגנוזה לך תשע מאות ושבעים

4   *Makkos* 23b.
5   *Yeshayahu* 42:21.
6   *Rambam*, commentary on Mishnah, *Makkos* 3:16:1.

וארבעה דורות קודם שנברא העולם אתה מבקש ליתנה לבשר ודם...אמר
לו הקדוש ברוך הוא למשה החזיר להן תשובה...אמר לפניו רבונו של
עולם תורה שאתה נותן לי מה כתיב בה אנכי ה' אלקיך אשר הוצאתיך
מארץ מצרים אמר להן למצרים ירדתם לפרעה השתעבדתם...מיד הודו לו
להקדוש ברוך הוא שנאמר ה' אדנינו מה אדיר שמך וגו'.

*And Rabbi Yehoshua ben Levi said: When Moshe ascended on
High to receive the Torah, the ministering angels said before
Hakadosh Boruch Hu: "Master of the Universe, what is one
born of a woman doing here among us?" Hakadosh Baruch Hu
said to them: "He came to receive the Torah." The angels said
before Him: "The Torah is a hidden treasure that was concealed
by you 974 generations before the creation of the world, and
you seek to give it to flesh and blood?"...Hakadosh Baruch Hu
said to Moshe: "Provide them with an answer..." Moshe said
before Him: "Master of the Universe, the Torah that You are
giving me, what is written in it?" God said to him: "'I am your
God Who brought you out of Egypt from the house of slavery.'"
Moshe said to the angels: "Did you descend to Egypt? Were
you enslaved to Pharaoh? Why should the Torah be yours?..."
Immediately they agreed with Hakadosh Baruch Hu that He
made the right decision to give the Torah to the people, as it is
stated: "Hashem our Master, how glorious is Your name in all
the earth."*

The Gemara relates the events that took place when Moshe went to
receive the Torah. The *malachim* wanted to keep the Torah with them,
and they asked Hashem why the Torah was being given to mankind.
They argued that the Torah should remain in the heavens just as it did
for the 974 generations before the world was created. Hashem told
Moshe to respond to the *malachim*. Moshe said, "The Torah says, 'I am
Hashem Who brought you out of *Mitzrayim*,' were you slaves to Pharaoh
in *Mitzrayim*? The Torah says, 'You shouldn't have any other gods.' Do
you live amongst other nations who worship idols? The Torah tells us to
remember Shabbos...to honor one's father and mother...not to kill...not
to steal...Do you work that you need a rest from it? Do you have a father

and mother that makes this commandment relevant to you? Do you have jealousy amongst you or a *yetzer hara* that could lead to murder...or robbery?" Immediately, the *malachim* agreed that mankind should have the Torah because they realized the Torah and mitzvos are guidelines for man—to benefit us.[7]

ואני קרבת אלקים לי טוב...

And for me, closeness to Hashem is good...

What is a *korban*? Loosely translated, a *korban* is a sacrifice that one would bring in the times of the Beis Hamikdash. However, the true meaning of *korban* comes from the root of *karov*—to become close.[8] When we "sacrifice" our will and desires to observe the mitzvos of Hashem, we are becoming closer to Him. The closer one is to another, the more they stand up for each other in times of need. When we are on the way to perform a mitzvah, we are in essence bringing a *korban* and becoming closer to Hashem. Of course, Hashem will protect those who are close to Him.

"*Shomer Hashem es kol ohavav*—Hashem protects all who love Him."[9] The more mitzvos we observe properly, the greater we grow and the closer to Hashem we become.[10]

To Summarize

We were put into this world to serve Hashem and make the world a better place. Fortunate for us, we were given a guide. The Torah and mitzvos that Hashem granted us are tools to support us in our mission.

---

7   *Shabbos* 88b.

8   The root of קרבן is קרב.

9   *Tehillim* 145:20.

10   There is a complex *sugya* that discusses the concept of שלוחי מצוה אינן ניזוקין—messengers of a mitzvah are not susceptible to harm. This chapter is focusing on the benefits, and not the rewards, we gain from the mitzvos in this world.

Points to Ponder

- Am I living like a robot and doing mitzvos because I have to?
- How can I "lighten the load" by appreciating mitzvos, even when I'm not in the mood to perform them?
- What is one mitzvah I can "take ownership of" and work on performing it to the best of my ability?

Jumping to Conclusions

I t was a long day, and my dear wife was working late, so I made dinner for the kids. With Daniel's help, I cut some vegetables and chicken, threw them together, added some spices, and placed the frying pan on the stove top. After some time, the food was ready for us to enjoy. I set up the table and served dinner. I was a bit taken aback when Daniel told me that he didn't want it. After all, he had helped me make it! I figured that it was the vegetables that weren't his taste, so I removed them and gave him the chicken. Once again, he said that he didn't want it, but this time he told me that it was because he doesn't like it. I was confused. I asked him, "How can you not like it if you haven't even tasted it?" He responded that he just didn't want it and that he wanted pretzels instead. So, I made a deal. If he eats two pieces of chicken, he can have pretzels. At first Daniel was hesitant, but then he quickly stuffed the chicken in his mouth. His face lit up, and he gave me a smile. He loved it! When he finished swallowing his chicken, he grabbed his plate, ran into the kitchen, and said, "Can I please have more?" I filled his plate with chicken, and again he finished the entire plate! He didn't even touch the pretzels!

Yes, it gave me great satisfaction that he liked my cooking and ate a healthy dinner. However, even more importantly, I learned a great lesson from this. Sometimes, we jump to conclusions and "eat with our eyes." I'm not only referring to food but to judging others as well.

We tend to judge based on the moment. "I don't like somebody because he/she looks like this" or "Mr. So-and-So is a bad person because I once saw him do such-and-such."

The Mishnah teaches:

אַל תָּדִין אֶת חֲבֵרְךָ עַד שֶׁתַּגִּיעַ לִמְקוֹמוֹ.[1]

Don't judge your fellow until you have reached their place.

The *Maharal* explains:

וְעַל זה אמר אל תדין את חבירך עד שתגיע למקומו, כלומר כי יש סבות הרבה לאדם ואם היתה אותה סבה בעצמה מתחדשת עליו כמו שהיא באה על חבירו היה עושה ג"כ מה שעושה חבירו, כי אין בטחון ואמונה לאדם פרטי מאחר שהוא בעל שנוי ולכך אין לו לדון על עצמו ומתחילה אמר אל תאמן בעצמך עד יום מותך, כי אפשר לאדם להיות משתנה בעצמו, ואמר אף דבר שהוא ענין זר שהאדם יאמר על זה המעשה כי דבר זה אין ראוי לעשות לאדם מאחר שהוא דבר זר, ואם כן יש לעלות על הדעת כי יש לאדם לדין אחר ולומר כי עשה מעשה שאין אדם אחר היה עושה, ומכל מקום אל ידין את חבירו עד שיגיע למקומו שאם הגיע לו הדבר מה שהגיע לחבירו והיה מתחדש עליו מה שהיה מתחדש על חבירו, אפשר שיהיה גם כן עושה אע"פ שהוא דבר זר שאין דרך לעשות, במה שהאדם הוא בעל שנוי אפשר שגם כן הוא היה עושה הדבר ההוא.[2]

On this, [Hillel] said, "Do not judge your friend until you are in his place." This means to say that there are many reasons for how a person acts, and if that same situation should happen upon him as it did to his friend, he would also act as his friend did. [The reason for this is that] there is no faith or trust [when it comes to] an individual, since he is [prone] to change. Therefore, he shouldn't judge [how he would act if he were in his friend's situation]. [The words] preceding state, "do not trust in yourself until your dying day," for it is possible that one can alter himself. And he said, even [in a situation where someone

---

1   *Avos* 2:4.

2   *Derech Chaim* 2:4.

does] something so odd that one would say [that it is such a strange act that no one would do such a thing]; therefore, one could assume that judging the other would be acceptable [in this case]. Nevertheless, he should not judge him until he is in his [friend's] place. For if the same situations would happen to him as they happened to his friend, it's possible that he would act the same way even though [the act that was done] was an odd one, that wouldn't be done [normally]. The reason for this is that [due to life situations], man is subject to change [at any time], and could possibly act in the same manner.

Don't judge another for sinning because although our lifestyle may have changed, it is possible we have committed a similar sin.

One reason people judge others is because they want to feel better about themselves. However, one can never know what they would have done had the situation been different. Two people can undergo the same exact situation, yet have totally different experiences and outcomes. Some soldiers return from war with post-traumatic stress disorder (PTSD), while their friends return just fine. There are stories of people who survived the Holocaust and had a much stronger connection to Hashem, while others did not.

When an officer is investigating a crime, the officer will look for as many witnesses as they can find. The reason for this is so that the officer can get as many angles on the circumstance as possible. Although the officer can receive the story from one person and call it a day, every person there witnessed it in their own way.

Although one may have done *teshuvah* and changed for the better, it doesn't give them the right to judge others who faced similar challenges and didn't perform a complete *teshuvah*.

The Gemara relates an incident with Rav Ashi who, when speaking of the three kings of Yisrael, said "Now we will discuss our friend Menasheh." Menasheh later appeared to Rav Ashi and said angrily, "How dare you compare us as equals?!" After a halachic dialogue, Rav Ashi asked, "If you are so wise, why did you engage in idol worship?" Menasheh responded, "Had you been there at that time, you would have lifted the hem of your cloak and run after me due to the fierce desire to engage in *avodah zarah*."[3] It is easy to judge others without fully looking into their situation. We never truly know another's situation unless we are deliberate in our discernment.

The Mishnah teaches us to be deliberate in judgment.[4] The *Rambam* explains that we should delay in reaching the verdict and not determine it quickly before fully understanding it, as it is possible that new matters will be revealed to our eyes that were previously not revealed. In our case, if we get to know people better before we judge them, we may actually like them more than we think! One of the stories that the Gemara relates to show the importance of judging favorably is as follows:

תנו רבנן הדן חבירו לכף זכות דנין אותו לזכות ומעשה באדם אחד שירד מגליל העליון ונשכר אצל בעל הבית אחד בדרום שלש שנים ערב יום הכפורים אמר לו תן לי שכרי ואלך ואזון את אשתי ובני אמר לו אין לי מעות אמר לו תן לי פירות אמר לו אין לי תן לי קרקע אין לי תן לי בהמה אין לי תן לי כרים וכסתות אין לי הפשיל כליו לאחוריו והלך לביתו בפחי נפש לאחר הרגל נטל בעל הבית שכרו בידו ועמו משוי שלשה חמורים אחד של מאכל ואחד של משתה ואחד של מיני מגדים והלך לו לביתו אחר שאכלו ושתו נתן לו שכרו אמר לו בשעה שאמרת לי תן לי שכרי ואמרתי אין לי מעות במה חשדתני אמרתי שמא פרקמטיא בזול נזדמנה לך ולקחת בהן ובשעה שאמרת לי תן לי בהמה ואמרתי אין לי בהמה במה חשדתני אמרתי שמא מושכרת ביד אחרים בשעה שאמרת לי תן לי קרקע ואמרתי לך אין לי קרקע במה חשדתני אמרתי שמא מוחכרת ביד אחרים היא ובשעה שאמרתי לך אין לי פירות במה חשדתני אמרתי שמא אינן מעושרות ובשעה שאמרתי לך אין לי כרים וכסתות במה חשדתני אמרתי שמא הקדיש כל נכסיו לשמים אמר ליה העבודה כך היה הדרתי כל נכסי בשביל הורקנוס בני שלא עסק בתורה וכשבאתי אצל חבירי בדרום התירו לי כל נדרי ואתה כשם שדנתני לזכות המקום ידין אותך לזכות.[5]

The Rabbanan taught in a Beraisa: One who judges another favorably is himself judged favorably. There was an incident

---

3   *Sanhedrin* 102b.

4   *Avos* 1:1.

5   *Shabbos* 127b.

with someone who descended from the Upper Galilee and was hired to work for a certain homeowner in the South for three years. On Erev Yom Kippur, the worker asked the homeowner for his pay so he could go and feed his wife and children. The homeowner said to him: "I have no money." He said to him: "In that case, pay me in the form of produce." The homeowner responded: "I have none." The worker said to him: "Pay me in the form of land." The homeowner said to him: "I have none." The worker said to him: "Pay me in the form of animals." He said to him: "I have none." The worker said to him: "Give me cushions and blankets." He said to him: "I have none." The worker slung his tools over his shoulder behind him and went to his home in anguish.

After Sukkos, the homeowner took the worker's wages in his hand, along with a burden that required three donkeys, one laden with food, one laden with drink, and one laden with types of sweets, and went to the worker's home. After they ate and drank, the homeowner gave him his wages.

The homeowner said to him: "When you said to me, 'Pay me my wages,' and I said, 'I have no money,' of what did you suspect me? [Did you suspect me of trying to avoid paying you?]" The worker answered, "I said, 'Perhaps the opportunity to purchase merchandise inexpensively presented itself, and you purchased it with the money that you owed me, and therefore you had no money available.'" The homeowner asked, "And when you said to me, 'Pay me in the form of animals,' and I said, 'I have no animals,' of what did you suspect me?" The worker answered, "I said, 'Perhaps the animals are hired to others.'" The homeowner asked, "When you said to me, 'Pay me in the form of land,' and I said, 'I have no land,' of what did you suspect me?" The worker answered, "I said, 'Perhaps the land is leased to others, and you cannot take the land from the lessees.'" The homeowner asked, "And when you said to me, 'Pay me in the form of produce,' and I said, 'I have no produce,' of what did you suspect me?" The worker answered, "I said, 'Perhaps you haven't separated maaser yet, and that's why you could not give them to me.'" The homeowner asked, "And when I said, 'I have no cushions or blankets,' of what did you suspect me?" The worker answered, "I said, 'Perhaps you made all of your property hekdesh and therefore have nothing available at present.'"

The homeowner said to him, "I swear by the service in the Beis Hamikdash that it was so. I had no money available at the time because I promised and made all of my property hekdesh on account of Horkenus, my son, who did not engage in Torah study. [The homeowner sought to avoid leaving an inheritance for his son.] And when I came to the chachamim in the South, they dissolved all my vows." At that point, the homeowner had immediately gone to pay his worker. Now the homeowner said, "And you, just as you judged favorably, so may Hashem judge you favorably."

This concept of judging others fairly and not jumping to conclusions is not just in the Mishnah and Gemara; it is, in fact, a *mitzvah d'Oraisa!* The *pasuk* says:

לֹא תַעֲשׂוּ עָוֶל בַּמִּשְׁפָּט...בְּצֶדֶק תִּשְׁפֹּט עֲמִיתֶךָ.⁶

Do not make any unfair decisions...with righteousness you shall judge My nation.

The Gemara discusses this *pasuk* and has two understandings of its meaning.

ת״ר, בצדק תשפוט עמיתך שלא יהא אחד יושב ואחד עומד אחד מדבר כל צרכו ואחד אומר לו קצר דבריך ד״א בצדק תשפוט עמיתך הוי דן את חבירך לכף זכות.⁷

---

6   *Vayikra* 19:15.

7   *Shevuos* 30a.

> *The Rabbanan taught: The pasuk states: "In righteousness shall you judge your nation." The court must ensure that there will not be a situation where one litigant is sitting and one litigant is standing, or a situation where one litigant says everything that he needs to say to present his case and one litigant, the judge says to him: "Shorten your statement." Alternatively, it is derived from the pasuk: "In righteousness shall you judge your colleague," that you should judge another favorably.*

The first explanation is that the *pasuk* is speaking to judges when deliberating a case in court. However, the second is that it applies to every person to judge others favorably.

In today's day and age, when much of our communication is done through texting or social media, many arguments occur because of simple misunderstandings. If you think someone is messaging something negative, give him/her a call to find out what he/she really means. It could just be your mood at the moment that causes you to perceive the message as something negative.

כל המעביר על מדותיו מעבירין לו על כל פשעיו שנאמר נושא עון ועובר
על פשע.[8]

> *Anyone who foregoes the misdeeds of others, Hashem will waive His judgment on him*

Try to judge others more positively and favorably. Not only will you view others in a more positive light, but others—and Hashem—will judge you in a favorable light as well.

To Summarize

We never know the full story. Although human mentality is to judge others, we should try to judge others favorably. When you find it difficult to find favorable judgment for others, consider how you would want to be judged if you were found in a compromising situation.

---

8   *Rosh Hashanah* 17a.

Points to Ponder

- What is one way I can work on becoming more understanding of others?
- How would I feel if someone judged me for something they didn't know fully?
- How can I focus on seeing people more positively?

Help!

Becoming a big boy isn't so simple. Many more responsibilities come upon you, from brushing your teeth to cleaning up after yourself. However, one responsibility that really proves that someone is a big boy is the ability to get dressed on one's own.

We would usually assist Daniel with getting dressed, but there were times that Daniel wanted to take on a greater responsibility by picking out his clothes and getting dressed all by himself without any supervision. Of course, we would afterward make sure that everything matched and was on properly. Once, Daniel wanted to wear a sweatshirt that was in his top drawer, but it was too high for him to reach. Luckily, he built up the courage to ask for help instead of climbing up the drawers, but I could tell that he didn't have the same satisfaction as getting dressed *all* by himself. I explained to him that he is still a very big boy, and that it is OK to ask others for help. One may think that asking for help shows a sign of weakness, but that is not true. I told Daniel that when you ask for help, it doesn't mean that you aren't a big boy, it's just the opposite! When you ask for help, not only are you a big boy, but you become a very big boy because you are now learning something new and will be able to build on it for next time. The lesson learned from this is that when one asks for help, it's not because they are weak but because they want to remain strong.

This is why one of the three things the world stands on is *gemilus chassadim*.[1] If everyone thought of themselves as independent beings, the world would cease to exist. We have to realize that interdependence is holding the world up. The Gemara teaches the well-known saying, "Companion or death."[2] We wouldn't be able to survive without the help of others.

When man was created, the *pasuk* says:

וַיֹּאמֶר ה׳ אֱלֹקִים לֹא טוֹב הֱיוֹת הָאָדָם לְבַדּוֹ אֶעֱשֶׂה לּוֹ עֵזֶר כְּנֶגְדּוֹ.[3]

And Hashem said: "It is not good that man should be alone, I will make him a helper opposite him."

Mankind cannot survive alone. The Mishnah asks, "If I am just for myself, then who am I?"[4] Our life mission must include helping others, and that is the only way we can truly fulfill our purpose.

Stephen Covey writes, "Life is, by nature, highly interdependent. To try to achieve maximum effectiveness through independence is like trying to play tennis with a golf club—the tool is not suited to reality."[5] One needs others to help in life.

יְהוֹשֻׁעַ בֶּן פְּרַחְיָה אוֹמֵר, עֲשֵׂה לְךָ רַב, וּקְנֵה לְךָ חָבֵר ...[6]

Yehoshua ben Perachya says, make for yourself a mentor and acquire a friend for yourself.

The Mishnah is teaching us that one should make a mentor and acquire a friend for himself, so that if one is ever in need of assistance he will have someone to call.

"We can all do so much more together than we ever can alone. Too often, though, we 'tough it out' rather than reaching out to ask for help

---

1   *Avos* 1:2.
2   *Taanis* 23a.
3   *Bereishis* 2:18.
4   *Avos* 1:14.
5   S.R. Covey, *The 7 Habits of Highly Effective People: Powerful Lessons in Personal Change* (New York: Simon & Schuster, 2004), p. 28.
6   *Avos* 1:6.

when we need it most. Fear gets the better of us while depriving others of a chance to show they care and share their gifts."[7]

When one recognizes this, one will have a much greater chance in becoming successful in what one is trying to accomplish, and we give others the opportunity to help out.

To Summarize

The more experience we gain, the more expectations and accountability we are given. Asking for help should not be a sign of weakness; rather, it is a sign of strength. Many people live with regrets because they were too weak to ask for assistance.

Points to Ponder

- Is it because of my pride that I'm not asking for help?
- How do I feel when someone asks me for assistance?
- How can I feel more comfortable asking for help when in need?

---

7   M. Warrell, "Asking for Help Reveals Strength, Not Weakness," accessed March 25, 2015. See https://bit.ly/3nxfFHu.

The Gift of Life

One Friday afternoon, the kids were taking a bath when suddenly Daniel slipped and started bleeding right above his eye. I took a look at the cut and decided to go to the hospital. Because of how deep it looked, I figured it would need stitches. With two hours before Shabbos, I was getting nervous that we weren't going to make it back home in time. Luckily for us, we knew a doctor in that hospital who was able to help expedite things. After a bit of waiting (and eight stitches later), we thankfully made it home for Shabbos.

When all was said and done, the children were asleep and we were able to sit back, kick our shoes off and relax. I then told my dear *eishes chayil* about a quote I recently saw. The quote was, "Life isn't tied with a bow, but it is still a gift." This is a powerful quote. Things happen that seem terrible and unplanned, but we have to appreciate that things could have been worse. Even someone who looks at the cup half-empty should be grateful that there is water in the cup!

There is a story said in the name of the Klausenberger Rebbe, that after the Holocaust, someone came over to him and said that he didn't want to have any connection to Judaism anymore because of what he'd witnessed. He related that every day, he would watch someone who had a pair of tefillin take people's last piece of bread before lending them his tefillin. The man said that if that is what Judaism is all about, then he wants to have no part in it. The Klausenberger Rebbe suggested to the man that instead of looking at the individual charging a piece of bread for tefillin, he should instead focus on all of the people who were willing to give up their last piece of bread just to put on tefillin for those few moments. That's what Yiddishkeit is all about; focusing on the positive in every situation brings *menuchas ha'nefesh*. There is so much positive in the world, yet people tend to focus on the bit of negative.

וְרָאָה הַכֹּהֵן וְהִנֵּה שְׂאֵת לְבָנָה בָּעוֹר וְהִיא הָפְכָה שֵׂעָר לָבָן וּמִחְיַת בָּשָׂר חַי בַּשְׂאֵת: צָרַעַת נוֹשֶׁנֶת הִוא בְּעוֹר בְּשָׂרוֹ וְטִמְּאוֹ הַכֹּהֵן לֹא יַסְגִּרֶנּוּ כִּי טָמֵא הוּא: וְאִם פָּרוֹחַ תִּפְרַח הַצָּרַעַת בָּעוֹר וְכִסְּתָה הַצָּרַעַת אֵת כָּל עוֹר הַנֶּגַע מֵרֹאשׁוֹ וְעַד רַגְלָיו לְכָל מַרְאֵה עֵינֵי הַכֹּהֵן: וְרָאָה הַכֹּהֵן וְהִנֵּה כִסְּתָה הַצָּרַעַת אֵת כָּל בְּשָׂרוֹ וְטִהַר אֵת הַנֶּגַע כֻּלּוֹ הָפַךְ לָבָן טָהוֹר הוּא:[1]

If the Kohen finds a white blemish on the skin that has turned some hair white, with a patch of discolored flesh in the blemish, it is chronic leprosy on the skin of his body, and the Kohen shall pronounce him tamei; he does not isolate him, for he is tamei. If the eruption spreads out over the skin so that it covers all the skin of the affected person from head to foot, wherever the Kohen can see. If the Kohen sees that the eruption has covered the whole body—he shall pronounce the affected person tahor; he is tahor, for he has turned all white.

The *pesukim* teach us that if one becomes afflicted with *tzaraas* on part of one's body, that person is impure. However, if someone became afflicted with *tzaraas* on their entire body, that person is pure. This is because the punishment fits the crime. A person decided to focus on the 2% negative in another person, and not on the 98% positive. This is why the punishment is *middah k'neged middah*. When one focuses on the negatives in this world, one becomes fully impure and separate from the community. Yet, those who focus on the positive of others, even though they may have conflicting views, are worthy of honor.

---

1   *Vayikra* 13:10–13.

As the Mishnah says:

אֵיזֶהוּ מְכֻבָּד? הַמְכַבֵּד אֶת הַבְּרִיּוֹת.[2]

Who is worthy of honor? One who honors others.

Honor comes to those who honor others. Focusing on the positive of life and recognizing that you are fortunate no matter where you find yourself helps one be grateful for what one has. It will help us appreciate the gift of life.

To Summarize

Life is a gift, so why waste it by being gloomy? Compare yourself to those who are less fortunate, and you will recognize the treasures you wake up with every day. Being grateful for what one has helps one see the sunshine in the rain.

Points to Ponder

- How do I focus on the good that comes my way?
- Do I feel different when focusing on the good over the bad?
- How can I find the good in a seemingly negative situation?

2   *Avos* 4:1.

LESSON 8

Drip Drop

מה היה תחלתו של רבי עקיבא. אמרו בן ארבעים שנה היה ולא שנה כלום.
פעם אחת היה עומד על פי הבאר אמר מי חקק אבן זו אמרו לא המים
שתדיר [נופלים] עליה בכל יום אמרו [לו] עקיבא אי אתה קורא אבנים
שחקו מים. מיד היה רבי עקיבא דן קל וחומר בעצמו מה רך פסל את
הקשה דברי תורה שקשה כברזל על אחת כמה וכמה שיחקקו את לבי
שהוא בשר ודם. מיד חזר ללמוד תורה.‏[1]

*What were the origins of Rabbi Akiva? They say that he was
forty years old and had still not learned anything. Once, he
was standing at the mouth of a well, and he said: "Who carved
a hole in this stone?" They said to him: "It is from the water,
which constantly [falls] on it, day after day." And they said:
"Akiva, don't you know this from the verse, 'Water erodes
stones'?" Rabbi Akiva immediately applied this, all the more
so, to himself. He said: "If something soft can carve something
hard, then all the more so the words of Torah, which are like
steel, can engrave themselves on my heart, which is but flesh
and blood." He immediately went to start studying Torah.*

---

1   *Avos d'Rabi Nosson* 6:2.

42

Chazal teach us the inspirational story of how Rabbi Akiva became the Tanna we know of today. At forty years old, he recognized that if something "as weak" as water can penetrate through something "as hard" as rock, so too, Torah can penetrate one's heart.

This midrash came to mind one day when Ayelet dropped her bottle of milk on the floor. Even though the milk dripped out slowly, after some time, it made a big puddle. The lesson here is that even something small and weak can penetrate a stone—if it is consistent.

וְשַׂמְתֶּם אֶת דְּבָרַי אֵלֶּה עַל לְבַבְכֶם וְעַל נַפְשְׁכֶם וּקְשַׁרְתֶּם אֹתָם לְאוֹת עַל יֶדְכֶם וְהָיוּ לְטוֹטָפֹת בֵּין עֵינֵיכֶם: וְלִמַּדְתֶּם אֹתָם אֶת בְּנֵיכֶם לְדַבֵּר בָּם בְּשִׁבְתְּךָ בְּבֵיתֶךָ וּבְלֶכְתְּךָ בַדֶּרֶךְ וּבְשָׁכְבְּךָ וּבְקוּמֶךָ: וּכְתַבְתָּם עַל מְזוּזוֹת בֵּיתֶךָ וּבִשְׁעָרֶיךָ:[2]

And place these words upon your heart and your soul, bind them as a sign on your hand, and they shall be a symbol between your eyes. And teach them to your children; speak to them when you are at home and when you are on your way; when you lie down and when you arise. And write them on the doorposts of your house and on your gates.

Rashi explains that this is referring to tefillin and *mezuzos*.[3] Why does the *pasuk* say, "And place these words on your heart and on your soul"? It should say to bring the words *into* your heart and *into* your soul! Based on the midrash of Rabbi Akiva, we could learn that if placed on one's heart and soul, the words of Torah will eventually seep through, becoming part of the person.[4]

Another lesson we can learn is that if a person is having a hard time understanding something, they should try reviewing it slowly and let

---

2   *Devarim* 11:18–20.

3   *Devarim* 11:18, s.v. *V'samtem es devarai.*

4   We don't want to force the words of Torah into a person, for they may see it as a burden and become turned away from Hashem. Placing the words of Torah onto one's heart and soul will allow a person to reestablish their relationship between himself and Hashem.

the words penetrate their mind, just like the water penetrated the rock over time. This is why the Mishnah tells us:

כַּךְ הִיא דַּרְכָּהּ שֶׁל תּוֹרָה, פַּת בְּמֶלַח תֹּאכַל, וּמַיִם בִּמְשׂוּרָה תִשְׁתֶּה...⁵

This is the path [to acquire] Torah; you shall eat bread with salt, and drink a small amount of water...

What does it mean to drink a small amount of water? I'd venture to say the Mishnah is teaching us to let the water seep in drop by drop.

The best way to be successful when making a *kabbalah* or working on self-improvement is by taking on something small and building on it. Rabbi Elimelech Biderman relates a story on this topic:

> *Once, on Shivah Asar B'Tamuz, a student saw the Rosh Yeshiva of Toldos Aharon, Rav Binyamin Rabinowitz, zt"l, learning eight hours straight without interruption! When asked how he did it, Rav Binyamin answered, "Do you think that when I was your age, I was studying eight hours straight? I started with a kabbalah that I wouldn't interrupt my learning for five minutes. I kept this kabbalah for several months. Then I added to those five minutes another five minutes. And for several months I didn't interrupt my learning for ten minutes straight. Then I added another five minutes. Now I'm an old man, and those five minutes accumulated, and I'm up to eight hours of learning Torah without interruption."⁶*

Another wonderful story to show the importance of taking one step at a time is of Rabbi Yaacov Yisroel Kanievsky, also known as the Steipler Gaon, who was forced to be a soldier in the Russian army. Although the soldiers tried to make the Steipler Gaon work on Shabbos, he never would. Even if they beat him, the Steipler Gaon wouldn't work on Shabbos because he never wanted to desecrate the holy day. There was a rotation where soldiers would stand guard by the entrance of

---

5   *Avos* 6:5.
6   Rabbi Elimelech Biderman, *Torah Wellsprings, Parashas Shemini.*

the camp. Due to the freezing cold weather in Russia, the guard who was on duty had a special coat. One Shabbos, it was the Steipler Gaon's turn to stand guard. When he came to his position, he noticed that the gentile soldier who stood guard before him had hung the coat on a tree. The Steipler Gaon did not want to violate the Rabbinic prohibition of removing something from a tree on Shabbos, so the Steipler Gaon told himself to give it five minutes before removing the coat from the tree, as this was a case of *pikuach nefesh*. After five minutes, the Steipler Gaon assured himself that he could wait another five minutes, and then another five minutes. Sure enough, each five-minute period accumulated until finally his shift was over. All the Steipler Gaon did was take five minutes at a time. I give this advice to my students when they have long, difficult tests—just take it five minutes at a time.

The key to success in accumulating the little drops into a big puddle, or becoming so powerful that it drills through a stone, is through consistency.

שַׁמַּאי אוֹמֵר, עֲשֵׂה תוֹרָתְךָ קֶבַע...[7]

Shammai says, make your Torah study fixed...

Be consistent in your learning, even if it is for five minutes a day. I've heard a beautiful *p'shat* from my father explaining that *Parashas Nitzavim* is before *Parashas Vayeilech* because one first has to stop, stand still, and reflect on the past in order to move forward. It's no wonder why many people check their rearview mirror before driving!

I would venture to say that another *p'shat* is that in order to move forward, one must first be secure in their ways. Without consistency, there will be no way that the water can penetrate the stone. Only when one is consistent can one move forward in the proper direction and accomplish the unbelievable.

---

7   *Avos* 1:15.

To Summarize

"Winners never quit and quitters never win." Persistence is key to one's success. Even when it is something small, if it is constant, it will become great. Learning one letter at a time with consistence can result in finishing many books. Be stable in your plan, and be consistent with your action.

Points to Ponder

- What is something small that I can take upon myself to strengthen my connection to Hashem?
- Do I appreciate things more when I slow things down?
- Do I realize that slow is better than no?

Teamwork Makes the Dreamwork

Daniel has been very acrobatic from a very young age, and he loves to do flips. This can be a distraction while attempting to get him dressed in the morning. What I did was give him the decision to either put his pants on by himself or that I would put them on for him. He continued to jump and do flips. I quickly caught him while he was upside down and asked if I should put his pants on him while he was upside down. Daniel thought it was hilarious and loved the idea of getting dressed upside down, i.e., in such a silly fashion.

The lesson I took from this instance is to make others feel part of the team and to give them a say in how they want to do things. When a leader makes the rest of the team feel valued and heard, the team will be successful even if the leader isn't around, because everyone knows their place and role. Therefore, they will continue to work in harmony.

One way to include others as part of the team is to compromise. Although Daniel wanted to practice his flips, he had to get dressed. Why not have him flip into his pants or put them on in acrobatic fashion? Compromise is the key to teamwork and success; it is what helps move people forward.

There's a little-known story of the game that the 1992 Dream Team lost. In 1992, the Olympics were played in Barcelona. This was the first year that NBA players were allowed to participate in the Olympic games (before then, only college players were allowed to participate). The Dream Team consisted of the best players in the NBA. The first time the team was together for practice, their coach, Chuck Daly, had them play against a college team. The Dream Team got crushed. "We got killed today," Michael Jordan said after the scrimmage game. "They beat us and they played well. We're so out of sync and so unsure about things that we feel comfortable with in normal situations. We don't have any continuity at all." Jordan's Chicago Bulls teammate Scottie Pippen concurred. "These young kids were killing us," Pippen said in NBA TV's document "The Dream Team," per the New York Times. "We didn't know how to play with each other."[1]

This experience of not working together opened the eyes of the players, as they went on to win the gold medal in the 1992 Olympics. Even though they were the best individual players in the world, without teamwork, they were a terrible team.

The *Nesivos Shalom* explains that the *rasha* mentioned in the Pesach Haggadah is only a *rasha* because he doesn't realize the importance of community.[2] Since the *rasha* excludes himself, he must fight against the *yetzer hara* on his own, and he feels that the challenge is so great that he gives in. We all have a *yetzer hara*, but when we have unity, we share the burden and weight.

The Mishnah warns us, "אַל תִּפְרֹשׁ מִן הַצִּבּוּר—do not separate from the community,"[3] and the Gemara elaborates on this saying:

---

1   "Dream Team 25 years: US Olympic legends 'killed' in little-remembered game," accessed August 09, 2017. See https://bit.ly/32ZkwHZ.

2   S.B. Ginsberg and S.N. Berezovsky, *Gems from the Nesivos Shalom: Chag Ha-Pesach, Sefiras Ha-Omer* (Lakewood, NJ: Israel Bookshop Publications, 2017), pp. 585–86.

3   *Avos* 2:5.

תנו רבנן בזמן שישראל שרויין בצער ופירש אחד מהן באין שני מלאכי
השרת שמלוין לו לאדם ומניחין לו ידיהן על ראשו ואומרים פלוני זה
שפירש מן הצבור אל יראה בנחמת צבור.[4]

*The Rabbanan taught in a Beraisa: when there's a time that
Yisrael is distressed and an individual separates from them,
two malachim who accompany a person place their hands on
his head and say, "This person who separates from the community will not see the comfort of the community."*

What is so wrong if one goes on their own path and follows their
own ways?

Distancing oneself from the community displays a sense of arro-
gance. The action of separating from others is in essence saying that
one doesn't need others.

The only way to fully receive the Torah is, as *Rashi* explains, *"k'ish
echad b'lev echad*—as one man with one heart."[5]

A single snowflake melts in a moment, yet when snowflakes come
together, they can close down a city. It is so important for us as a nation
to stand together.

When Haman approached Achashveirosh to eliminate the Jewish
nation, he used these words:

יֶשְׁנוֹ עַם אֶחָד מְפֻזָּר וּמְפֹרָד בֵּין הָעַמִּים בְּכֹל מְדִינוֹת מַלְכוּתֶךָ.[6]

*There is a nation that is scattered and spread out among the
other nations throughout your kingdom...*

The way we combat Haman's request is by performing the four mitzvos of Purim since each one of those creates a form of unity. We gather
in shul to listen to the *Megillah. Mishlo'ach manos* and *matanos l'evyonim*
create bonds between man and friend.

---

4   *Taanis* 11a.
5   *Shemos* 19:2, s.v. *Vayichan sham Yisrael.*
6   *Esther* 3:8.

אַבַּיֵי בַּר אָבִין וְר׳ חֲנִינָא בַּר אָבִין מַחְלְפֵי סְעוּדָתַיְיהוּ לַהֲדָדֵי.[7]

Abaye bar Avin and Rabbi Chanina bar Avin would exchange their Purim meals with one another.

The Gemara teaches that Abaye bar Avin and Rabbi Chanina bar Avin would take turns hosting their Purim meals.[8] With this, the Gemara teaches that it is better to eat the *mishteh* together with others than alone.[9]

שִׁמְעוֹן הַצַּדִּיק הָיָה מִשְּׁיָרֵי כְנֶסֶת הַגְּדוֹלָה. הוּא הָיָה אוֹמֵר, עַל שְׁלֹשָׁה דְבָרִים הָעוֹלָם עוֹמֵד, עַל הַתּוֹרָה וְעַל הָעֲבוֹדָה וְעַל גְּמִילוּת חֲסָדִים.[10]

Shimon HaTzaddik was from the remainders of the Knesses Hagedolah. He would say, "The world stands on three things: on Torah, on service, and on giving of loving kindness."

One of the three things the world stands on is showing kindness toward others. The way to build a team and become one is through giving to others. The word *ahavah*—love—has the root word *hav*—give. *Ahavah* has the same *gematria* as *echad*—one.[11] The more one loves another, the more one gives. The greater the love we give each other, the more complete we are.

When we daven as a community, our *tefillos* are answered as a community. What one is lacking, the other fills in. On food or drink upon which we make the *berachah* of *Shehakol niheye bi'dvaro*—that all was created with His word—we recite a *berachah* afterward, saying, "*Borei nefashos rabos v'chesronan*—Hashem created living things with abundance and deficiencies." As a unit, we fill in for each other.

Toward the end of davening is a special reading about the *ketores*. The *ketores* consists of eleven different spices, such as cinnamon and

---

7   *Megillah* 7b.
8   *Rashi*, s.v. *Michalfei seudaseihu*: זה אוכל עם זה בפורים של שנה זו ובשניה סועד חברו עמו —One ate with the other on Purim this year, and the following year his friend feasted with him.
9   *Chiddushei Anshei Shem.*
10   *Avos* 1:1.
11   The middle letters of אהבה is הב; אהבה = 13 = אחד.

frankincense. However, there is one spice that has a terrible odor, which is the *chelbenah*. One may wonder why this foul spice is included in the *ketores*, which contains only pleasant spices. The answer is because the spices represent different types of people. The *chelbenah* is included because every Jew is a child of Hashem, even those who may have a "foul odor."

"ואם חיסר אחת מכל סממניה חייב מיתה"—one is liable for death if he misses one of the spices."[12]

If one doesn't include others in their life, it is like a puzzle that is missing pieces; it will never be complete.

On a similar note, the *arba minim* that we shake on Sukkos each represent a different type of person, and yet all have to be held together when performing the mitzvah, or one will not fulfill one's obligation. The way we will merit Mashiach speedily in our days is the way we received the Torah, and that was with unity. Teamwork really does make the dreamwork.

To Summarize

We were all created to play on the same team. We may have different positions, but that is what makes the team. There are many great individuals, but they can't compare to great teams. Shared success is true success, and without unity and teamwork, there will be no shared success.

Points to Ponder

- What is one way I can become more of a team player in my social network/family/work environment, etc.?
- What type of team would I like to be a part of?
- What would my role be and why?

---

12   *Kerisos* 6a.

What's That Smell?

We once had a clogged pipe in our house, and it backed up our plumbing. The bathroom began to smell pretty bad, causing the smell to slowly creep out from the bathroom to the rest of the house. Even after calling the plumber to clean out the pipes, the entire house stunk really badly. We decided to go out for dinner and return later, when hopefully the smell would be a bit more manageable. After dinner, the smell was still unbearable, so we went to sleep at my parent's house. We stopped off at our house to pick up pajamas, and I ran in to get them. When I reached the car, the kids told me that I stunk as well. Right then, I thought of the well-known *mashal* of one who walks into a perfume shop—that even if he doesn't spray any perfume on himself, he'll nonetheless walk out smelling like perfume.

This example teaches us that we must be careful with whom we associate ourselves with. If one associates oneself with bad friends, he will be known as part of the bad group, even if he doesn't do anything wrong. The same is when someone associates oneself with a positive group of people; one will be regarded as part of the group whether or not one participates in those activities.

יוֹסֵי בֶּן יוֹעֶזֶר אִישׁ צְרֵדָה אוֹמֵר, יְהִי בֵיתְךָ בֵית וַעַד לַחֲכָמִים.[1]

Yosi ben Yoezer from Tzereidah says, "Let your house be a meeting place for the wise."

נִתַּאי הָאַרְבֵּלִי אוֹמֵר, הַרְחֵק מִשָּׁכֵן רַע, וְאַל תִּתְחַבֵּר לְרָשָׁע.[2]

Nitai HaArbeli says, "Distance yourself from a bad neighbor, and don't associate with the wicked."

This is why the Mishnah advises to let your home be a meeting place for the wise. Even if one doesn't understand their conversation at first, one can still pick up some of their lingo and manners. This also applies to those who surround themselves with negativity; hence, the Mishnah guides us to distance ourselves from an evil neighbor and to refrain from any association with a wicked person.

When discussing lending and interest between non-Jews, the Gemara asks, "Why did the *Rabbanan* decree that a Jew shouldn't lend or invest with gentiles? Lest the Jew learn from their actions."[3] When Jews are constantly interacting with gentiles, we may be negatively influenced by them.

Influence is a very powerful tool that can be used for both constructive and destructive purposes. The best way to be influenced by positive people is to be around them and associate with them. The more we connect with the Torah, the greater success we will have overcoming the influences of society and the *yetzer hara*.

כך הקב"ה אמר להם לישראל בני בראתי יצר הרע ובראתי לו תורה תבלין ואם אתם עוסקים בתורה אין אתם נמסרים בידו...תנא דבי ר' ישמעאל בני אם פגע בך מנוול זה משכהו לבית המדרש.[4]

Hakadosh Baruch Hu said to B'nei Yisrael, "I created an evil inclination, and I created Torah as its antidote. If you are

---

involved in Torah, you will not be ensnared in his [the yetzer hara's] hand…" It was taught in the school of Rabbi Yishmael: *"My son, if this corrupted one confronts you, drag him to the beis ha'midrash."*

If we feel that the *yetzer hara* is having a negative influence on us, the Gemara instructs that we pull the *yetzer hara* into the *beis midrash*. The power of the *yetzer hara's* influence is so great that we wouldn't be able to combat it alone—we need the antidote of Torah to overcome the power of the *yetzer hara*.

A wonderful example of how one's influence can change the mindsets of others is Reginald Rose's play called *Twelve Angry Men*. The play is about a jury that is almost unanimous of the decision on a homicide trial. Eleven of the twelve jurors are decided on a guilty verdict. One juror began to plant the seed of reasonable doubt, and in the end, he persuades all of the other jurors to change their verdict. Even one individual can have a major influence on others.

אונקלוס בר קלונימוס איגייר שדר קיסר גונדא דרומאי אבתריה משכינהו בקראי איגיור הדר שדר גונדא דרומאי [אחרינא] אבתריה אמר להו לא תימרו ליה ולא מידי כי הוו שקלו ואזלי אמר להו אימא לכו מילתא בעלמא ניפיורא נקט נורא קמי פיפיורא פיפיורא לדוכסא דוכסא להגמונא הגמונא לקומא קומא מי נקט נורא מקמי אינשי אמרי ליה לא אמר להו הקב"ה נקט נורא קמי ישראל דכתיב (שמות יג, כא) וה' הולך לפניהם יומם וגו' איגיור [כולהו] הדר שדר גונדא אחרינא אבתריה אמר להו לא תשתעו מידי בהדיה כי נקטי ליה ואזלי חזא מזוזתא [דמנחא אפתחא] אותיב ידיה עלה ואמר להו מאי האי אמרי ליה אימא לן את אמר להו מנהגו של עולם מלך בשר ודם יושב מבפנים ועבדיו משמרים אותו מבחוץ ואילו הקב"ה עבדיו מבפנים והוא משמרן מבחוץ שנאמר (תהלים קכא, ח) ה' ישמר צאתך ובואך מעתה ועד עולם איגיור תו לא שדר בתריה.⁵

Onkelos bar Klonimus converted to Judaism. The Roman emperor sent a troop of Roman soldiers after him to seize Onkelos and bring him to the emperor. Onkelos drew them

---

toward him with pesukim that he cited and learned with them, and they converted. The emperor then sent another troop of Roman soldiers after him and said to them: "Do not say anything to him so that he cannot convince you with his arguments." The troops followed this instruction and took Onkelos with them.

When they were walking, Onkelos said to the troop of soldiers, "I will say a mere statement to you: A minor official holds a torch before a high official, the high official holds a torch for a duke, a duke for the governor, and the governor for the ruler. Does the ruler hold a torch before the common people?" The soldiers said to Onkelos: "No." Onkelos said to them: "Yet Hakadosh Baruch Hu holds a torch before the Jewish People, as it is written: 'And Hashem went before them by day in a pillar of cloud, to lead them the way, and by night in a pillar of fire, to give them light.'" They all converted. The emperor then sent another troop of soldiers after him to bring Onkelos and said to them, "Do not converse with him at all." The troops followed this instruction and took Onkelos with them. While they grabbed him and were walking out (of his house), Onkelos saw a mezuzah that was placed on the doorway. He placed his hand upon it and said to the soldiers, "What is this?" They said to him, "You tell us." Onkelos said to them, "The standard practice throughout the world is that a king of flesh and blood sits inside his palace, and his servants stand guard, protecting him from the outside; but with regard to Hakadosh Baruch Hu, His servants, the Jewish People, sit inside their homes, and He guards over them from outside, as it is stated, 'Hashem shall guard your going out and your coming in, from now and forever'" (Tehillim 121:8). Upon hearing this, those soldiers also converted to Judaism. After that, the emperor sent no more soldiers after him.

This Gemara demonstrates how one man, Onkelos, the nephew of the Roman Emperor and a convert to Judaism, influenced the wicked

Romans to convert to Judaism and wrote one of the most influential commentaries on the Torah.

לֹא יִפָּטֵר אָדָם מֵחֲבֵרוֹ...אֶלָּא מִתּוֹךְ דְּבַר הֲלָכָה.⁶

Elsewhere, the Gemara teaches that one should only take leave of another with a *d'var halachah*. In this manner, whenever he thinks of his friend, he will think of that halachah. Every individual can have a major influence on another. Make sure it is a positive one.

To Summarize

Influence is a very powerful tool. We can be influenced by others just by associating with them. To be a positive influence, one must connect with a positive source, even if the individual is not yet holding at that level. Over time, one begins to act and speak like those around him if he lets his guard down.

Points to Ponder

- Am I easily influenced by my surroundings?
- How do I react when I am in a situation that jeopardizes my morals?
- Do I try to make others happy and forget about my own happiness?

---

6   *Berachos* 31a.

LESSONS AT THE PARK

Keep Pumping!

One summer day, I was at the park with Daniel. It was a bit crowded then, and all of the swings were taken, so Daniel waited very patiently for a swing. Finally, a swing became available, and Daniel hopped on. He asked if I could push him, to which I courteously obliged!

After a few minutes, Daniel noticed that the boy two swings over was going really high. He pointed it out to me, and I responded, "That boy is pumping; do you know how to pump?" And he began pumping.

At that moment, a powerful life lesson entered my mind (which inspired this book): In life, one must continue to work and "pump" their way to the highest one can be. However, once a person stops pumping, even for a moment, one begins to slow down. It is important for one to continue putting in the effort, even if it doesn't seem like one is attaining new heights.

The Mishnah tells us, "לְפוּם צַעֲרָא אַגְרָא—One is rewarded according to the effort he puts in."[1]

As my Rosh Yeshivah, Rabbi Ahron Kaufman, once explained, "Life is trying to go up on a downward escalator." The moment one feels satisfied with where one is, that's the moment one begins to descend.

---

1   *Avos* 5:26.

אֵיזֶהוּ עָשִׁיר? הַשָּׂמֵחַ בְּחֶלְקוֹ.[2]

Who is rich? He who is happy with his portion.

ויש לומר כי אין ראוי שיהיה מתואר האדם בשם עשיר כאשר יש לו רבוי
ממון אשר הוא באוצר או בתיבתו כי דבר זה אינו שייך אל האדם ואין
העושר מצד עצמו ואין ראוי שיקרא עשיר בשביל זה, רק מי ששמח בחלקו
שכאשר הוא שמח בחלקו והוא עשיר בדעת זהו העשיר שהוא עשיר מצד
עצמו, לא כאשר הוא עשיר ברבוי ממון שהוא בתיבתו שאין זה העושר
באדם מצד עצמו כלל ואין ראוי שיקרא האדם עשיר, וכאשר שמח בחלקו
והוא עשיר בדעת אז הוא עשיר מצד עצמו.[3]

*And there are those who say it is not fitting for a person to be
labeled as a rich man just because he has lots of riches in his
vault or treasure houses. This is [due to the fact] that those
riches are really not intrinsically part of him, so it is not fitting
that he be called wealthy, but rather one who is happy with his
lot [should be labeled wealthy]. For when one is happy with his
lot and rich in knowledge, he is intrinsically wealthy. Unlike
the person who has lots of [external] riches in his vaults, for
this wealth is not part of the person at all, and therefore it is
not fitting to label him "wealthy." When a person is satisfied
with his lot and is rich in knowledge, [only] then is he wealthy
in his own right.*

The *Maharal* explains the Mishnah by saying that the emphasis is on
his portion. The Mishnah doesn't say "he who is happy with what he
has," but rather "his portion," i.e., what one worked for. Those who invest their time, effort, and life truly earn their portion, making it their
own "portion."

The Mishnah says, "If I am not for myself, who will be for me?"[4] One
must put in effort to grow. It is like someone lifting weights; no one

---

2   Ibid. 4:1.

3   *Maharal, Derech Chaim* 4:1.

4   *Avos* 1:14.

can lift them for you to help you become stronger; you must put in the effort and lift them yourself in order to gain strength.

We are judged on our effort in this world:

לֹא עָלֶיךָ הַמְּלָאכָה לִגְמֹר, וְלֹא אַתָּה בֶן חוֹרִין לִבָּטֵל מִמֶּנָּה.⁵

You are not required to complete your work, but you are not free to give up on it.

We are rewarded based on the effort we put into something, not the results of those efforts. The Torah is infinite; there is no way humans can complete such a task. However, we are not free to give up on it. The more effort we put in, the greater the outcome.

The Gemara teaches that the road to success is through effort:

ואמר ר' יצחק אם יאמר לך אדם יגעתי ולא מצאתי אל תאמן לא יגעתי ומצאתי אל תאמן יגעתי ומצאתי תאמן.⁶

Rabbi Yitzchak said, if a person tells you that they worked and did not find success, don't believe them. If a person tells you that they did not work, yet found success, do not believe them. However, if a person tells you that they have worked and found success, believe them.

It is very easy to judge others on their external achievements and awards they display. Although these accomplishments take a great feat, there are so many internal battles others may be going through that we see as minute and insignificant. One who puts in effort to overcome a struggle has achieved something far greater than one who didn't face the challenge at all.

הוּא הָיָה אוֹמֵר: אוֹרֵחַ טוֹב מַהוּ אוֹמֵר? כַּמָּה טְרָחוֹת טָרַח בַּעַל הַבַּיִת בִּשְׁבִילִי...אֲבָל אוֹרֵחַ רַע מַהוּ אוֹמֵר? מַה טּוֹרַח טָרַח בַּעַל הַבַּיִת זֶה?...כָּל טוֹרַח שֶׁטָּרַח בַּעַל הַבַּיִת זֶה, לֹא טָרַח אֶלָּא בִּשְׁבִיל אִשְׁתּוֹ וּבָנָיו.⁷

---

5   Ibid. 2:21.

6   *Megillah* 6b.

7   *Berachos* 58a.

> *Ben Zoma would say, "What does a good guest say? 'Look at how much effort my host has done on my behalf…' However, what does a bad guest say? 'What effort did the host show on my behalf?…All the effort my host has put in was only for his wife and children.'"*

A good guest recognizes the effort put into the meal, as opposed to a bad guest who believes that the food he received was given without any effort. The *Sifsei Chachamim* explains that a good guest focuses on the efforts of the host and not the final product, whereas a bad guest focuses only on the food he took, i.e., the final product.

Winston Churchill once said, "Continuous effort—not strength or intelligence—is the key to unlocking our potential." Effort is the key to success. Only one who keeps pumping will be able to reach the sky.

To Summarize

Putting in the effort is what defines one's character. Effort is something that isn't always seen by others. It is a battle within oneself that can ultimately make one great. Many people give up on their dreams because it takes too much work, but it is the effort—not the outcome—that characterizes a person.

Points to Ponder

- What are the things I put effort into?
- What motivates me to put in the effort?
- How can I put more effort into things I'm not presently so interested in?

Magic Money

As a parent, one "exciting" part of going to the park is the ice cream truck waiting in the parking lot. Upon leaving the park one day, Daniel asked me for some ice cream, which led to the following conversation.

"How are you going to get ice cream, Daniel?"

"With money," he said.

"Where are you going to get the money from?" I continued.

"From our pockets," came the reply.

I asked him if he can show me the money he has in his pockets, which he couldn't seem to find.

From here, I learned two lessons:

- First, my children don't need their own money to buy ice cream as long as I have money in my pockets. My children have such faith in me that I will supply them with what they want. So too, the children of Hashem don't need anything of our own since we rely on our Father in Heaven. For example, when Eliana was learning to walk, she would lean on someone for support. It would be very cruel for the person to walk away, because then Eliana would fall. We can apply the same lesson to our relationship with Our Father; Hashem can't just walk away when we lean on Him. If we fully believe that Hashem will support us, He will.

- Second, sometimes we take things for granted. Just take a look around you and realize that so much had to happen for everything to exist. Things don't just happen; money doesn't just come out of one's pockets.

It is said in the name of Rav Shach that when he would make a *berachah* on an orange, it would strengthen his *emunah*. When Rav Shach saw an orange, he thought of the tiny seed that was planted and then had to rot in order to begin to grow roots. After the roots grew, the stem began to push out of the ground. After time, the tiny seed grew into a tree and started to grow fruit. As the fruit grew, the orange started off green, telling the harvesters that it is not ready to be picked. The leaves grow over the fruit to protect it from the sun. Finally, when it is at the perfect time, the orange has a beautiful color, telling the harvesters that it is ready to be plucked. Once it's plucked and opened, the orange has a white rind protecting the fruit. After peeling the peel and rind, the orange has sections so that the juice and pulp don't squirt out. The amazing creations of nature go on and on, which show how impossible it is not to recognize *hashgachah pratis*—Divine Providence.

Sometimes, we see people walking on the side of highways. I often wonder how that person ended up there. It turns out that everyone has a story—how we got to where we are and where we are going.

Imagine being on a boat, passing by an island, when you see a person on the island without any possessions. The first thing you might wonder is how this person got there. Maybe a fish spat him out onto dry land![1]

Everything in this world has a story and process. Where you are at this exact moment and where you are going is all part of *hashgachah pratis*.

זָכוֹר אֵת אֲשֶׁר עָשָׂה לְךָ עֲמָלֵק בַּדֶּרֶךְ בְּצֵאתְכֶם מִמִּצְרָיִם: אֲשֶׁר קָרְךָ בַּדֶּרֶךְ...[2]

---

1   *Yonah* 2:11.
2   *Devarim* 25:18–19.

Remember what Amalek did to you on your way when you left Mitzrayim. That he happened upon you on your way…

B'nei Yisrael were attacked by Amalek in the desert. The *pasuk* tells us to remember what Amalek did to us when we left *Mitzrayim* and heading to Eretz Yisrael. The *pasuk* uses the phrase, "That he happened upon you on your way." The essence of Amalek is to make one think that things "just" happen—that everything is one big coincidence and there is no greater Source that controls it all.

בָּרוּךְ אַתָּה ה'…שֶׁעָשָׂה לִי כָּל צָרְכִי.

Blessed are You, Hashem…who fulfills all of my needs.

In *Birchos Ha'shachar*, we say the *berachah* of *She'asah li kol tzarki*. We are recognizing that everything comes from Hashem. Those who don't recognize this have no right to complain when they feel Hashem doesn't support them.

אֵיזֶהוּ עָשִׁיר? הַשָּׂמֵחַ בְּחֶלְקוֹ.[3]

Who is rich? He who is happy with his portion.

The reason for this is because a rich person has all he needs. When we recognize that Hashem supports us with all of our needs, we will be truly rich and content. We can rely on Hashem to continue assisting us and always be there to lean on.

To Summarize

Everything in this world has purpose and meaning. Hashem is the one who sees the full picture, and we are part of it. Coincidence is nothing but an illusion. When we realize that Hashem is in control of the world, we will not have so much worry of what will be and how we are going to be supported.

---

3 Ibid. 4:1.

Points to Ponder

- What are some of the small things that make me happy?
- How can I show gratitude to those who give to me?
- How can I make the most of my situation?

LESSON 3

Who's Judging?

שַׁמַּאי אוֹמֵר...וֶהֱוֵי מְקַבֵּל אֶת כָּל הָאָדָם בְּסֵבֶר פָּנִים יָפוֹת.[1]

Shammai says...accept everyone with a cheerful face.

While at the park one summer day, I noticed that Ayelet was smiling at everyone, and this reminded me of the Mishnah that tells us to greet everyone with a pleasant face. I took her out of the stroller and brought her to the playground, where she immediately made a new friend who was two years older. They got along very nicely and were very cute together. This was the first time either of them had seen each other, yet there was beautiful chemistry between them. As the saying goes, "A smile is contagious."

My first thought was, why would they want to play together? They are so different and are at different stages of life. Then I realized that all they see is another person who wants to have fun and play. Ayelet doesn't care if the other child is her age, older or younger; she will get along because they want to have fun. She isn't judging what the other child looks like or what his or her personality is.

---

1   *Avos* 1:15.

The Mishnah teaches:

רַבִּי אוֹמֵר, אַל תִּסְתַּכֵּל בַּקַּנְקַן, אֶלָּא בְמַה שֶׁיֵּשׁ בּוֹ.²

Rebbi says, don't look at the vessel, rather what is in it.

The Western saying for this is "Don't judge a book by its cover." One cannot rely on what a person looks like to see one's knowledge or personality.

I learned a tremendous lesson from this: to stop being judgmental. We all want to be happy and enjoy life. For this to happen, we need to work together and "synergize." As Stephen Covey puts it, "Synergy is the highest activity in all of life…simply defined, it means that the whole is greater than the sum of its parts."³ When we recognize that, yes, we are all different, but we are all connected, it will make the world a better place and bring the *geulah*. Before B'nei Yisrael left *Mitzrayim*, they showed unity through the *Korban Pesach*. The *pasuk* says, "The whole community of *Yisrael* shall offer it."⁴

למה נאמר, לפי שהוא אומר בפסח מצרים "שה לבית אבות," שנמנו עליו למשפחות, יכול אף פסח דורות כן? ת"ל כל עדת ישראל יעשו אתו.⁵

Why is this stated? Since it speaks of the Pesach in Mitzrayim, "a lamb for the house of their fathers," it means that they partake on it with their families. One may think that this is so regarding the Korban Pesach of future generations. Therefore, the Torah states, "All of the congregation of Yisrael may partake in it."

Rashi comments that everyone, not only immediate family members, can join one another to partake in the *Korban Pesach*. The point is that when we have unity, we have freedom.

---

2   Ibid. 4:27.

3   *The 7 Habits*, p. 274.

4   *Shemos* 12:47.

5   Rashi, ibid., s.v. *Kol Adas Yisrael ya'asu o'so.*

We see this again at *Matan Torah*. It is written, "וַיִּחַן שָׁם יִשְׂרָאֵל נֶגֶד הָהָר—and Yisrael camped there opposite the mountain."[6] *Rashi* comments that B'nei Yisrael were "*k'ish echad b'lev echad*—like one person with one heart."[7] Through unity, we received the Torah.

Rabbi Akiva says that a great principle of the Torah is "*V'ahavta l'reiacha kamocha*—love your fellow as you love yourself."[8] Everyone can find good qualities within themselves; however, the struggle comes when trying to find the positive in others.

The word *ahavah*—love—has the same *gematria* as *echad*—one.[9] When we love one another, we become one. When we become one, we love each other. When we stop judging others and looking at the flaws of others, we will be happier and closer to those around us.

The Mishnah teaches:

הַחוֹשֵׂךְ עַצְמוֹ מִן הַדִּין, פּוֹרֵק מִמֶּנּוּ אֵיבָה.[10]

One who stays away from judgment removes themselves from hatred...[11]

Let us put our differences aside and come together for the greater picture—to serve Hashem as one person with one heart.

---

6 *Shemos* 19:2.

7 *Rashi*, ibid., s.v. *Vayichan sham Yisrael*.

8 *Vayikra* 19:18, s.v., *V'ahavta l'reiacha kamocha*.

9 אהבה = 13 = אחד.

10 *Avos* 4:7.

11 There are times when it's appropriate to judge, as we see all over *Torah She'bichsav* and *Torah She'baal Peh*, such as "שֹׁפְטִים וְשֹׁטְרִים תִּתֶּן לְךָ—Appoint judges" (*Devarim* 16:18), "שִׁפְטוּ יָתוֹם—Judge the orphan" (*Yeshayahu* 1:17), and "וֶהֱוֵי דָן אֶת כָּל הָאָדָם לְכַף זְכוּת—Judge every person on the side of merit" (*Avos* 1:6). However, we must understand that there are times to judge and times to refrain from judgment. Most of the cases that the Torah brings about judging are in reference to one whose occupation is as a legal judge. There are times when a regular person must judge as well. As the Mishnah (*Avos* 1:7) guides us, "הַרְחֵק מִשָּׁכֵן רָע—Distance oneself from a bad neighbor." The only way to know if one has a bad neighbor is to judge. This is why the Torah guides us on how to judge, such as "Judge every person on the side of merit." The lesson of this story is that if we focus more on the common goal and less on the judging of one another, we will be much happier people. Of course, this story happened with parent supervision. Children, especially young, should be supervised at all times when playing and meeting new people. In general, children should be cautious when making new friends.

To Summarize

How one judges others reflects how they see themselves. One who judges based on appearance can miss out on many opportunities. When we love others the way we love ourselves, we tend to judge them more favorably. With peace and love, we will have unity.

Points to Ponder

- When I judge someone negatively, am I just seeing one of my flaws in them?
- How many potential friends did I lose because of judging others?
- Did I really gain by judging others?

Not Afraid to Cry

Taking all of your children to the park is not as easy as one may think, especially when they are at very different stages of their growth. On one such occasion, Daniel wanted to play in the sprinklers, but Ayelet was too little. I told Daniel that he could go play in the sprinklers and that I would be around with Ayelet, as I was able to watch him from where we were standing. A short while later, Daniel came out of the sprinklers and began looking for me. He was calling my name, "Daddy, Daddy!" yet he couldn't see me. I called back, "Daniel, we're over here!" but he still didn't hear me. He began to cry, so I picked up Ayelet and ran over to comfort him and show him that I was right there.

When a child is lost and can't find their parents, when they are sad or hurt, they don't care to let it all out and shed a few tears. They aren't super-conscious of where they are or who's there and watching, even if it is their best friend. They aren't worried what people are going to say or how they are going to be perceived. The lesson I learned is that what other people think of you is none of your business. If you do what you feel is the proper thing to do at that time, don't worry what others will say.

אף על פי שהתשובה והצעקה יפה לעולם בעשרה הימים שבין ראש השנה ויום הכפורים היא יפה ביותר ומתקבלת היא מיד.[1]

---

1   *Rambam, Mishneh Torah, Hilchos Teshuvah* 2:6.

Even though it is always beneficial to cry out and repent, in the ten days between Rosh Hashanah and Yom Kippur, it is exceedingly better, and the supplication is immediately accepted.

The *Rambam* teaches us that it is always beneficial to cry out to Hashem. Hashem may be more accepting during different times of the year, but the gates of tears are always open.

קוֹל בְּרָמָה נִשְׁמָע נְהִי בְּכִי תַמְרוּרִים רָחֵל מְבַכָּה עַל בָּנֶיהָ.[2]

A cry is heard in Ramah, wailing, bitter weeping—Rachel weeping for her children.

וּמָרְדֳּכַי יָדַע אֶת כָּל אֲשֶׁר נַעֲשָׂה וַיִּקְרַע מָרְדֳּכַי אֶת בְּגָדָיו וַיִּלְבַּשׁ שַׂק וָאֵפֶר וַיֵּצֵא בְּתוֹךְ הָעִיר וַיִּזְעַק זְעָקָה גְדֹלָה וּמָרָה.[3]

When Mordechai learned all that had happened, Mordechai tore his clothes and put on sackcloth and ashes. He went through the city, crying out loudly and bitterly.

וְכֵן יַעֲשֶׂה שָׁנָה בְשָׁנָה מִדֵּי עֲלֹתָהּ בְּבֵית ה׳ כֵּן תַּכְעִסֶנָּה וַתִּבְכֶּה וְלֹא תֹאכַל: וַיֹּאמֶר לָהּ אֶלְקָנָה אִישָׁהּ חַנָּה לָמֶה תִבְכִּי וְלָמֶה לֹא תֹאכְלִי וְלָמֶה יֵרַע לְבָבֵךְ הֲלוֹא אָנֹכִי טוֹב לָךְ מֵעֲשָׂרָה בָּנִים: וַתָּקָם חַנָּה אַחֲרֵי אָכְלָה בְשִׁלֹה וְאַחֲרֵי שָׁתֹה וְעֵלִי הַכֹּהֵן יֹשֵׁב עַל הַכִּסֵּא עַל מְזוּזַת הֵיכַל ה׳: וְהִיא מָרַת נָפֶשׁ וַתִּתְפַּלֵּל עַל ה׳ וּבָכֹה תִבְכֶּה.[4]

This happened year after year: Every time she went up to the House of the Hashem, the other would taunt her so that she cried and would not eat. Her husband Elkanah said to her, "Chanah, why are you crying and why aren't you eating? Why are you so sad? Am I not more devoted to you than ten sons?" After they had eaten and drunk at Shiloh, Chanah rose. The Kohen, Eli, was sitting on the seat near the doorpost of the

---

2   *Yirmiyahu* 31:15.

3   *Esther* 4:1.

4   *Shmuel I* 1:7, 10.

Heichal of Hashem. In her bitterness, she prayed to Hashem, weeping all the while.

וַיִּשְׁמַע אֱלֹקִים אֶת קוֹל הַנַּעַר וַיִּקְרָא מַלְאַךְ אֱלֹקִים אֶל הָגָר מִן הַשָּׁמַיִם וַיֹּאמֶר לָהּ מַה לָּךְ הָגָר אַל תִּירְאִי כִּי שָׁמַע אֱלֹקִים אֶל קוֹל הַנַּעַר בַּאֲשֶׁר הוּא שָׁם.[5]

Hashem heard the cry of the lad, and an angel of Hashem called to Hagar from heaven and said to her, "What troubles you, Hagar? Fear not, for Hashem has heeded the cry of the lad where he is."

כִּשְׁמֹעַ עֵשָׂו אֶת דִּבְרֵי אָבִיו וַיִּצְעַק צְעָקָה גְּדֹלָה וּמָרָה עַד מְאֹד וַיֹּאמֶר לְאָבִיו בָּרֲכֵנִי גַם אָנִי אָבִי.[6]

When Eisav heard his father's words, he burst into a great and bitter sobbing, and said to his father, "Bless me, too, Father!"

וַיִּתְפַּלֵּל אֵלָיו וַיֵּעָתֶר לוֹ וַיִּשְׁמַע תְּחִנָּתוֹ וַיְשִׁיבֵהוּ יְרוּשָׁלַם לְמַלְכוּתוֹ וַיֵּדַע מְנַשֶּׁה כִּי ה' הוּא הָאֱלֹקִים.[7]

He prayed to Him, and He granted his prayer, heard his plea, and returned him to Yerushalayim to his kingdom. Then Menasheh knew that Hashem alone was God.

Throughout *Tanach*, we find people crying out to Hashem, such as Rachel Imeinu, Mordechai HaTzaddik, and Chanah, the mother of Shmuel HaNavi. Even those who were *rasha'im*, such as Yishmael, Eisav, and Menasheh cried out for Hashem's mercy. In the Haggadah, we recall what happened in *Mitzrayim*, as the *pasuk* says, "וַנִּצְעַק אֶל ה'—and they cried out to Hashem."[8]

---

5   *Bereishis* 21:17.

6   Ibid. 27:34.

7   *Divrei Hayamim II* 33:13.

8   *Devarim* 26:7.

The Gemara teaches us that the gates of tears are never locked.[9] It says in *Tehillim*:

שִׁמְעָה תְפִלָּתִי ה' וְשַׁוְעָתִי הַאֲזִינָה אֶל דִּמְעָתִי אַל תֶּחֱרָשׁ.[10]

Hear my prayer, Hashem; listen to my cry; do not disregard my tears.

Each time someone cried out to Hashem, their *tefillos* were answered. Even nowadays, it is a great *zechus* to go to the *kever* of Rachel Imeinu because she continuously cries out for *Klal Yisrael*. There are many stories of people who *daven* there and whose *tefillos* are answered. Whether for a *shiduch*, health, *shalom bayis*, or children, Rachel Imeinu is crying for us. We see in *Megillas Esther* that the salvation only began after Mordechai and the Jewish nation began crying out to Hashem.

וַיַּעַן עֵלִי וַיֹּאמֶר לְכִי לְשָׁלוֹם וֵאלֹקֵי יִשְׂרָאֵל יִתֵּן אֶת שֵׁלָתֵךְ אֲשֶׁר שָׁאַלְתְּ מֵעִמּוֹ...וַיְהִי לִתְקֻפוֹת הַיָּמִים וַתַּהַר חַנָּה וַתֵּלֶד בֵּן וַתִּקְרָא אֶת שְׁמוֹ שְׁמוּאֵל כִּי מֵה' שְׁאִלְתִּיו.[11]

Eli answered, "Then go in peace, and may the God of Yisrael grant you what you have asked of Him."...Chanah conceived, and at the turn of the year bore a son. She named him Shmuel, meaning, "I asked Hashem for him."

Shortly after Chanah davened and cried for a child, Eli HaKohen blessed her that she would be granted whatever she asked for. Sure enough, Chanah, a barren woman, conceived and gave birth to a son. One doesn't need to be on the spiritual level of Rachel Imeinu or Chanah to have their cries answered, as we see that those who were wicked also had their cries answered.

וַיִּכְלוּ הַמַּיִם מִן הַחֵמֶת וַתַּשְׁלֵךְ אֶת הַיֶּלֶד תַּחַת אַחַד הַשִּׂיחִם: וַתֵּלֶךְ וַתֵּשֶׁב לָהּ מִנֶּגֶד הַרְחֵק כִּמְטַחֲוֵי קֶשֶׁת כִּי אָמְרָה אַל אֶרְאֶה בְּמוֹת הַיָּלֶד וַתֵּשֶׁב מִנֶּגֶד

---

9   *Bava Metzia* 59a.
10   *Tehillim* 39:13.
11   *Shmuel I* 1:17–20.

וַתִּשָּׂא אֶת קֹלָהּ וַתֵּבְךְּ: וַיִּשְׁמַע אֱלֹקִים אֶת קוֹל הַנַּעַר וַיִּקְרָא מַלְאַךְ אֱלֹקִים אֶל הָגָר מִן הַשָּׁמַיִם וַיֹּאמֶר לָהּ מַה לָּךְ הָגָר אַל תִּירְאִי כִּי שָׁמַע אֱלֹקִים אֶל קוֹל הַנַּעַר בַּאֲשֶׁר הוּא שָׁם: קוּמִי שְׂאִי אֶת הַנַּעַר וְהַחֲזִיקִי אֶת יָדֵךְ בּוֹ כִּי לְגוֹי גָּדוֹל אֲשִׂימֶנּוּ.[12]

When the water was gone from the canister, she left the child under one of the bushes, and she went and sat down at a distance, two bowshots away; for she thought, "Let me not look on as the child dies." And sitting from afar, she burst into tears.

God heard the cry of the boy, and an angel of Hashem called to Hagar from heaven and said to her, "What troubles you, Hagar? Fear not, for God has heeded the cry of the boy where he is. Come, lift up the boy and hold him by the hand, for I will make a great nation of him."

After Yishmael was sent out of the house of Avraham and Sarah, he became dehydrated and couldn't move. His mother, Hagar, left him to die. Yet Hashem heard his cry; he was saved and was promised that he would become a great nation.

וַיַּעַן יִצְחָק וַיֹּאמֶר לְעֵשָׂו הֵן גְּבִיר שַׂמְתִּיו לָךְ וְאֶת כָּל אֶחָיו נָתַתִּי לוֹ לַעֲבָדִים וְדָגָן וְתִירֹשׁ סְמַכְתִּיו וּלְכָה אֵפוֹא מָה אֶעֱשֶׂה בְּנִי: וַיֹּאמֶר עֵשָׂו אֶל אָבִיו הַבְרָכָה אַחַת הִוא לְךָ אָבִי בָּרֲכֵנִי גַם אָנִי אָבִי וַיִּשָּׂא עֵשָׂו קֹלוֹ וַיֵּבְךְּ: וַיַּעַן יִצְחָק אָבִיו וַיֹּאמֶר אֵלָיו הִנֵּה מִשְׁמַנֵּי הָאָרֶץ יִהְיֶה מוֹשָׁבֶךָ וּמִטַּל הַשָּׁמַיִם מֵעָל.[13]

Yitzchak answered, saying to Eisav, "But I have made him master over you: I have given him all his brothers for servants and sustained him with grain and wine. What, then, can I still do for you, my son?" And Eisav said to his father, "Have you but one blessing, Father? Bless me, too, Father!" And Eisav wept aloud. And his father Yitzchak answered, saying to him, "See, your abode shall enjoy the fat of the earth and the dew of heaven above."

---

12   *Bereishis* 21:15–18.

13   Ibid. 27:37–39.

When Yitzchak gave his children *berachos*, Yaakov received the *berachah* that Yitzchak thought would go to Eisav. When Eisav asked for a *berachah*, Yitzchak told him that he doesn't have any more *berachos* to give. Eisav begged and cried for just one *berachah*, and only then was Yitzchak able to give him a *berachah*.

וַיָּשָׁב וַיִּבֶן אֶת הַבָּמוֹת אֲשֶׁר נִתַּץ יְחִזְקִיָּהוּ אָבִיו וַיָּקֶם מִזְבְּחוֹת לַבְּעָלִים וַיַּעַשׂ אֲשֵׁרוֹת וַיִּשְׁתַּחוּ לְכָל צְבָא הַשָּׁמַיִם וַיַּעֲבֹד אֹתָם...וַיִּתְפַּלֵּל אֵלָיו וַיֵּעָתֶר לוֹ וַיִּשְׁמַע תְּחִנָּתוֹ וַיְשִׁיבֵהוּ יְרוּשָׁלַם לְמַלְכוּתוֹ וַיֵּדַע מְנַשֶּׁה כִּי ה' הוּא הָאֱלֹקִים.[14]

He rebuilt the altars that his father Chizkiyahu had demolished; he erected altars for the Baals and made sacred posts. He bowed down to all the host of heaven and worshiped them...He prayed to Him, and He granted his prayer, heard his plea, and returned him to Yerushalayim to his kingdom. Then Menasheh knew that Hashem alone was God.

Menasheh the king served every idol in the book, but when he was captured by the king of Ashur, he cried to Hashem and was returned to his throne in Yerushalayim.

Sometimes, we cry out to Hashem, and our cries are not answered right away. We may feel that our cries don't have any influence or power, but as it says in *Tehillim*: "נֹדִי סָפַרְתָּה אָתָּה שִׂימָה דִמְעָתִי בְנֹאדֶךָ הֲלֹא בְּסִפְרָתֶךָ—You keep count of my wanderings; put my tears into Your flask, into Your record."[15]

Hashem has a flask that he saves our tears in and keeps them for a time that we will truly need them. Remember that crying is not a sign of weakness; rather, it shows that one has heart.

To Summarize

Tears have power that one can only dream of. Tears can open any gate and deliver any message. Throughout *Tanach*, we see people, good and evil, cry their hearts out and have their requests answered. One

---

14   *Divrei Hayamim II* 33:3, 13.
15   *Tehillim* 56:9.

shouldn't feel embarrassed or ashamed to cry out to Hashem. These tears are what Hashem treasures.

Points to Ponder

- Do I hold back my tears? If so, why?
- Why do I cry?
- How do I feel after crying?

One Fish, Two Fish

O ne summer, I took Daniel fishing in one of the local parks. As we
approached the water, he asked me, "Daddy, where are all the
fishies? I cannot see them." I explained to him that they were
underwater, which is why we cannot see them. I immediately thought
of the paragraph we say every night after *Shema*. In the paragraph of
Hamalach Hagoel, the *berachah* that Yaakov Avinu gave to his grandchildren, Menasheh and Ephraim, we say the words, "וְיִדְגּוּ לָרֹב בְּקֶרֶב הָאָרֶץ—
and may they multiply abundantly like fish, in the midst of the land."[1]
Why did Yaakov Avinu choose fish as an example of multiplying in the
midst of the land? I would think that an animal that lives on the land,
such as bunny rabbits, would be more suitable.

כַּדָּגִים הַלָּלוּ שֶׁפָּרִים וְרָבִים וְאֵין עַיִן הָרַע שׁוֹלֶטֶת בָּהֶם.

*Like fish, which are fruitful and multiply, and which the evil
eye cannot affect.*

רבי יוסי ברבי חנינא אמר מהכא: "וידגו לרב בקרב הארץ," מה דגים שבים
מים מכסין עליהם ואין עין הרע שולטת בהם.[2]

---

1   *Bereishis* 48:16.
2   *Berachos* 20a; *Bereishis* ibid., *Rashi* s.v. *Veyidgu*, and many other places.

Rabbi Yosi bar Rabbi Chanina said from here: "And may they multiply in the midst of the earth," just as the fish in the sea—water covers them and the evil eye has no dominion over them.

However, Chazal explain that Yaakov Avinu was blessing his grandchildren, saying, just as the sea covers the fish so that *ayin hara* doesn't affect them, you will be impervious to the evil eye.

We can learn a valuable lesson from this: not to be showy or flashy with our possessions. There are so many unnecessary *machlokos* that come from others showing off their possessions. As a consequence of showing off one's possessions, others may look at them negatively, which brings an *ayin hara* on oneself. Just like the Mishnah warns:

רַבִּי אֶלְעָזָר הַקַּפָּר אוֹמֵר, הַקִּנְאָה וְהַתַּאֲוָה וְהַכָּבוֹד מוֹצִיאִין אֶת הָאָדָם מִן הָעוֹלָם.[3]

Rabbi Elazar HaKapar says, jealousy, desires, and honor removes one from this world.

When one runs after these things, one brings *ayin hara* on oneself.

I have a rule in all of my classes. Students know that there are two things we don't discuss with others: grades and paychecks. The reason for this is because there is no positive outcome from sharing one's grades with others.[4] It only causes jealousy and resentment. That will bring *ayin hara* to someone.

ודברים האלו כלן כלן דברי שקר וכזב הן והם שהטעו בהן עובדי כוכבים הקדמונים לגויי הארצות כדי שינהגו אחריהן. ואין ראוי לישראל שהם חכמים מחכמים להמשך בהבלים אלו ולא להעלות על לב שיש תועלת בהן...כל המאמין בדברים האלו וכיוצא בהן ומחשב בלבו שהן אמת ודבר חכמה אבל התורה אסרתן אינן אלא מן הסכלים ומחסרי הדעת.[5]

---

3   *Avos* 4:21.

4   Even if one feels good that they did the best in their class, causing them to feel good and confident, it usually comes at the expense of others who didn't perform as well. This type of feeling isn't real positivity.

5   *Rambam, Mishneh Torah, Hilchos Avodah Zarah* 11:16.

All of these things are false and phony, and it was with such
that the ancient idolaters misled the peoples of many lands
so that they would be following them. And it is unbecoming
to Israel who are exceedingly wise to be attracted by these
absurdities, nor to even imagine that they are of any conse-
quence...Whoever believes in these matters, and their like, and
suppose that there is wisdom and truth in them, save that the
Torah disallowed them, such are none other than among the
foolish and ignorant.

People believe *segulos* prevent *ayin hara* from harming them. According to the *Rambam*, believing that a *segulah* has powers of its own is tantamount to believing in an idol. This would not be the case, though, were one to believe that the *segulah* is merely a conduit for one to be reminded of Hashem's dominion in said area.

האי מאן דעייל למתא ודחיל מעינא בישא, לנקוט זקפא דידא דימיניה
בידא דשמאליה וזקפא דידא דשמאליה בידא דימיניה, ולימא הכי: אנא
פלוני בר פלוני מזרעא דיוסף קאתינא, דלא שלטא ביה עינא בישא,
שנאמר: "בן פרת יוסף בן פרת עלי עין וגו'", אל תקרי "עלי עין", אלא
"עולי עין".[6]

One who enters a city and fears the evil eye should hold the
thumb of his right hand in his left hand and the thumb of his
left hand in his right hand and recite the following: "I, so-
and-so son of so-and-so, come from the descendants of Yosef,
over whom the evil eye has no control, as it is stated: 'Yosef is
a fruitful vine, a fruitful vine by a fountain; its branches run
over the wall.'" Do not read it as alei ayin; rather, read it as olei
ayin, who rise above the eye [and the evil eye has no dominion
over him].

The Gemara discusses remedies for one who fears *ayin hara*; however, part of the remedy is quoting a *pasuk*. When one quotes the *pasuk*, they

---

6   *Berachos* 55b.

are connecting themselves to the Torah. *Segulos* are real and can benefit a person, as they are discussed throughout the *Torah Shebichsav* and *Torah She'baal Peh*. However, this is as long as one remembers that the *segulah* is merely a reminder that Hashem is in control.

והיה כאשר ירים משה ידו וגבר ישראל וג' וכי ידיו של משה עושות
מלחמה או שוברות מלחמה אלא לומר לך כל זמן שהיו ישראל מסתכלין
כלפי מעלה ומשעבדין את לבם לאביהם שבשמים היו מתגברים ואם לאו
היו נופלים.⁷

"And it came to pass, when Moses held up his hand, Israel prevailed, etc." Did the hands of Moshe wage war or break to wage war? Rather, this teaches that as long as Yisrael would look upward and subject their hearts to their Father in heaven, they prevailed, and if not they fell.

During the war with Amalek, when Moshe's arms were raised, B'nei Yisrael prevailed, and when Moshe's arms were lowered, Amalek prevailed. The Mishnah asks, "Was it really the hands of Moshe that caused B'nei Yisrael to prevail or fall? The Mishnah answers that it was when B'nei Yisrael would look up and turn their eyes and hearts to their Father in heaven that they would prevail.

כיוצא בדבר אתה אומר עשה לך שרף ושים אותו על נס והיה כל הנשוך
וראה אותו וחי וכי נחש ממית או נחש מחיה אלא בזמן שישראל מסתכלין
כלפי מעלה ומשעבדין את לבם לאביהם שבשמים היו מתרפאין ואם לאו
היו נימוקים.

Similarly, "Make for yourself a fiery serpent and mount it on a pole. And if anyone who is bitten shall look at it, he shall live." Did the serpent kill or did the serpent keep alive? Rather, when Yisrael would look upward and subject their hearts to their Father in heaven, they were healed, and if not their [flesh] would melt away.

<hr>

7   *Rosh Hashanah* 3:8.

The Mishnah continues this topic and discusses when B'nei Yisrael were in the desert and were plagued with serpents biting them. They recognized their mistakes and wanted to do *teshuvah*. Hashem told Moshe to make a copper serpent and put it on a pole, and whoever would gaze at the serpent would be healed. The Mishnah asks, "Was it really the serpent who healed?" Did merely gazing at a copper serpent take away any pain or negative feeling, giving life? The Mishnah answers, "Rather, when B'nei Yisrael would turn their eyes and hearts toward their Father in heaven, they were saved.

We see later on in history that Chizkiyahu HaMelech destroyed this copper snake that Moshe had made and also the *Sefer Refuos*—Book of Remedies. *Rashi* commentates that people were mistaken by going after it.[8] This means that Jews began bringing offerings to the snake and had used the *Sefer Refuos* as a remedy of healing while forsaking davening to Hashem for healing.

אמר אביי השתא דאמרת סימנא מילתא היא יהא רגיל איניש למיכל ריש
שתא קרא ורוביא כרתי סילקא ותמרי.[9]

Abaye said: Now that you have said that a sign is a substantial matter, a person should be accustomed to eat, at the start of the year, gourd, fenugreek, leeks, beets, and dates.

The Gemara discusses certain omens or *simanim* to eat on Rosh Hashanah.

One is not obligated to actually eat any of the *simanim*; however, they should still say the *Yehi Ratzon*. The point is the prayer, not the food:

- If one eats a jar of honey, it does not guarantee one a sweet year.
- Holding the Torah for the third or sixth *hakafah* on Simchas Torah does not guarantee *parnasah*.

One must remember that these *simanim* and *segulos* act as a reminder to *daven* to Hashem.

---

8   *Pesachim* 56a.
9   *Krisus* 6a.

We should also remember the paragraph we say before *Hamalach Hagoel* when going to bed, namely, the *parshah* of *V'ahavta*, in which we say that we should love Hashem with all of our heart, soul, and possessions.[10] When we have this love toward Hashem, we will recognize that everything comes from Hashem and that He gives every being their own special package. With this in mind, there is no reason to show off your belongings or to be jealous of what others have.

וכנוני ימא יסגון בגו בני אנשא על ארעא.[11]

And the fish of the sea flourish among the people of the land.

(נ)וַיְהִי בִּנְסֹעַ הָאָרֹן וַיֹּאמֶר מֹשֶׁה קוּמָה ה' וְיָפֻצוּ אֹיְבֶיךָ וְיָנֻסוּ מְשַׂנְאֶיךָ מִפָּנֶיךָ: וּבְנֻחֹה יֹאמַר שׁוּבָה ה' רִבְבוֹת אַלְפֵי יִשְׂרָאֵל. (נ)[12]

When the Ark would travel, Moshe would say: "Arise Hashem! Let Your enemies be scattered, and may Your foes flee before You!" And when it rested, he would say: "Return, Hashem, to Yisrael's myriads of thousands!"

ואין מים אלא תורה.[13]

And [the reference to] water [refers] only to Torah.

In the *pasuk* of *Hamalach Hagoel*, *Targum Onkelos* translates the word "*v'yidgu*" as "*nunim*," fish in Aramaic. In *Parashas Behaaloscha*, there are two letter *nuns* that act as parentheses around the *parashah* of "*va'yehi binsoa ha'aron*." This teaches that just as fish (*nunim*) are protected from *ayin hara* when they are in water, so too, when one is immersed in Torah, which is compared to water, one will be protected from *ayin hara*.

---

10   *Devarim* 6:5.
11   *Targum Onkelos, Bereishis* 48:16.
12   *Bamidbar* 10:35–36.
13   *Bava Kama* 17a.

To Summarize

Modesty is what prevents one from *ayin hara*. Advertising our possessions to the public only brings animosity toward others. Fish are covered by the water, and that is why they are so numerous. So too, we will be plentiful and have much blessing when we act modestly.

Points to Ponder

- How can I have nice things but protect myself from *ayin hara*?
- How can I be happy for my friends when they get something new instead of wishing I had their fortune?
- How can I use what I have to become closer to Hashem?

The Right Bait

Fishing gives you time to relax, reflect, and think about life. However, there are many valuable life lessons we can learn from fish and fishing itself. Every time I walk into a bait and tackle shop, I am amazed by the variety of bait, lures, and tackle there are.

Similarly, when it comes to capturing an audience's attention or when teaching a class, people use the term "hooking them in." It sounds simple enough; all you have to do is get the audience's attention, right? That is part of it; however, just getting their attention for the moment doesn't do the job.

Ask a parent who is watching multiple children at once; each child needs to show their mother how they hop, skip, and jump, but the mother can only focus on one at a time. Besides for hooking the audience in, the teacher or speaker has to maintain their attention throughout their class, lecture, or speech. This is where the right bait comes in. Bait may get the attention of a fish for a moment, but if it doesn't like what it sees, the fisherman will lose the attention of the fish.

The same is true when it comes to an audience. Getting the attention is the easy part, but hooking them in comes down to the right bait, as each person may need a different bait. It is important to know what type of "bait" one will hook onto. Only then will the teacher or speaker be able to have undivided attention throughout the entire class or lecture.

The first Jewish child to leave the path of Torah was Eisav.[1] Many *gedolim* discuss this topic and begin with the *pasuk* from *Mishlei*:

חֲנֹךְ לַנַּעַר עַל פִּי דַרְכּוֹ גַּם כִּי יַזְקִין לֹא יָסוּר מִמֶּנָּה.[2]

Educate a child according to his way, and he will not stray even in old age.

"חנוך לנער על פי דרכו"—דרכו הוא. ובזה דורש הפסוק חינוך אינדבידואלי בהחלט, התכלית של חיי תורה ומצוות היא כללית, אבל הדרכים המובילות אל הרמה הטהורה של קיום התורה והמצוות, מתחלפות לפי תכונותיו וכשרונותיו של החניך, לפי נטיותיו וכוחותיו השכליים והנפשיים, על כן לא כל שיטה מתאימה לכל חניך וחניך.[3]

"Educate the child according to his way"—his way. With these words, the pasuk is demanding definite individual education. The purpose, [goal,] of a life of Torah and mitzvos is general, but the paths leading to the pure level of fulfillment of Torah and mitzvos vary according to the capabilities and traits of the individual pupil, according to his inclinations and his intellectual and emotional strengths. Therefore, not every method is suitable to each and every pupil.

Rav Shimshon Raphael Hirsch explains this *pasuk* by saying that the way for a child to reach great heights is if the child is educated according to their uniqueness and individuality, i.e., according to the child's physical and mental strength.

השיטה האחידה בחינוך ובהוראה, שהשתמשו בה לגבי שני האחים, מבלי להתחשב בהבדלים שבכשרונותיהם ובתכונותיהם, גרמה לאותו ניגוד מוחלט שהיה קיים אצל שני החניכים בדרכי חייהם כאשר גדלו והיו לאנשים. אילו הושם לב בילדותם להבדלי תכונותיהם וכשרונותיהם, אפשר היה לחנך את שניהם אף כי היו נשארים שונים זה מזה—להיות

---

1   See the *Masok Midvash, Zohar, Parashas Va'era* 32a and *Sarei Me'os, Manhig* 6 for why Yishmael wasn't considered a Jew.

2   *Mishlei* 22:6.

3   Rav Shimshon Raphael Hirsch, *Yesodos Hachinuch* 53.

ראויים שיקבלו על עצמם את ברית אברהם וכו', וכך גרם חינוכו הבלתי
מותאם לאופיו, שהזניח עשיו את תפקידה של משפחת אברהם. שכן מילוי
התפקיד נתגלה לפני עשיו הילד רק באופן חד צדדי, בלימוד ספרים ובקיום
מצוות ביתיות, על כן אמר עשיו לנפשו, כי כשם שאין בו נטייה לצורה זו
של התקרבות לתכליתו של אברהם, כך אין לו בכלל אפשרות להגיע
לדרגה אנושית נעלה זו, לכן ציפה עשיו הילד בכליון עינים לרגע שבו יוכל
לפרוק את עולו של בית המדרש מעל צווארו, להתפרץ החוצה, אל חיי
החופש ביער ובשדה, ולנתק עצמו מכל קשר עם בית אברהם ותורתו,
אשר נועדה לבעלי תכונות ונטיות אחרות, שלא היו לו.[4]

*The identical approach used with the two brothers in their
education and rearing, without taking into consideration
the differences in their abilities and personalities, caused the
definitive opposing lifestyles of the two as they grew up and
became adults. Had attention been paid during their childhood
to the differences in their personalities and abilities, it would
have been possible to educate both of them, even though they
would have remained different from one another, to be fitting
of accepting upon themselves the covenant of Avraham, etc.
Thus, the education that was not fitting to his personality was
the cause for Eisav to forsake the heritage of Avraham's family.
The fulfilling of the heritage [tradition] appeared to Eisav,
the child, as one-sided; [that of] studying [the holy] books and
fulfilling the duties of domestic life. Therefore, Eisav felt that
just as he has no inclination to this form of approach to the
purposeful [and meaningful] way of Avraham, he has no ability to reach that lofty human level [of moral self-refinement].
Eisav the child yearned for the moment that he would be free
to remove the [spiritual] yoke of the beis midrash from upon his
neck, to break free to the freedom of [the hunter's life in] the
forest and field. [He yearned] to break [for all time] his bond
with Avraham's covenant and Torah, [which he thought] were*

---

4   Ibid., 72.

meant for people with different inclinations and personalities than his.

Rav Hirsch explains further that an educator or parent cannot look at all of their children the same; this was the flaw in Eisav's education. Yaakov and Eisav grew up in the same home, went to the same yeshiva, and even had the same educators. They were given the same bait. It worked for Yaakov, but not for Eisav. Had Eisav been taught according to *his* way, he could have potentially been one of the Avos. If each child's education focused on their individualities, every child can be successful.

הוּא הָיָה אוֹמֵר, בֶּן חָמֵשׁ שָׁנִים לַמִּקְרָא, בֶּן עֶשֶׂר לַמִּשְׁנָה, בֶּן שְׁלֹשׁ עֶשְׂרֵה לַמִּצְוֹת, בֶּן חֲמֵשׁ עֶשְׂרֵה לַתַּלְמוּד...[5]

He would say: At five years of age, the study of Chumash; at ten, the study of Mishnah; at thirteen, subject to the mitzvos; at fifteen, the study of Talmud.

פירוש לפי דעתי שכל עשר שנים האדם משתנה, וראיה לזה שמצאנו "בן עשר שנים למשנה בן עשרים לרדוף בן ל' לכח בן ארבעים לבינה כו'", הרי שנות האדם משתנים מעשר לעשר. אבל כל עשר שנים הם כמו זמן אחד ושעה אחת. ובאותן עשר שנים שהיתה מיתה—ידאג, דהיינו חמשה לפני מיתת אבותיו וחמשה לאחריה, דכל אלו עשר שנים הם זמן אחד ושעה אחת.[6]

The explanation, in my opinion, is that every ten years a person changes. As proof to this, we find in Pirkei Avos, "Ten years old to learning Mishnah, twenty years old ready to pursue, thirty years old to strength, forty years old to understanding, etc." [We see from this] that a person's life changes from decade to decade. However, every ten years is [like one unit of] time. Within the span of ten years that a death occurred, one should worry; meaning, five years before his parent's death and

---

5   *Avos* 5:22.

6   *Gur Aryeh, Bereishis* 27:2.

five years after, as the ten years are [considered] as one [unit of] time.

On this topic, the *Maharal* references the Mishnah in *Avos* that discusses the proper age and level for *chinuch*, emphasizing the importance of building a strong foundation. The *Maharal* says that fools do the opposite and try to build without a foundation.

Parents would be amazed at how well they can connect with their children if they focus on each child as an individual. It is an unfortunate mistake that parents and educators make of having a fixed mindset when educating children—just like the way they grew up.

The *pasuk* states, "חֲנֹךְ לַנַּעַר עַל פִּי דַרְכּוֹ גַּם כִּי יַזְקִין לֹא יָסוּר מִמֶּנָּה—Educate a lad according to his way so that he does not deviate in old age."

If one raises and educates children with one mindset, they will fail to reach everyone, and it is guaranteed that children will go off the *derech*. Albert Einstein once said, "Everybody is a genius. But if you judge a fish by its ability to climb a tree, it will live its whole life believing that it is stupid." Just like different fish require different bait, so too, each individual requires their own unique education and connection.

The lesson of using the proper bait can also be applied to making friends. The Mishnah advises us to acquire a friend.[7] Rav Ovadiah Mi'Bartenura comments:

וַאֲפִלּוּ אַתָּה צָרִיךְ לִקְנוֹתוֹ בְּדָמִים יְקָרִים וּלְפַזֵּר עָלָיו מָמוֹן כְּדֵי שֶׁתִּקְנֶה אַהֲבָתוֹ.

Even if one must acquire with sentimental possessions and spend a large sum of money to acquire his love.

In order to make friends, we sometimes have to compromise and give more than we would like. Although we prefer using a certain bait, in order to become closer to someone else, we need to switch baits and try something new.

---

7   *Avos* 1:6.

We learn in *Chovos Halevavos*:

וכן אמרו חז"ל והוי דן את כל האדם לכף זכות והוי מקבל את כל האדם
בסבר פנים יפות ואמרו מאד מאד הוי שפל רוח ואמרו יהי אדם רך כקנה
ואל יהי קשה כארז לפיכך זכה קנה לחתוך ממנו קולמוס לכתוב בו ס"ת
תפילין ומזוזות.[8]

*Our sages taught, judge every man favorably, receive every
person with a cheerful countenance, and be very, very lowly
of spirit, and one should always be flexible as a reed and not
unyielding as a cedar. This is why the reed has merited to
have made from it a quill to write a Sefer Torah, tefillin, and
mezuzos.*

When we recognize that every person is unique, and when we are
understanding and flexible to others' needs, we can be more sensitive
toward others and merit to have and be a good friend.

To Summarize

Hooking an audience requires plenty of skill and technique, but most
importantly, it requires the right bait. This applies to education as well.
Students and children will be attracted to the bait that is to their individual liking. Everyone has something they enjoy and appreciate, so use
that as bait to connect with them. By using the bait that they prefer,
they will hook on, and then you can reel them in.

Points to Ponder

- How can I connect to those who aren't like me?
- How can I find the unique qualities of others?
- How can I find my own uniqueness?

---

8   *Chovos Halevavos* 6:10:8.

Chutes and Ladders

While watching my children play on the playground, I observed Daniel climbing up a ladder leading to a slide and sliding back down to the bottom, time and time again. I noticed that the top of the slide was the highest point of the park, and so in one moment, one could go from the highest point to the lowest point.

This reminded me of the Mishnah:

הוּא הָיָה אוֹמֵר, אַל תְּהִי בָז לְכָל אָדָם, וְאַל תְּהִי מַפְלִיג לְכָל דָּבָר, שֶׁאֵין לְךָ אָדָם שֶׁאֵין לוֹ שָׁעָה וְאֵין לְךָ דָבָר שֶׁאֵין לוֹ מָקוֹם.[1]

Do not look down on any man, and do not disregard anything. For there is no man who does not have his hour, and nothing that does not have its place.

Often, people who are in high places become very haughty and don't treat others kindly. However, there are times when the tides turn and those "other" people find themselves as the ones in high places, while the haughty people have been brought low. On a simple level, one should never look down on anyone because that low person could easily turn around to be you.

---

1   *Avos* 4:3.

An example of this is when Shmuel HaNavi went to anoint Dovid as king. After seeing the appearance of Dovid's older brothers, Shmuel thought that one of them must be the son of Yishai that Hashem wanted him to anoint as king over Yisrael. However, the pasuk says:

וַיֹּאמֶר ה' אֶל שְׁמוּאֵל אַל תַּבֵּט אֶל מַרְאֵהוּ...כִּי הָאָדָם יִרְאֶה לַעֵינַיִם וַה' יִרְאֶה לַלֵּבָב.[2]

And Hashem said to Shmuel, "Pay no attention to his appearance or stature...man only sees what is visible to the eyes, but Hashem sees what is in the heart."

Shmuel HaNavi didn't think that Dovid was the chosen one because Dovid was red and resembled Eisav, as the verse says, "He was red, had nice eyes, and handsome."[3] Dovid seemed like a simple shepherd out in the fields watching the flock.[4] Yet, as we read every Shabbos after the *haftarah* and sing during Motza'ei Shabbos *zemiros*, it is from Dovid that Mashiach will come.

בכל דור ודור חייב אדם לראות את עצמו כאילו הוא יצא ממצרים.[5]

In every generation, one is obligated to see himself as if he left Mitzrayim.

When B'nei Yisrael left *Mitzrayim*, one of the first commandments they learned was how to treat a slave. The question is, they were just slaves—shouldn't they know how (and how not!) to treat a slave? Yes, but even B'nei Yisrael, who were just freed from slavery, could easily become desensitized when they would be free people. This is why each individual is commanded to see himself as if he came out of *Mitzrayim*.

Sometimes, we may begin at the bottom and make it to the top, but we shouldn't forget how it felt to be at the bottom.

---

2   *Shmuel I* 16:7.
3   Ibid., v. 12.
4   Ibid., v. 11.
5   *Pesachim* 116b.

There is a well-known *mashal* said in the name of the Dubno Maggid of a man who used to be very poor until one day his fortune changed when he found a sack of gold coins! After some time, this man became extremely wealthy, and people began to come to his mansion to collect tzedakah. Before he would give tzedakah to anyone, he would open a small closet near his front door, take a glance, and then proceed with giving the pauper tzedakah. One day, a pauper asked what he was looking at in his closet every time someone came to collect money. He invited him in and showed the pauper an outfit of tattered clothes. The man explained that these were his clothes that he would wear every day when he lived on the streets. Before he gave tzedakah, he reminded himself of where he came from.

There is another well-known story of a man who was in Auschwitz during the Holocaust. Every morning, he would wake up early before the Nazis would come into the barracks, go to the corner, and put on a soldier's beret. One morning, someone in his barracks saw him doing this and asked what he was doing. This man responded that he was a high-ranking officer in the army before the war began. He puts on this beret to remind him of who he is, and it gives him confidence and motivation to survive.

It may take some time to climb the ladder to get to the top, but remember how fast it takes to fall back down.

דַּע מֵאַיִן בָּאתָ, וּלְאָן אַתָּה הוֹלֵךְ.[6]

Know from where you came and to where you are going.

The Mishnah reminds us to always remember where we came from and where we are going. When we keep this in mind, we will become better people.

---

6   *Avos* 3:1.

To Summarize

Life has its ups and downs, and it can be a struggle. Those whom we see on top can come tumbling down, and those whom we see on the bottom can rise on up. Don't get too comfortable with the monetary things in life because things may change. Whatever level one may be on, focus on bettering yourself so you can be the best you through all of the twists and turns life may bring.

Points to Ponder

- What is something I can do to remember where I came from?
- Was there a time I reached a goal and recognized that the road there wasn't all rainbows and butterflies? How can I use that to my advantage for future goals?
- Do I remember to thank those who helped me get to where I am today?

Picking Flowers

I once heard my father explain that there are two types of people in the world:

- Type A takes negatives and transforms them into positives.
- Type B takes something positive and makes it negative.

We dip twice at the Pesach seder to commemorate our slavery and freedom:

- The first time we dip is by *karpas*, when we take a vegetable and dip it into saltwater.
- The second time we dip is by *maror*, when we dip the *maror* into the *charoses*.

Notice how they are "opposites":

- At *karpas*, we take a sweet vegetable and dip it into salty water. This is similar to those who transform positive into negative.
- *Maror*, on the contrary, is when we take the bitter *maror* and dip it into the sweet *charoses*. This is similar to those who take something negative and transform it into something positive.

Thomas Edison is a great example of someone taking something negative and making it positive. Edison had a hearing impairment that made it difficult for him to socialize with others. Instead of giving up on himself, he used his time alone and hearing deficiency to work on his inventions.

I was reminded of this powerful lesson when Talia handed my wife a handful of dandelions. Dandelions are weeds that most people try to kill so that they don't ruin their garden. However, Talia took these unfavorable weeds and made them into a beautiful bouquet. She took the negative and made it positive.

וְכַאֲשֶׁר יְעַנּוּ אֹתוֹ כֵּן יִרְבֶּה וְכֵן יִפְרֹץ וַיָּקֻצוּ מִפְּנֵי בְּנֵי יִשְׂרָאֵל.[1]

But the more they were oppressed, the more they increased and spread out, so that the [Egyptians] came to dread B'nei Yisrael.

את פיתום ואת רעמסס, רב ושמואל חד אמר פיתום שמה ולמה נקרא שמה רעמסס שראשון ראשון מתרוסס וחד אמר רעמסס שמה ולמה נקרא שמה פיתום שראשון ראשון פי תהום בולעו.[2]

"Pisom and Ramses": Rav and Shmuel—One says that Pisom was its real name, and why was it called Ramses? Because as the buildings were constructed, they collapsed one by one and needed to be rebuilt. And one says that Ramses was its real name, and why was it called Pisom? Because the opening of the abyss swallowed each building that they constructed one by one, and it sunk into the ground.

The more B'nei Yisrael were oppressed in *Mitzrayim*, the more we thrived. The *Mitzrim* forced us to build the cities of Pisom and Ramses, which would sink into the ground. However, as *Rashi* comments, we had to build the cities over and over again.[3]

Shlomo HaMelech tells us that a righteous person falls seven times and gets back up. One may think that they are ascending great heights, and all of a sudden, they fall to the bottom. If an individual stays down, he will never become anything. At the end of the day, Pisom and Ramses were storage houses for Pharaoh's treasures, and B'nei Yisrael were

---

1   *Shemos* 1:12.
2   *Sotah* 11a.
3   Ibid., s.v., *Rishon rishon misroses.*

successful.[4] It takes time and is very difficult, but perseverance and resiliency in not giving up is who we are as a people. We take negative and turn it into positive, and that's how one overcomes obstacles.

There are many things in life that try to break us. When one sins and does *teshuvah*, he could learn from his mistakes and become stronger. It doesn't matter if it's the *yetzer hara* or other people trying to bring one down; one can take those same stumbling blocks and use them to become stronger.

It is said in the name of Rebbetzin Sarah Schenirer, the mother of the Beis Yaakov movement and the reason girls have Jewish education today, that there were many people who were opposed to her views when she began. People would throw stones at her, but she responded by saying, "With these stones, I will build my foundation." Meaning, the stones and negativity that is thrown my way will only be stepping stones for my growth.

The *Mitzrim* forced us to build cities and work the fields. We had to survive through immense torture, but that is what made us into a nation. We used those hardships and turned them into positive, for without suffering there is no joy. Without darkness one can't truly appreciate the light. Don't say that there is a light at the end of the tunnel, rather recognize that the light is in the tunnel. Yes, on the surface it may seem dark, but in reality, we just have to open our eyes and see the light. When we say in the morning the *berachah* of *Pokeach ivrim*—opening the eyes of the blind—we are not only thanking Hashem for helping those who are physically blind but also for helping us see things we haven't seen before, such as a situation in a bright and positive paradigm instead of a negative and dark perspective.[5]

---

4   *Shemos* 1:11; see *Rashi*.

5   Obviously, one must consistently work on oneself to attain great levels of *emunah* and *bita-chon*. However, one must realize that these levels are attainable for even the simplest person. Many times, we only recognize how a "negative" event was truly positive much later. As the saying goes, "It's much easier to connect the dots once there are dots." We are coming into a world that has been around long before us and will be around long afterward. We cannot judge what Hashem does since we truly don't know. Hashem was, is, and always will be. Only He can be the true judge.

My father once gave a *mashal* of a surgeon about to perform an amputation. After his

חַיָּב אָדָם לְבָרֵךְ כו': מַאי "חַיָּב לְבָרֵךְ עַל הָרָעָה כְּשֵׁם שֶׁמְּבָרֵךְ עַל הַטּוֹבָה"?
אִילֵימָא כְּשֵׁם שֶׁמְּבָרֵךְ עַל הַטּוֹבָה "הַטּוֹב וְהַמֵּטִיב", כָּךְ מְבָרֵךְ עַל הָרָעָה
"הַטּוֹב וְהַמֵּטִיב", וְהָתְנַן עַל בְּשׂוֹרוֹת טוֹבוֹת אוֹמֵר "הַטּוֹב וְהַמֵּטִיב", עַל
בְּשׂוֹרוֹת רָעוֹת אוֹמֵר "בָּרוּךְ...דַּיַּין הָאֱמֶת"! אָמַר רָבָא: לֹא נִצְרְכָה, אֶלָּא
לְקַבּוֹלִינְהוּ בְּשִׂמְחָה.6

*"One is obligated to recite a blessing": What does it mean?...If
we say [it means] that just as one recites a blessing for the good,
"Who is good and does good," so too one [should] recite...for
the bad, "Who is good and does good," didn't we learn in our
Mishnah that over good tidings one recites, "Who is good and
does good," while over bad tidings one recites, "Blessed...the
true Judge?" Rava said: It was only necessary to instruct us to
accept bad tidings with the same joy.*

The Gemara teaches that one is obligated to make a *berachah* on
something bad just as they would on something good. When something positive happens in one's life, they make the *berachah* of *Hatov
V'Hametiv*—Who is good and causes good. When something seemingly negative happens in one's life, one makes the *berachah* of *Dayan
Ha'emes*—the true Judge. Rava says that the statement of the Mishnah
is to instruct us to accept the bad with the same joy with which we accept the good from Hashem.

The more *emunah*, faith, one has, the more one recognizes that everything is from Hashem. If we recognize that everything comes from
Hashem, then there is nothing bad since Hashem is *kulo tov*—entirely
good. As finite beings, we may not recognize that what seems bad is
really good. It is like when children get a shot; they just see the needle
and not the good that comes from it. Just as we trust the doctor when

---

preparations, he began to make the incision when the patient began yelling at the surgeon.
"How can you do such a thing?! I came into the hospital to get better, and now you are ampu-
tating my limb!" The surgeon replied, "Are you a doctor? This amputation will save the rest
of your body and your life!" So too, we are like the patient. We are not Hashem, and we don't
understand why certain things happen, but we do know that all Hashem does is for the best.

6   *Berachos* 60b.

giving us a shot, let's trust that it is for our benefit when Hashem gives us a "shot."

To Summarize

As we see regarding world events, things can be seen positively or negatively. There are those who, in moments of joy, will focus on the negative. There are times when things seem so down that one cannot see any sign of redemption, yet we must still try to find the good. One can take a sour fruit, such as lemons, and create a beautiful, tasty lemon meringue pie. It's not just about what life gives you, but it is what you do with it.

Points to Ponder

- How can I take what I see as negative and use it positively?
- What are some ways to see the negatives in others as positives?
- How do I feel when I am able to take something negative and see it as a positive?

Looking Back

As children grow, they want to become more independent and do things on their own. One example of this is when they play at the playground. As soon as the parent lets go of their hand, children are off running toward the slides, swings, or wherever they set their eyes on. However, most of the time, along with this independence, children are constantly looking back over their shoulder to confirm that their parents are still there. As soon as children lose sight of the one who is supposed to be there for them, they begin to get nervous, look around, and perhaps even cry. This isn't limited to children playing at the park, but occurs also as children get older—and even sometimes with adults.

People want independence; however, they constantly look for somebody to lean on.

I was once speaking to a principal about how his responsibilities differ from an assistant-principal position. He told me that one major difference is that as a principal, he can't shift the responsibility or pass it on to the next person—"the buck stops here." An assistant principal can always go to the principal if there is an issue, but a principal has to make the final decision. We must all be like a principal for our principles.

וַיֹּאמֶר הָאָדָם הָאִשָּׁה אֲשֶׁר נָתַתָּה עִמָּדִי הִוא נָתְנָה לִּי מִן הָעֵץ וָאֹכֵל:
וַיֹּאמֶר ה׳ אֱלֹקִים לָאִשָּׁה מַה זֹּאת עָשִׂית וַתֹּאמֶר הָאִשָּׁה הַנָּחָשׁ הִשִּׁיאַנִי
וָאֹכֵל...וַיְשַׁלְּחֵהוּ ה׳ אֱלֹקִים מִגַּן עֵדֶן לַעֲבֹד אֶת הָאֲדָמָה אֲשֶׁר לֻקַּח מִשָּׁם.[1]

The man said, "The woman You put at my side—she gave me of
the tree, and I ate." And Hashem said to the woman, "What is
this you have done!" The woman replied, "The serpent deceived
me, and I ate."...So Hashem banished him from the garden of
Eden, to work the soil from which he was taken.

וַיֹּאמֶר קַיִן אֶל הֶבֶל אָחִיו וַיְהִי בִּהְיוֹתָם בַּשָּׂדֶה וַיָּקָם קַיִן אֶל הֶבֶל אָחִיו וַיַּהַרְגֵהוּ:
וַיֹּאמֶר ה׳ אֶל קַיִן אֵי הֶבֶל אָחִיךָ וַיֹּאמֶר לֹא יָדַעְתִּי הֲשֹׁמֵר אָחִי אָנֹכִי?...וְעַתָּה
אָרוּר אָתָּה...כִּי תַעֲבֹד אֶת הָאֲדָמָה לֹא תֹסֵף תֵּת כֹּחָהּ לָךְ נָע וָנָד תִּהְיֶה
בָאָרֶץ...וַיָּשֶׂם ה׳ לְקַיִן אוֹת לְבִלְתִּי הַכּוֹת אֹתוֹ כָּל מֹצְאוֹ.[2]

Kayin said to his brother Hevel when they were in the field;
Kayin charged his brother Hevel and killed him. Hashem said
to Kayin, "Where is your brother Hevel?" And he said, "I do
not know. Am I my brother's keeper?"...Therefore, you shall be
more cursed than the ground...If you work the earth, it shall
no longer yield its strength to you. You shall become a constant
wanderer on earth...And the Lord set a sign for Kayin lest any
finding him should smite him.

וַיֹּאמֶר לֶמֶךְ...כִּי אִישׁ הָרַגְתִּי לְפִצְעִי וְיֶלֶד לְחַבֻּרָתִי...כִּי שִׁבְעָתַיִם יֻקַּם קָיִן.[3]

And Lemech said..."I have slain a man for wounding me, and
a lad for bruising me...If Kayin is avenged sevenfold, then
Lamech seventy-sevenfold."

שהיה למך סומא ותובל קין מושכו, וראה את קין ונדמה לו כחיה ואמר
לאביו למשך בקשת והרגו.[4]

---

1   *Bereishis* 3:12–13, 23.
2   Ibid. 4:8–9, 11–15.
3   Ibid. 4:23–24.
4   Ibid., *Rashi, s.v. Shema'an koli.*

Lemech was blind and Tuval-Kayin used to lead him. He saw Kayin and thought he was an animal. He therefore told his father to draw the bow, and thus Lemech killed him.

The Torah has many episodes of people shifting responsibility. Two examples happened in the beginning of Creation:

- At the sin of the *eitz ha'daas*, Adam blames Chavah, who blames the snake. This severe act resulted in an expulsion from Gan Eden.
- A short time after, Kayin kills his brother Hevel, and when he is approached by Hashem, Who asks, "Where is your brother?" Kayin responds, "Am I my brother's keeper?" After that, Hashem curses Kayin and sentences him with a harsh punishment. We see later that the curse was fulfilled when Lemech killed Kayin.

It is much easier to shift the blame and avoid responsibility, but as we see, it comes with negative consequences. Let's take a look at some true leaders who stepped up to take responsibility.

וַיֹּאמֶר מֶלֶךְ סְדֹם אֶל אַבְרָם תֶּן לִי הַנֶּפֶשׁ וְהָרְכֻשׁ קַח לָךְ...אִם מִחוּט וְעַד שְׂרוֹךְ נַעַל וְאִם אֶקַּח מִכָּל אֲשֶׁר לָךְ וְלֹא תֹאמַר אֲנִי הֶעֱשַׁרְתִּי אֶת אַבְרָם:[5]

Then the king of Sodom said to Avram, "Give me the people, and take the possessions for yourself."..."I will not take so much as a thread or a sandal strap of what is yours; you will not say, 'It is I who made Avram rich.'"

אַחַר הַדְּבָרִים הָאֵלֶּה הָיָה דְבַר ה' אֶל אַבְרָם בַּמַּחֲזֶה לֵאמֹר אַל תִּירָא אַבְרָם אָנֹכִי מָגֵן לָךְ שְׂכָרְךָ הַרְבֵּה מְאֹד:[6]

Sometime later, the word of Hashem came to Avram in a vision. He said, "Fear not, Avram, I am a shield to you; Your reward shall be very great."

Avraham Avinu stood up and helped his nephew Lot many times, such as when it came to the war of the five kings against four kings.

---

5   *Bereishis* 14:21–23.
6   Ibid. 15:1.

Although Avraham refused to accept anything from the king of Sodom, we see that Hashem came to Avraham and told him that He will protect him and he will have a great reward.

וַיֵּשֶׁב יִשְׂרָאֵל בַּשִּׁטִּים וַיָּחֶל הָעָם לִזְנוֹת אֶל בְּנוֹת מוֹאָב: וַתִּקְרֶאןָ לָעָם לְזִבְחֵי אֱלֹהֵיהֶן וַיֹּאכַל הָעָם וַיִּשְׁתַּחֲווּ לֵאלֹהֵיהֶן...וַיַּרְא פִּינְחָס בֶּן אֶלְעָזָר בֶּן אַהֲרֹן הַכֹּהֵן וַיָּקָם מִתּוֹךְ הָעֵדָה וַיִּקַּח רֹמַח בְּיָדוֹ: וַיָּבֹא אַחַר אִישׁ יִשְׂרָאֵל אֶל הַקֻּבָּה וַיִּדְקֹר אֶת שְׁנֵיהֶם אֵת אִישׁ יִשְׂרָאֵל וְאֶת הָאִשָּׁה אֶל קֳבָתָהּ וַתֵּעָצַר הַמַּגֵּפָה מֵעַל בְּנֵי יִשְׂרָאֵל:[7]

While Yisrael was camped at Shittim, the people profaned themselves by acting with licentiousness with the daughters of Moav, who invited the people to the sacrifices for their god. The people ate and worshiped their gods...When Pinchas, son of Elazar, son of Aharon the Kohen, saw this, he got up and, taking a spear in his hand, he followed the Jew into the chamber and stabbed both of them, the Jew and the woman, through the belly. Then the plague against the Israelites was ceased.

אמר רבי שמעון בן לקיש פינחס הוא אליהו. א"ל הקב"ה אתה נתת שלום בין ישראל וביני בעולם הזה אף לעתיד לבא אתה הוא שעתיד ליתן שלום ביני לבין בני שנאמר הנה אנכי שולח לכם את אליה הנביא לפני בוא יום ה' וגו' והשיב לב אבות על בנים.[8]

Rabbi Shimon ben Lakish said, "Pinchas is Eliyahu." The Holy One, blessed be He, said to [Eliyahu], "You brought peace between Israel and Me in this world; so too, in the coming world, you will be the one to make peace between Me and my children." As it says, "Behold, I will send you Eliyahu the Prophet before the coming of the [great and awesome] Day of God. That he may turn the heart of the fathers back to the children."

---

7   *Bamidbar* 25:1–8.
8   *Yalkut Shimoni, Parashas Pinchas* 771:21.

When Pinchas saw the terrible *aveiros* that B'nei Yisrael were committing in the *midbar*, even while they were punished and plagued by Hashem, he stood up and killed Zimri along with Cozbi, the non-Jewish Midianite woman he was with. This courageous act resulted in calming the wrath of Hashem and thus ending the plague. The midrash teaches that Hashem told Pinchas that since he brought peace to B'nei Yisrael, he will bring peace in the future as Eliyahu HaNavi.

וַתֹּאמֶר נָעֳמִי לִשְׁתֵּי כַלֹּתֶיהָ לֵכְנָה שֹּׁבְנָה אִשָּׁה לְבֵית אִמָּהּ...וַתֹּאמַרְנָה לָּהּ
כִּי אִתָּךְ נָשׁוּב לְעַמֵּךְ...וַתֹּאמֶר נָעֳמִי שֹּׁבְנָה בְנֹתַי...שֹּׁבְנָה בְנֹתַי...וַתִּשֶּׂנָה
קוֹלָן וַתִּבְכֶּינָה עוֹד וַתִּשַּׁק עָרְפָּה לַחֲמוֹתָהּ וְרוּת דָּבְקָה בָּהּ: וַתֹּאמֶר הִנֵּה שָׁבָה
יְבִמְתֵּךְ אֶל עַמָּהּ וְאֶל אֱלֹהֶיהָ שׁוּבִי אַחֲרֵי יְבִמְתֵּךְ: וַתֹּאמֶר רוּת אַל תִּפְגְּעִי בִי
לְעָזְבֵךְ לָשׁוּב מֵאַחֲרָיִךְ...[9]

Naomi said to her two daughters-in-law, "Turn back, each of you to her mother's house."...And they said to her, "No, we will return with you to your people."...But Naomi replied, "Turn back, my daughters!...Turn back, my daughters..." They broke into weeping again, and Orpah kissed her mother-in-law farewell. But Rus clung to her...So she said, "See, your sister-in-law has returned to her people and her gods. Go follow your sister-in-law." But Rus replied, "Do not urge me to leave you, to turn back and not follow you..."

Naomi repeatedly urged Rus and Orpah to turn back, which they both refused originally. However, Orpah gave in, as the midrash reveals that she lost all hope and went to the lowest of levels.[10] Rus, who did not look back and took accountability for her choice of becoming a Jew, was *zocheh* to be the great-grandmother of Dovid HaMelech and have Mashiach descend from her.

When one turns back, one loses sight as to what is ahead. One who takes responsibility for his actions recognizes that the mistakes are to

---

9   *Rus* 1:8–17.
10   *Midrash Lekach Tov, Rus* 1:15:1.

be learned from, not to be dwelled upon. When one cannot let go of the past, they will have much difficulty moving forward.

וְלִפְנֵי מִי אַתָּה עָתִיד לִתֵּן דִּין וְחֶשְׁבּוֹן, לִפְנֵי מֶלֶךְ מַלְכֵי הַמְּלָכִים הַקָּדוֹשׁ בָּרוּךְ הוּא:[11]

Before Whom are you destined to give an account and reckoning? Before the King, the King of kings, Hakadosh Baruch Hu.

The Mishnah tells us that at the end of our days, we will be held accountable for all of our actions. There is no shifting the responsibility or passing the problem onto someone else. We can't always look back and rely on others to have our back, making sure we are safe. Yes, we should have people to rely on, as the Mishnah teaches, "Make for yourself a *rav* (mentor) and acquire yourself a friend."[12] Still, at the end of the day, the buck stops by each individual; we have to answer why we listened and followed others' advice.

Hal Elrod once said, "The moment you take responsibility for everything in your life is the moment you can change anything in your life."

The Mishnah tells us:

הַכֹּל צָפוּי, וְהָרְשׁוּת נְתוּנָה וּבְטוֹב הָעוֹלָם נִדּוֹן.[13]

Everything is foreseen, yet freedom of choice is granted, and the world is judged with goodness.

Although everything is foreseen by Hashem, the choices we make are still ours, and we control how much goodness the world will be judged with based on our actions.

The point is that we are responsible for all of our actions. Take control and own up to your choices. "אִם אֵין אֲנִי לִי, מִי לִי"—if I am not for me, who will be for me?"[14] If I don't take accountability for my own actions, no one else will.

---

11 *Avos* 3:1.
12 Ibid. 1:6.
13 Ibid. 3:15.
14 Ibid. 1:14.

In life, change is consistent. There are many reasons why people may want to shy away from change;[15] however, it is inevitable. When confronting change, people often say, "Way back in the good ole' days…" or "When I was younger…" I believe one reason people speak this way is because when they are able to revisit times of the past, it takes their mind off the present, similar to passing the buck. Yet, when they come back to reality, they are still in the same situation and have to adapt to the changes around them.

Of course, it is very important to reflect on the past in order to enhance your future. The problem becomes when one dwells in the past and tries to avoid what may be in the future. This is when people get fixed into their ways, and it is very difficult to change. When Lot and his family were saved from Sodom, the *malach* warned them,

אַל תַּבִּיט אַחֲרֶיךָ וְאַל תַּעֲמֹד בְּכָל הַכִּכָּר הָהָרָה הִמָּלֵט פֶּן תִּסָּפֶה.[16]

Do not turn around or stop anywhere in the fields; run to the hills lest you be swept away.

However, the wife of Lot turned as the city was burning, and she became a pillar of salt, fixed in place.[17] She was punished because she turned around to look back. There was no reason for her to look back; she should have focused on the future. Perhaps at a later point in time she could have reflected on the past to improve her ways, but at that moment, she sinned by looking back.

…אָמַר אֱלֹקִים פֶּן יִנָּחֵם הָעָם בִּרְאֹתָם מִלְחָמָה וְשָׁבוּ מִצְרָיְמָה…הֲלֹא זֶה הַדָּבָר אֲשֶׁר דִּבַּרְנוּ אֵלֶיךָ בְמִצְרַיִם לֵאמֹר חֲדַל מִמֶּנּוּ וְנַעַבְדָה אֶת מִצְרַיִם כִּי טוֹב לָנוּ עֲבֹד אֶת מִצְרַיִם מִמֻּתֵנוּ בַּמִּדְבָּר…וַיֹּאמְרוּ אֲלֵהֶם בְּנֵי יִשְׂרָאֵל מִי יִתֵּן מוּתֵנוּ בְיַד ה' בְּאֶרֶץ מִצְרָיִם…[18]

---

15   R.M. Kanter, "Ten Reasons People Resist Change," accessed August 07, 2014.
      See https://hbr.org/2012/09/ten-reasons-people-resist-chang.html.

16   *Bereishis* 19:17.

17   Ibid., v. 26.

18   *Shemos* 13:17, see *Rashi, s.v. Bir'osam milchamah*; 14:12; 16:3, see *Rashi, s.v. Mi yitein museinu*.

Hashem said, "Lest the people have a change of heart when they see war, and return to Mitzrayim."...."Is this not the very thing we told you in Mitzrayim, saying, 'Let us be, and we will serve the Egyptians, for it is better for us to serve the Egyptians than to die in the wilderness'?"...B'nei Yisrael said to them, "If only we had died by the hand of Hashem in the land of Mitzrayim..."

זָכַרְנוּ אֶת הַדָּגָה אֲשֶׁר נֹאכַל בְּמִצְרַיִם חִנָּם אֵת הַקִּשֻּׁאִים וְאֵת הָאֲבַטִּחִים וְאֶת הֶחָצִיר וְאֶת הַבְּצָלִים וְאֶת הַשּׁוּמִים...וְלָמָה ה' מֵבִיא אֹתָנוּ אֶל הָאָרֶץ הַזֹּאת לִנְפֹּל בַּחֶרֶב נָשֵׁינוּ וְטַפֵּנוּ יִהְיוּ לָבַז הֲלוֹא טוֹב לָנוּ שׁוּב מִצְרָיְמָה: וַיֹּאמְרוּ אִישׁ אֶל אָחִיו נִתְּנָה רֹאשׁ וְנָשׁוּבָה מִצְרָיְמָה...וְלָמָה הֶעֱלִיתֻנוּ מִמִּצְרַיִם לְהָבִיא אֹתָנוּ אֶל הַמָּקוֹם הָרָע הַזֶּה לֹא מְקוֹם זֶרַע וּתְאֵנָה וְגֶפֶן וְרִמּוֹן וּמַיִם אַיִן לִשְׁתּוֹת:[19]

"We remember the fish that we used to eat free in Egypt, the cucumbers, the melons, the leeks, the onions, and the garlic...Why is Hashem taking us to that land to fall by the sword? Our wives and children will be disgraced! It would be better for us to go back to Egypt!" And they said to one another, "Let us head back for Egypt."...Why did you make us leave Egypt to bring us to this wretched place, a place with no grain or figs or vines or pomegranates? There is not even water to drink!"

Throughout their journey in the desert, we find in numerous places that B'nei Yisrael complained, wanting to return to *Mitzrayim*. Why would they want to return to a life of torture, pain, and suffering? It doesn't make sense that after becoming free from such a difficult lifestyle they would want to return to such living conditions. Rather, they were afraid of change and the responsibilities they would be held accountable for. Their desire is comparable to those who wish to stay young forever and avoid any responsibility that comes with adulthood. However, this is not the reality. Our eyes were positioned to see what is

---

19   *Bamidbar* 11:5, 14:3–4, 20:5.

ahead of us. Someone who constantly has their head turned will find it very difficult to hurdle the challenges, as well as to enjoy the good times that lie ahead.

We must reflect on the past but must focus on the future.

To Summarize

Reflecting on your past to improve your future is a wonderful thing. However, dwelling on your past will only hinder your future. Looking back toward others for things you've done will slow the process of becoming the best you can be. Accepting accountability for your words and actions will help you move on and progress.

Points to Ponder

- How do I keep moving forward while glancing in the rearview mirror every once in a while?
- Why is it important for my future that I learn from the past yet continue to move on?
- Are there things that I hold onto that are preventing me from moving forward?

The Climb

As my children advance to the next stages in life, I feel that it is important for them to learn how to do things on their own, allowing them to be independent. With this in mind, one day at the park, while pushing Daniel on the swings, I stopped pushing and told him to get back up to the same height as before.

This reminded me of a beautiful *mashal* I saw in the *Nesivos Shalom*, explaining the significance and importance of the days between Pesach and Shavuos. There was a man who decided that he wanted to become a mountain climber. One day, he hired a mentor to guide and teach him how to master climbing. The next morning, the mentor led the way, assisting and guiding the man to the top of the mountain. The man was delighted as he looked on at the beautiful scenery with an amazing feeling of accomplishment. The following day, as they were getting ready to climb another mountain, the mentor told the man that today it was the man's turn to lead the way.

The same is true with us from the days of Pesach until Shavuos. On Pesach, Hashem guides us and brings us to the top of the mountain, where we bask in the beautiful scenery with amazing feelings of accomplishment, faith, and success. For example, the Seder begins with *Kadesh*, when we sanctify ourselves. Each step of the Seder we advance another level, reaching the highest step of the Seder—*Nirtzah*—when we ask for acceptance and conclude with *l'shanah haba'ah b'Yerushalayim*—the ultimate redemption. We also eat matzah, which is called *"nehama d'meheimenusa*—bread of faith[1]—since we are on such a high level. We also relive the events from slavery to freedom that we describe in the Haggadah.

However, during the days of *Sefirah*, Hashem tells us that it is our turn to lead the way back to those great heights. We are like that mountain climber working to bring ourselves back to those levels of achievement.[2]

Although it may be difficult and feel impossible at times, it is the climb that gives one true satisfaction. One who climbs a mountain will feel much better about reaching the top than one who was dropped off by a helicopter. Life is all about the mountains one climbs. It isn't easy, but it is worth it. Whether it be an internal mountain to climb or an external, it is all about the climb.

We see this when B'nei Yisrael were reminded that they traveled in the desert for forty years.

וְזָכַרְתָּ אֶת כָּל הַדֶּרֶךְ אֲשֶׁר הֹלִיכְךָ ה׳ אֱלֹקֶיךָ זֶה אַרְבָּעִים שָׁנָה בַּמִּדְבָּר לְמַעַן עַנֹּתְךָ לְנַסֹּתְךָ לָדַעַת אֶת אֲשֶׁר בִּלְבָבְךָ הֲתִשְׁמֹר מִצְוֹתָיו אִם לֹא: וַיְעַנְּךָ וַיַּרְעִבֶךָ וַיַּאֲכִלְךָ אֶת הַמָּן אֲשֶׁר לֹא יָדַעְתָּ וְלֹא יָדְעוּן אֲבֹתֶיךָ לְמַעַן הוֹדִעֲךָ כִּי לֹא עַל הַלֶּחֶם לְבַדּוֹ יִחְיֶה הָאָדָם כִּי עַל כָּל מוֹצָא פִי ה׳ יִחְיֶה הָאָדָם: שִׂמְלָתְךָ לֹא בָלְתָה מֵעָלֶיךָ וְרַגְלְךָ לֹא בָצֵקָה זֶה אַרְבָּעִים שָׁנָה: וְיָדַעְתָּ עִם לְבָבֶךָ כִּי כַּאֲשֶׁר יְיַסֵּר אִישׁ אֶת בְּנוֹ ה׳ אֱלֹקֶיךָ מְיַסְּרֶךָ: וְשָׁמַרְתָּ אֶת מִצְוֹת ה׳ אֱלֹקֶיךָ לָלֶכֶת בִּדְרָכָיו וּלְיִרְאָה אֹתוֹ: כִּי ה׳ אֱלֹקֶיךָ מְבִיאֲךָ אֶל אֶרֶץ טוֹבָה אֶרֶץ נַחֲלֵי מָיִם עֲיָנֹת וּתְהֹמֹת יֹצְאִים בַּבִּקְעָה וּבָהָר: אֶרֶץ חִטָּה וּשְׂעֹרָה וְגֶפֶן וּתְאֵנָה וְרִמּוֹן אֶרֶץ זֵית שֶׁמֶן וּדְבָשׁ: אֶרֶץ אֲשֶׁר לֹא בְמִסְכֵּנֻת תֹּאכַל בָּהּ לֶחֶם לֹא תֶחְסַר כֹּל בָּהּ אֶרֶץ אֲשֶׁר אֲבָנֶיהָ בַרְזֶל וּמֵהֲרָרֶיהָ תַּחְצֹב נְחֹשֶׁת: וְאָכַלְתָּ וְשָׂבָעְתָּ וּבֵרַכְתָּ אֶת ה׳ אֱלֹקֶיךָ עַל הָאָרֶץ הַטֹּבָה אֲשֶׁר נָתַן לָךְ:[3]

Remember the long way that Hashem your God has made you travel in the wilderness these past forty years, in order to test you through hardships to learn what was in your hearts, whether you would keep His commandments or not. He put you

---

1   *Zohar, Parashas Bo.*

2   Ginsberg and Berezovsky, *Nesivos Shalom: Chag Ha-Pesach, Sefiras Ha-Omer*, pp. 585–86.

3   *Devarim 8:2–10.*

through the hardship of hunger and then gave you manna to eat, which neither you nor your fathers had ever known, in order to teach you that man does not live on bread alone, but that man may live on anything that Hashem decrees…For Hashem your God is bringing you into a good land, a land with streams and springs and fountains issuing from plain and hill. A land of wheat and barley, of grapes, figs, and pomegranates. A land of olive trees and honey. A land where you may eat food without scarcity, where you will lack nothing; a land whose rocks are iron and from whose hills you can mine copper. When you have eaten your fill, give thanks to Hashem your God for the good land which He has given you.

The entire journey of B'nei Yisrael was a climb up a long and steep mountain in order to reach the ultimate sweet feeling of accomplishment, victory, and satisfaction in having a land of their own. Had Hashem led them straight to Eretz Yisrael, B'nei Yisrael would not have had the same recognition and appreciation toward Hashem. Although Hashem was eager to bring B'nei Yisrael into Eretz Yisrael, their troublesome behaviors showed that they weren't ready to enter the land expeditiously. Therefore, Hashem had to delay their entry to their lot. This gave them the opportunity to learn the lessons needed, one step at a time, while ascending their climb—entering Eretz Yisrael.

Hashem had to teach B'nei Yisrael the lessons before they reached the top of their mountain.

Once one reaches the top of one's mountain, one can then sit back, reflect, and appreciate the view of all the work and effort that was put into their climb.

ובפני...צדיקים נדמה להם כהר גבוה.[4]

And for the righteous, [the yetzer hara] to them is compared to a high mountain.

---

4   *Sukkah* 52a.

אֵיזֶהוּ גִבּוֹר, הַכּוֹבֵשׁ אֶת יִצְרוֹ.[5]

Who is considered strong? One who overcomes his evil inclination.

The Gemara teaches that the *yetzer hara* is compared to a mountain. One who is strong climbs the mountain and overcomes it.

To Summarize

Life is a constant climb to the top. The climb is the process, and the view is the result. One who wishes for a greater view will have more to climb. Whether it's an outward or internal battle, overcoming the obstacles and reaching the top makes the view all worth it.

Points to Ponder

- What do I find challenging about the obstacles ahead of me?
- What is one step that, if taken, would move me forward?
- How do I feel when I imagine myself moving forward and taking that first step to climb the mountain?

---

5   *Avos* 4:1.

LESSONS FROM SCHOOL

Red Light, Green Light

D aniel knows what the colors of the traffic lights mean; red means stop, yellow means slow down, and green, of course, means go. One day, I was stopped at a traffic light while driving my children to school. As soon as the traffic light turned green, Daniel yelled, "Go!" and so I went. This reminded me of the words *"v'im lo achshav, eimasai?"*[1]

This may seem like a silly and outlandish example, but how many times in life do we have an opportunity waiting for us to go forward, yet we push it off hoping that the opportunity will come around again? Rabbeinu Yonah commentates on this Mishnah, saying;

שלא יאמר אני היום עסוק במלאכתי למחר אפנה ואעסוק ואתקן עצמי. כי שמא לא תפנה ואפי׳ אם יפנה היום ההוא חלף עבר ובטל אותו ממלאכת ה׳ ולא יוכל לשלמו כל ימיו כי כל הימים אשר הוא חי על האדמה חייב הוא לתקן עצמו ולעסוק במצות ואין לו רשות ליבטל ממלאכתו ואפי׳ שעה אחת. ועוד יש בכלל זה הלשון אם לא עכשיו בימי נערות אימתי אם עד זקנה ושיבה יניחנה לא יוכל לעשותה. ועל ענין זה אמר דוד ע״ה (תהלים קמ״ד י״ב) אשר בנינו כנטעים מגדלים בנעוריהם. ר״ל כי הנטע בעודנו קטן אדם יכול לגדלו להיות עץ ישר ולא יהיה עקום אך לאחר שגדל בעקומו היותו קשה הוא מאד לתקן. וכן האדם בעודנו קטן בקל הוא להיות בדרך

טוב ולסור מן הרע אבל אם הזקין ברשעו קשה בעיניו להניחה כמו שכתוב
(משלי כ"ב ו') חנך לנער על פי דרכו גם כי יזקין לא יסור ממנה.[2]

*And there is also included in this expression, "If not now [in
the days of my youth], then when?" If I leave it until my old
age, I will not be able to do it. And about this matter, Dovid
[HaMelech], peace be upon him, stated (Tehillim 144:12),
"For our sons are like saplings, well-tended in their youth."
He meant to say that when the sapling is small, a person can
grow it to be a straight tree and not be crooked. However, after
it grows crooked, it is very difficult to fix. And so [too], when
a person is still young, it is easy for him to be on a good path
and to turn from evil, but when he grows old with his evil, it is
difficult in his eyes to leave it, as it is written (Mishlei 22:6),
"Teach a lad according to his way; also when he will grow old,
he will not swerve from it."*

Hashem is constantly bringing opportunities to our doorstep, giving
us a choice to either pursue them or to pass them by. The choices we
make will define whom we become later in life. People who focus on the
short-term and immediate opportunities will lose out and regret the
long-term and everlasting ones. However, those who seek the long-term
opportunities will look back and be content with the choices made.

Habit number three in Steven Covey's famous *The 7 Habits of Highly
Effective People* is to "put first things first." Covey quotes Goethe,
stating, "Things which matter most must never be at the mercy of
things which matter least."[3] Those who mainly focus their attention
on things that have little value long-term will miss out in the end since
they will not be able to fit all of the long-term and important things
in. For example, if a student decides to hang out with friends instead
of studying for the upcoming exam, the student is focusing on a short-
term opportunity (i.e., fun), causing the student to miss out on the
greater opportunity (i.e., doing well on the test and getting a better

---

2   Rabbeinu Yonah, *Avos* ibid.
3   Covey, *The 7 Habits*, p. 94.

job). However, a student who focuses on studying and recognizes the long-term importance will have many more opportunities to hang out with friends later.

Reflect on your younger years; think about how many of your close friends then are still your close friends now. Most people don't even speak to friends from their younger years anymore. As people age, they go their own ways. Think about all the decisions you either made or didn't because of those friends. Isn't it amazing how most of us are the way we are because of the decisions we made when we hung around those we barely know anymore?

איזהו חכם הרואה את הנולד.[4]

Who is wise? One who envisions what will be.

Chazal describe a wise person as one who "sees what will be," i.e., foresees the consequences of his actions. One puts everything aside and focuses on the opportunities that will make them a better person. Rabbeinu Gershom comments on this Gemara, saying,

המבין מלבו מה שעתיד להיות קורות שעתידים לבא ונזהר מהן.

Understand from your heart what the future [of your actions] will bring and be careful.

I once heard of a study in which nurses shared some of the regrets their elderly patients had told them before they passed away. Most of the regrets were related to missed opportunities. We go through our lives with opportunities to accomplish great things every day. Are we going to look back and feel satisfied with our accomplishments or regret, wishing that we didn't push certain things off?

Let us see the light and recognize that it's "go" time!

---

4   *Tamid* 32a.

To Summarize

Success rarely comes to those who are passive. If one wants to achieve his goals, he must be proactive. Pushing off tasks could lead to failure. We only have a limited amount of time in this world, and if we don't put our priorities first, then we may not have time for them later. Put first things first, and focus on what is really important.

Points to Ponder

- What is something important that I constantly push off and regret it every time?
- How can I overcome and beat procrastination?
- How can I make the most of my time in this world?

It's Not Fair, but It's All Good

One Erev Shabbos, Daniel was the "Shabbos Abba" in school. When Daniel was the Shabbos Abba, I would bring in some treats that Daniel could give out to his class for the Shabbos party. This time, I brought some cupcakes for the class. There were a few extra, so Daniel gave some to his *moros*, but there was still one more extra cupcake. I told Daniel that since he was the Shabbos Abba, he could have it. One of the children in the class noticed that Daniel got two while everyone else only got one and exclaimed, "That's not fair! I also want two cupcakes!" The *moros* calmed the child down, explained the situation, and all was good. As I was leaving, it occurred to me that this child wasn't losing anything. He was upset because Daniel got an *extra* one. The experience made me think about how often people complain that others have more, and that life isn't fair.

וַיִּקַּח קֹרַח בֶּן יִצְהָר בֶּן קְהָת בֶּן לֵוִי...וַיָּקֻמוּ לִפְנֵי מֹשֶׁה וַאֲנָשִׁים מִבְּנֵי יִשְׂרָאֵל חֲמִשִּׁים וּמָאתָיִם נְשִׂיאֵי עֵדָה קְרִאֵי מוֹעֵד אַנְשֵׁי שֵׁם:[1]

Korach, son of Yitzhar, son of Kehas, son of Levi, took...and they stood before Moshe and men from among the children of Israel, two hundred and fifty heads of the assembly, distinguished men of name.

---

1   *Bamidbar* 16:1–2.

Korach began his revolt against Moshe and Aharon out of jealousy. He was a tremendous and powerful person, had a very important leadership role, and many followers. Moshe and Aharon did not take anything away from his position by receiving theirs. Yet, Korach came to believe that Moshe and Aharon took his role away. The *Ibn Ezra* explains what is meant by the commandment of *lo sachmod*—do not be jealous.[2]

אנשים רבים יתמהו על זאת המצוה. איך יהיה אדם שלא יחמוד דבר יפה בלבו כל מה שהוא נחמד למראה עיניו. ועתה אתן לך משל. דע כי איש כפרי שיש לו דעת נכונה והוא ראה בת מלך שהיא יפה לא יחמוד אותה בלבו שישכב עמה. כי ידע כי זה לא יתכן. ואל תחשוב זה הכפרי שהוא כאחד מן המשוגעים שיתאוה שיהיו לו כנפים לעוף לעוף השמים...כי הרגילוהו מנעוריו לדעת שהיא אסורה לו. ככה כל משכיל צריך שידע כי אשה יפה או ממון לא ימצאנו אדם בעבור חכמתו ודעתו. רק כאשר חלק לו השם.[3]

Many people have wondered about this commandment, how is it that a man not covet in his heart that which is beautiful [and] all that which appears pleasant in his eyes. I will give you a parable. You should know that a villager who thinks correctly and sees that the king's daughter is beautiful will not covet her in his heart…as he knows that this is impossible. And this villager will not think like one of the lunatics that desires that he should have wings to fly in the sky, when it is not possible…So must every enlightened person know that a beautiful woman or money is not attained by a person because of his wisdom or knowledge; rather it is from that which Hashem apportioned to him.

The *Ibn Ezra* explains that people question how it's possible not to want something that they find favorable in their heart. He compares this to a villager who shouldn't be jealous of a king's possessions or wishing to have wings to fly; it's just not possible. When we see that we lack something that another person has, we must recognize that each

---

2   *Shemos* 20:14.

3   *Ibn Ezra, Shemos* 20:14.

individual receives their personal package from Hashem. If my friend has something and I don't, it should feel so distant from me that I don't desire it. If I was meant to have it, Hashem would incorporate it into my package. It could be that later in life I may acquire it, but at this moment it shouldn't even be a thought for me.

Why can't people just be happy with what they have and not constantly look at how much more another person has? If somebody has $100 and the next person has $101, the one with $100 isn't losing anything! Yes, certain things in life may not seem fair, but it is still good.

As my father says, "The reason people feel that the grass looks greener on the other side is because they forget to water their own grass." If you're going to look at someone else, don't look at someone with more than you and wish to have what they have; look at someone with less than you and appreciate what you do have. In other words, focus on what you have and be happy with it. The Mishnah teaches that one who is happy and content with what they have is truly considered wealthy.[4]

When one thinks of a pauper, they think of someone on the street asking for money. When thinking of a wealthy person, one thinks of someone relaxing happily in paradise. However, someone who has all of the money in the world but is dissatisfied is more like the pauper constantly looking for money or their next meal. So too, one who barely has anything and is content with what they have is more comparable to the wealthy person relaxing in paradise, because he has no worries of needing more. He recognizes that everything comes from Hashem.

Further on in *Pirkei Avos*, the Mishnah states:

הַקִּנְאָה וְהַתַּאֲוָה וְהַכָּבוֹד מוֹצִיאִין אֶת הָאָדָם מִן הָעוֹלָם.[5]

Jealousy, desire, and honor remove a person from this world.

Is this really so? There are many people who are full of jealousy, desire, and honor yet seem to be doing very well. What does the Mishnah mean that these three things remove a person from this world?

---

4   *Avos* 4:1.
5   Ibid. 4:21.

One answer can be learned from the Gemara in *Nedarim*.[6] The Gemara quotes a *Beraisa* that teaches that a pauper is considered to be dead. As stated earlier, one who is constantly looking for more and is not happy with his lot is considered poor. According to this, the Mishnah now makes sense. One who is constantly jealous, chasing desires, or running after honor is unhappy with their portion, and therefore they are considered poor. One who is poor is considered dead and removed from this world.

Rabbeinu Bachya teaches in *Chovos Halevavos*:

ומהן כי הבוטח בה' לא ימנעינו רב הממון מבטח בה' מפני שאיננו סומך
על הממון והוא בעיניו כפקדון צוה להשתמש בו על פנים מיוחדים ובענינים
מיוחדים לזמן קצוב. ואם יתמיד קיומו אצלו לא יבעט בעבורו ולא יזכיר
טובתו למי שצוה לתת לו ממנו ולא יבקש עליו גמול הודאה ושבח אבל
הוא מודה לבוראו יתברך אשר שמהו סבה לטובות. ואם יאבד הממון ממנו
לא ידאג ולא יאבל לחסרונו אך הוא מודה לאלקיו בקחתו פקדונו מאתו
כאשר הודה בנתינתו לו וישמח בחלקו ואיננו מבקש היזק זולתו ולא יחמוד
אדם בממונו כמו שאמר החכם (משלי יג, כה) צדיק אוכל לשובע נפשו.[7]

*Another advantage for one who trusts in Hashem is that hav-
ing a great deal of money won't prevent him from trusting in
Him since he does not rely on his money. Rather, he sees it as
a deposit that he has been commanded to use in certain ways
and for certain purposes, for a limited amount of time. If it is
in his possession for a while, he does not become arrogant on its
account. He does not remind those he gave tzedakah to of the
kindness he performed for them since he was only performing
his mission. He does not wish to be recognized and praised,
rather he acknowledges the Creator, blessed be He, for having
appointed him as a means of good.*

*If he loses his money, he will not mourn and grieve the loss.
Rather, he recognizes that Hashem collected His deposit, just
as he recognized when Hashem gave it to him. He is happy with*

---

6   *Nedarim* 64b.
7   *Chovos Halevavos* 4, introduction.

his portion, doesn't want to harm anyone, and does not desire anyone's property. As the Wise Man [Shlomo HaMelech] said: "A righteous man eats only until he is content [and the stomach of the wicked is lacking]" (Mishlei 13:25).

The point is that true happiness is recognizing that everything comes from Hashem. This is demonstrated on Sukkos when we move out of our "secure" homes into the *sukkah*. Our actions show that we are leaving our physical comfort zone and are moving into a spiritual comfort zone. We display our complete faith and trust in Hashem by implying that we only need the bare minimum to serve Him with true, authentic *simchah*.

To Summarize

As my father says, "The grass is greener on the other side because we forget to water our own grass." People who are always looking at others tend to forget about all that they have. Life may not seem fair, but when we realize Hashem is in control, we don't need to worry about what is fair or not. Being content with what one has is a true blessing.

Points to Ponder

- How can I show more appreciation for what I have?
- When I recognize all that I have, do I still envy what others have?
- Do I use what I have properly?

Less Could Be Better

Daniel got a new toy and loved playing with it so much that he wanted to bring it to school to share it with all his friends. However, even though the thought is great and wonderful, it is not always the best idea to bring something you value very much to school. Daniel is definitely a big "mitzvah boy" and loves to share, but I tried explaining that this may not be such a good idea. After a short "back and forth," he agreed to leave his toy at home.

This made me think of what the Mishnah says, "*Marbeh nechasim, marbeh daagah*—The more possessions, the more worries."[1] Daniel leaving his toy at home would allow him to play with the toys at school without the extra responsibility and worry of making sure his toy was in a safe place.

My family and I have moved many times. Each time while packing or unpacking, we find things that we haven't used in years, yet we can't let go of them. It shows how much we could really live without. Plus, the less one has, the easier it is to move.

Often, one may think that those who are very wealthy or in high positions have less worries. In fact, it is just the opposite. Take a look at how many security cameras they have around their house; they sometimes even require bodyguards to protect them.

---

1   *Avos* 2:7.

Rabbeinu Yonah writes,

אל יחשוב כי על כבוד עושרו ורוב נכסיו יבלה ימיו בטוב ושנותיו בנעימים.
והוא דואג עליהם כל השנה כולה. שאל אותו ויגדך עשיריך ויאמרו לך:[2]

Don't think that because of one's money and possessions, he will live a calm life. Rather, he will worry about his possessions all year round. Ask him and he will tell you.

We know that everyone is tested by Hashem according to their portion. But, really, we all know that we silently ask for more *parnasah* and sustenance, that Hashem test us with wealth rather than poverty. But, of course, we also add that we'll certainly give *maaser* from our new wealth, in addition to all the wonderful things we'll buy with all the new money we get. Perhaps, though, we should take a step back and recognize that we already have so much to be thankful for and that we could serve Hashem with all that we have.

It is said in the name of the Chafetz Chaim that when his wife passed away, he asked the *Chevra Kadisha* to bury her next to someone who lived a life of poverty. The Chafetz Chaim explained that the *pasuk* states, "כִּי יַעֲמֹד לִימִין אֶבְיוֹן—Because He stands on the right of a pauper..."[3] Since Hashem is side by side with the pauper, he wanted his wife to be buried there as well.

The Mishnah asks, "אֵיזֶהוּ עָשִׁיר הַשָּׂמֵחַ בְּחֶלְקוֹ—Who is considered truly wealthy? One who's happy with their portion."[4] There is a way to be wealthy without all of the worries: when we recognize and appreciate all that we have, we will realize that we don't need anything else.

A well-known story is told of Reb Zusha of Anipoli that demonstrates real happiness.

A group of *chassidim* came to the *Noam Elimelech* asking how they can make the *berachah* of tragedy—*Dayan Ha'emes*—with the same enthusiasm as the *berachah* for fortunate things—*Ha'tov V'Hameitiv*.[5]

---

2   Rabbeinu Yonah, *Avos* ibid.

3   *Tehillim* 109:31.

4   *Avos* 4:1.

5   See *Berachos* 5:1.

The *Noam Elimelech* told them that he was unable to answer the question and that they should go visit his brother, Reb Zusha, in the city of Anipoli, since he would be able to answer their question. Upon searching for Reb Zusha in Anipoli, they were directed to an old beat-up shack with broken windows and holes in the roof. They were nervous to knock too hard on the door lest it fall right off its hinges. After knocking gently, a barefoot man wearing torn clothing answered the door. "This was Reb Zusha?" they wondered. They told him that his brother, the *Noam Elimelech*, sent them to him to ask their question. Reb Zusha told them that he is unable to answer their question because he never had a bad day in his life!

We see from this story that when one acknowledges that everything comes from Hashem, not only will one not have extra worries, but even things that may at first seem negative will be appreciated as well!

To Summarize

The more possessions one has, the more worries come along with them. Constantly focusing on one's possessions can prevent someone from living a free and extraordinary life. One should focus on investing their time in learning because that is something that gives one benefit in this world and the next. Connecting to Hashem is what brings true happiness.

Points to Ponder

- What is something that I hold on to but can live without?
- What are some possessions that aren't necessary in my home that I could give to a *gemach* or to tzedakah?
- How often do I thank Hashem for what I have?

Building Blocks

Daniel came home from school one day and told me all about a tower he built out of blocks together with his friends. He told me that when he was building the tower, it kept falling down, but after some time and assistance, Daniel figured out how to make the bottom bigger so the building could be taller. This taught me a great lesson of how important setting a foundation is.

אומר לך כלל תבין אותו בכל הפרשיות הבאות בענין אברהם יצחק ויעקב
והוא ענין גדול הזכירוהו רבותינו בדרך קצרה ואמרו (תנחומא, ט) כל מה
שאירע לאבות סימן לבנים.[1]

I will tell you a general principle—understand it in all of the coming sections about Avraham, Yitzchak and Yaakov, and it is a great matter. Our rabbis mentioned it in a brief way and said (Midrash Tanchuma 9), "Everything that occurred to our forefathers is a sign for the children."

There is a concept of *maaseh avos siman l'banim*—the actions of the fathers are a sign for the children. Children learn from their elders and follow their ways. Parents are the rock and foundation for their

---

1   *Ramban, Bereishis* 12:6.

children.[2] The Gemara says that bricks are called *livnei* because they build and last for one's children's children.[3]

Our children see and hear what we do and say. The saying "education begins at home" means the way the parents act is how the children will act. Parents are role models. If children learn something in school and observe the opposite being done at home, children will not fully value what they learn in school.

...וְהַחוּט הַמְשֻׁלָּשׁ לֹא בִמְהֵרָה יִנָּתֵק.[4]

A threefold chain is not readily broken.

מִי שֶׁהוּא תַּלְמִיד חָכָם, וּבְנוֹ וּבֶן בְּנוֹ, שׁוּב אֵין תּוֹרָה פּוֹסֶקֶת מִזַּרְעוֹ, וְכֵן הוּא אוֹמֵר, "לֹא יָמוּשׁוּ מִפִּיךָ וּמִפִּי זַרְעֲךָ וּמִפִּי זֶרַע זַרְעֲךָ".[5]

Whoever is a Torah scholar, as well as his son and his grandson, the Torah will never break off from his seed, as it states, "[My words] will not leave from your mouth nor from the mouth of your offspring nor from the mouth of your offspring's offspring."

Shlomo HaMelech teaches that something threefold isn't broken easily. *Rashi* adds that if there are three generations in a row that are *talmidei chachamim*, it's guaranteed that Torah won't be removed from that family.

The way one instills and plants these roots within their children is by acting the proper way. Children learn more through our actions than from our words. "It's not the study that is essential, but rather the action,"[6] or as the Western saying goes, "Actions speak louder than words."

---

2   The word for "stone" in Hebrew is אֶבֶן. The first two letters 'א and 'ב spell אָב—father; the second letter 'ב and third letter ן spell בֵּן—child.

3   *Shabbos* 77b. In Hebrew, the word *livnei*, bricks, can also mean "for the sons."

4   *Koheles* 4:12.

5   *Koheles* 4:12; *Rashi*, s.v. *V'im yiskefo ha'echad*.

6   *Avos* 1:18.

...לְאִילָן שֶׁעֲנָפָיו מְרֻבִּין וְשָׁרָשָׁיו מֻעָטִין, וְהָרוּחַ בָּאָה וְעוֹקַרְתּוֹ וְהוֹפַכְתּוֹ עַל פָּנָיו...לְאִילָן שֶׁעֲנָפָיו מֻעָטִין וְשָׁרָשָׁיו מְרֻבִּין, שֶׁאֲפִלּוּ כָל הָרוּחוֹת שֶׁבָּעוֹלָם בָּאוֹת וְנוֹשְׁבוֹת בּוֹ אֵין מְזִיזִין אוֹתוֹ מִמְּקוֹמוֹ... [7]

...To a tree whose branches are many and roots few, and a wind comes and uproots it and turns it on its face...to a tree whose branches are few and roots are many, that even if all of the winds in the world come and blow it, it will not move from its place...

The Mishnah teaches that a tree whose roots are few and branches are many will be blown away when a wind comes. However, a tree with many roots and few branches won't budge, even if all of the winds in the world try to blow it away.

The word *"even"* has the same *gematria* as *"gan"*—garden.[8] The way we nourish our garden is the way our beautiful flowers will blossom. We are the foundation for the future generations. We could either set a proper foundation that will be rooted within our children, or a weak foundation that will be easily blown away by the winds of the world. The choice is ours.

To Summarize

Any building made to last must have a solid foundation. This holds true in education as well. When we raise our children, we must recognize that we are laying the foundation for them to build on for the rest of their lives. We are the cornerstone and support that help them develop into healthy, strong-rooted members of Klal Yisrael. This foundation will enable our children to pass the *mesorah* down to the following generations.

Points to Ponder

- How can I start planting the seeds now for my future garden?
- Do my actions speak louder than my words?
- What are three things that are essential to me in my world?

---

7   Ibid. 3:22.

8   אבן = 53 = גן.

Growin' Up

One day, when dropping Daniel off at school, he turned to me and said, "Every day we are growing." I stopped walking to comprehend his thought; where did it come from? I realized that he was referring to physical growth; he is constantly looking at the "older kids" and wants to be big like them.

However, one could look at "every day we are growing" in a spiritual sense as well—to get higher and closer spiritually. We shouldn't be so focused on everyone else's growth, whether it's physical, monetary, or even spiritual growth. If we focus on the best that we can be, we will then be able to say, "Every day *we* are growing."

If we act properly, we have the ability to grow every moment. There are many examples of this:

- When one davens with *kavanah* and has the proper understanding of *tefillah*, one understands that no *tefillah* is alike. Each *tefillah* should be said with a new *kavanah*. On Monday, a person is on Step One, but after he davened and strengthened his *emunah*, one moves to Step Two. On Tuesday, he starts on Step Two and advances to Step Three, and so on.

- Each day of the *omer*, we move up a level in spirituality. However, one should know that there are levels within each level; each individual is on their own level. Moshe could be on one level while

Rachel is on another. Yet each has the potential to grow to the best one can be.

- When we keep Shabbos properly, it elevates the following week. Every day we look forward to Shabbos, as we say daily, *"Ha'yom yom…l'Shabbos."* If Shabbos elevates the week, then by the following Shabbos, we begin on a higher level.

As we have mentioned above, every time we do something positive, we ascend a level.

The Gemara teaches that once we go up in *kedushah*, we don't descend.[1] This principle is said in reference to lighting *Neiros Chanukah*. We ignite the lights of Chanukah to brighten the world from its darkness. The amazing thing about light is that one candle can ignite another without diminishing its flame. *Kedushah* is the same way; it can spread without diminishing from one's self.

הִלֵּל אוֹמֵר, הֱוֵי מִתַּלְמִידָיו שֶׁל אַהֲרֹן, אוֹהֵב שָׁלוֹם וְרוֹדֵף שָׁלוֹם, אוֹהֵב אֶת הַבְּרִיּוֹת וּמְקָרְבָן לַתּוֹרָה.[2]

Hillel says, be from the students of Aharon, love peace and run after peace, love people and bring them closer to the Torah.

שַׁמַּאי אוֹמֵר…וֶהֱוֵי מְקַבֵּל אֶת כָּל הָאָדָם בְּסֵבֶר פָּנִים יָפוֹת.[3]

Shammai says…"and receive every person with a cheerful face."

The Mishnah teaches that the way to bring people close to Torah is through peace and love. Furthermore, the Mishnah states that one should greet others with a pleasant face. A smile is contagious, just like the flame of *kedushah*.

The greater the flame, the greater level we ascend to. A flame is something that has physical characteristics such as heat and color, yet it also has spiritual characteristics, such as that it goes against gravity.

---

1   *Shabbos* 21b.
2   *Avos* 1:12.
3   Ibid. 1:15.

Human nature is to give in to the animalistic characteristics and desires of one's physical body. Yet, as moral people with a *neshamah*—soul—we have a conscience to follow the proper ways of the Torah. Fire is constantly growing and spreading, trying to reach the greatest heights. We, too, should be working on making this world of physicality into one of spirituality. The *pasuk* states, "נֵר ה׳ נִשְׁמַת אָדָם—The flame of Hashem is the soul of man."[4]

In a marriage, the husband and wife work to grow and build a family together. The words *ish*—man—and *isha*—woman—have the letters of Hashem, *yud* and *hei*, within them. They also have the letters *aleph* and *shin*, which spells *aish*—fire.[5] If one wants to be successful in their growth, one must be passionate like a fire. When Hashem sees that one is striving to be one's best, Hashem will help out. It is brought down that the month of Elul is an acronym for the words "*Ani l'dodi v'dodi li*—I am to my beloved and my beloved is to me."[6] When we take the first step toward our spouse, friend, business partner, Hashem, etc., the other party will take a step toward you. Taking the first step shows peace and growth. As mentioned before, a smile is contagious. The first smile leads to many more, like a fire spreading from one candle to the next. When there is *shalom bayis*, there is growth, just as each fire continues to grow while giving to the other.

Our mission in this world is to grow. We must continue to strive toward great heights and utilize what we have for *avodas Hashem*.

To Summarize

Growing isn't just something we do physically, but spiritually as well. Every time we overcome a challenge, great or simple, we are growing. Like a fire, we are made of physical features as well as spiritual components. By channeling our animalistic desires and using them to hone in on our spiritual being, we will have much growth.

---

4   *Mishlei* 20:27.
5   איש, אשה.
6   *Shir Hashirim* 6:3. אלול = אני לדודי ודודי לי.

Points to Ponder

- How am I focusing on becoming the best I can be?
- What is something small I can take upon myself to grow closer to Hashem?
- How am I like a fire—spreading warmth and love to others?

Awe

...אָמַר רַב נַחְמָן בַּר יִצְחָק מֵהָכָא: "עִבְדוּ אֶת ה' בְּיִרְאָה וְגִילוּ בִּרְעָדָה". מַאי "וְגִילוּ בִּרְעָדָה"? אָמַר רַב אַדָּא בַּר מַתְנָא אָמַר רַבָּה: בִּמְקוֹם גִּילָה שָׁם תְּהֵא רְעָדָה...מָר בְּרֵיהּ דְּרָבִינָא עֲבַד הִילּוּלָא לִבְרֵיהּ, חַזִנְהוּ לְרַבָּנָן דַּהֲווֹ קָבָדְחִי טוּבָא אַיְיתִי כָּסָא דְּמוֹקְרָא בַּת אַרְבַּע מְאָה זוּזֵי, וְתַבַּר קַמַּיְיהוּ, וְאַעֲצִיבוּ. רַב אַשִׁי עֲבַד הִילּוּלָא לִבְרֵיהּ, חַזִנְהוּ לְרַבָּנָן דַּהֲווֹ קָא בָדְחִי טוּבָא. אַיְיתִי כָּסָא דְּזוּגִיתָא חִיוָּרְתָּא, וְתַבַּר קַמַּיְהוּ, וְאַעֲצִיבוּ.[1]

...Rav Nachman bar Yitzchak said from here, "Serve the Lord in fear and rejoice with trepidation." What is the meaning of rejoice with trepidation? Rav Adda bar Masna said in the name of Rabbah: "Where there is rejoicing, there should be trembling"...Mar, son of Ravina, made a wedding for his son, and he saw the Rabbanan, who were excessively joyous. He brought a valuable cup worth four hundred zuz and broke it before them, and they became sad. Rav Ashi made a wedding for his son and he saw the Rabbanan, who were excessively joyous. He brought a cup of extremely valuable white glass and broke it before them, and they became sad.

---

1   *Berachos* 30b–31a.

The Gemara in *Berachos* discusses what it means to "rejoice with trepidation." The Gemara brings a few examples of instances showing those rejoicing without the proper mindset and someone coming to remind them to have trepidation. Two of the examples occurred by weddings, in which expensive glasses were smashed to regain their mindset.

When teaching this Gemara, many students asked why this was an appropriate approach to regain the mindset of "rejoice with trepidation." Immediately, I thought of my dear children. There are times when children are acting wild and full of energy, and they may act without thinking or play ball in the house. Simply telling children not to act in this manner may not always work; if there is a lack of supervision, the child may become a bit reckless. However, as soon as something breaks, the fun stops and the children then recognize what they have done.

This is how I understood the Gemara: "Trepidation" acts as the supervision and boundary. When one lacks a sense of trepidation, one goes astray. Sometimes a drastic action must be taken, such as breaking a glass, in order to regain focus.

"רֵאשִׁית חָכְמָה יִרְאַת ה' שֵׂכֶל טוֹב"—The beginning of wisdom is having fear of Hashem."[2]

As the wisest of all men, Shlomo HaMelech says, "The fear of Hashem is the beginning of knowledge."[3] The Mishnah teaches, "If one is lacking *yirah*, they cannot have *chochmah*."[4]

One can only begin to have true wisdom when one recognizes that everything comes from Hashem. There may be a doctor who is the best in the world in their field and studied in school for many years, pulled all-nighters every other night in order to learn all of the wonderful things the body has within it. But the moment that the doctor opens his eyes

---

2   *Tehillim* 111:10.

3   *Mishlei* 1:7.

4   *Avos* 3:17. Although there may be wonderful, nice, and intelligent people, they are lacking the ability to grow spiritually closer to Hashem. One who has the fear of Hashem and attaches oneself to Torah will not only have wonderful qualities and characteristics (*Avos* 6:1) but will have the opportunity to become closer to Hashem.

and recognizes that everything comes from Hashem, the doctor has an entirely new perspective on life.

In order to have boundaries, one must maintain a sense of trepidation at all times. People drive very differently next to police cars because it is the fear of getting caught that keeps them in check. Compare it to how they drive when they are late or when they think no one is around. This is how we must act at all times since Hashem is always watching.

One summer, the camp photographer got married and left a week before camp concluded. I was asked to take pictures and videos around the camp for the final week. I found it amazing how people would behave so differently when they knew that they were on camera.

וְהִסְתַּכֵּל בִּשְׁלשָׁה דְבָרִים וְאִי אַתָּה בָא לִידֵי עֲבֵרָה, דַּע מַה לְמַעְלָה מִמְּךָ, עַיִן רוֹאָה וְאֹזֶן שׁוֹמַעַת, וְכָל מַעֲשֶׂיךָ בַּסֵּפֶר נִכְתָּבִין.[5]

Consider three things and you will not come to sin: Know what there is above you—an eye that sees, an ear that hears, and all of your actions are written in a book.

הִסְתַּכֵּל בִּשְׁלשָׁה דְבָרִים וְאִי אַתָּה בָא לִידֵי עֲבֵרָה. דַּע מֵאַיִן בָּאתָ, וּלְאָן אַתָּה הוֹלֵךְ, וְלִפְנֵי מִי אַתָּה עָתִיד לִתֵּן דִּין וְחֶשְׁבּוֹן. מֵאַיִן בָּאתָ, מִטִּפָּה סְרוּחָה, וּלְאָן אַתָּה הוֹלֵךְ, לִמְקוֹם עָפָר רִמָּה וְתוֹלֵעָה. וְלִפְנֵי מִי אַתָּה עָתִיד לִתֵּן דִּין וְחֶשְׁבּוֹן, לִפְנֵי מֶלֶךְ מַלְכֵי הַמְּלָכִים הַקָּדוֹשׁ בָּרוּךְ הוּא.[6]

Consider three things and you will not come to sin: Know where you come from, and to where you are going, and to Whom you will give an account and reckoning. From where do you come from? From a putrid drop. And to where are you going? To a place of dirt, worms, and maggots. And before Whom will you give an account and reckoning? Before the King of all kings, Hakadosh Baruch Hu.

---

5   Ibid. 2:1.
6   Ibid. 3:1.

ובעבור הענוה, תעלה על לבך מדת היראה, כי תתן אל לבך תמיד: מאין
באת, ולאן אתה הולך; ושאתה רמה ותולעה בחייך, ואף כי במותך; ולפני
מי אתה עתיד לתן דין וחשבון, לפני מלך הכבוד.[7]

*Through humility you will also come to fear God. It will cause
you to always think about "where you came from and where you
are going," and that while alive you are only like a maggot and
a worm as after death, and before Whom you will eventually
stand for judgment, the Glorious King.*

Both of these Mishnayos tell us that if we consider three things, we
will not come to sin because of the awe and trepidation of Hashem.
This is equivalent to the Gemara mentioned earlier about rejoicing with
trepidation.

ר' מתיא בן חרש אומר לא בא הכתוב אלא לאיים עליו כדי שתהא תורה
ניתנת באימה ברתת וביזיע שנאמר, עבדו את ה' ביראה וגילו ברעדה מאי
וגילו ברעדה אמר רב אדא בר מתנה אמר רב במקום גילה שם תהא
רעדה.[8]

*Rabbi Masya ben Charash says: The pasuk only comes to in-
timidate so that the Torah would be delivered with awe, with
quaking, and with trembling, as it is stated: "Serve Hashem
with awe and rejoice with trepidation." What is the meaning of
"and rejoice with trepidation"? Rav Adda bar Masna said that
Rav said: Where there is the joy [of fulfilling a mitzvah], there
will be the trepidation [of the awe of Heaven] there.*

מתן תורה של לוחות דכתיב פקודי ה' ישרים משמחי לב.[9]

*Concerning the laws of the Torah, it is written, "The precepts of
Hashem are just, rejoicing the heart."*

---

7   *Igeres HaRamban* 4.
8   *Yoma* 4b.
9   Ibid., *Rashi s.v. Bimakom gilah*, quoting *Tehillim* 19:9.

Fear and joy may seem to contradict one another, but in reality, they don't. The Gemara in *Yoma* interprets the *pasuk* of "rejoice with trepidation" differently than the previous Gemara. The Gemara in *Yoma* alludes that wherever there is joy in fulfilling a mitzvah, there will be *yiras Shamayim* there as well. *Rashi* quotes the *pasuk*, saying, "The principles of Hashem are just, the joyousness of the heart..."[10]

As it says in *Tehillim*, "אַשְׁרֵי אִישׁ יָרֵא אֶת ה' בְּמִצְוֹתָיו חָפֵץ מְאֹד—Happy is the one who fears Hashem."[11]

הָאַהֲבָה וְהַיִּרְאָה שֶׁהֵם הַמְקָרְבִים וּמַדְבִּיקִים הָאָדָם בְּבוֹרְאוֹ...וְהִנֵּה הַיִּרְאָה הַזֹּאת הִיא מְטַהֶרֶת אֶת הָאָדָם מֵחֹשֶׁךְ חׇמְרִיּוּתוֹ וְגוּפָנִיּוּתוֹ וּמַשְׁרֶה עָלָיו הַשְׁרָאַת הַשְּׁכִינָה...[12]

About the matter of love and awe, that they bring a man close and to cleave to his Creator...And note that this awe purifies a person from the darkness of his materialism and his physicality, and brings the Divine Presence to rest upon him.

The *Maharal* elaborates on the benefits one receives when one has fear and awe toward Hashem. He teaches how one can reach levels of purity when having the proper mindset of trepidation.

Let us always have Hashem on our mind and not only will we be happier and more successful people, but we will be children with a great relationship to our Father in Heaven.

To Summarize

The Torah teaches us to "rejoice with trepidation." It may seem contradictory that one should always be happy yet at the same time have

---

10 On this, the *Radak* says, "כי החכם ישמח על שכלו—A wise person rejoices in his knowledge" (*Radak, Tehillim* 19:9). When his knowledge takes over his body, there is no comparable joy. We are constantly told to put mind over matter. There are three filters in one's body: מוח לב כליות—the mind, the heart, and the kidneys. When one places the filters in this order, they are in control and are like a מלך—a king. However, when one has their filters backward (כליות לב מוח) they are like כלם—nothing.

11 *Tehillim* 112:1.

12 *Derech Hashem*, chap. 4, *B'Ahavah v'yirah*.

trepidation. Chazal explain that these two emotions don't conflict with one another. One can be very happy and simultaneously conscious that Hashem is constantly in front of him. Having the balance of these two emotions will heighten one's level of purity.

Points to Ponder

- Do I live with trepidation of Hashem?
- What are some boundaries I have or can set to increase my *yiras Hashem*?
- How do I feel when Hashem is on my mind?

LESSON 7

Fun Times

When my children come home from school, I love to know how their day was and what they learned. Every day I ask, "How was your day in school? What did you learn in school today?" followed by, "Can you tell me more about it?"

There was a point when, every day, Ayelet would tell me that she didn't learn anything. So I asked, "Did you do any projects today? Did you play with anyone today?" She would then begin to tell me about her jam-packed fun day. What she didn't realize was how much she was learning! I realized from this that learning **can be** fun!

I once heard an educator say: "I know that I had a successful day when my students had fun and didn't realize how much they were learning."

I'm not sure what age it is where learning turns to work and a burden, but I find it somewhat heartbreaking when I hear students say that school is so boring. Anyone who has had any interaction with children can attest that they pick up and learn from how you speak and act. They will imitate you verbally or try to mimic your actions. They learn so much so quickly when they are alert and interested. However, when they are uninterested, just like adults, their minds turn off and they start looking at the clock, waiting to get out.

As we mentioned earlier, Einstein once said, "Everybody is a genius. But if you judge a fish by its ability to climb a tree, it will live its whole life believing that it is stupid." Shlomo HaMelech writes, "חֲנֹךְ לַנַּעַר עַל פִּי דַרְכּוֹ—

Educate a child according to his way."[1] An educator's job is to help each student bloom into the beautiful flower they can become. In order to do this, the educator must dial into each student's ability and use it to help the student learn. Unfortunately, in many education systems, educators forget the students are our future. Many schools have been teaching subjects instead of students.

There is a well-known story of Rav Avraham Pam, who would teach the same Gemara every year. Someone once asked him how it doesn't get old and boring to teach the same topic year in and year out. Rav Pam looked at him and said, "Every year I have new students, and I must teach the Gemara differently."

When educators are passionate to build connections and enhance their students' lives with knowledge, they are less focused on the content and more attuned with their students. They don't just teach bell to bell, but every moment they have is another opportunity to be involved, educate, and invest in our future.

On the *pasuk* brought above, Rabbi Shimshon Raphael Hirsch says: "*darko hu*—is his way,"[2] not the schools, not the textbook, not the other students, not any way other than that specific individual's way.

One way to have students enjoy learning is a process called participative leadership, which is defined as "sharing of problem solving by consulting with team members before making a decision."[3]

In his book, *Drive*, Daniel Pink discusses autonomy as one of the three methods to help motivate employees. Through research, Pink proves from various companies that when there is flexibility at work, not only will employees feel more committed to their employers and organizations, but they will be more productive as well.[4]

Participative leadership allows students to excel in their own way and to hone in on their talents. When children are in preschool, they

---

1   *Mishlei* 22:6.

2   *Yisodos Hachinuch* 53.

3   Stephen J. Sauer, "Taking the Reins: The effect of new leader status and leadership style on team performance," *American Psychological Association*, 96 (2011), pp. 574–87.

4   D.H. Pink, *Drive: The Surprising Truth about What Motivates Us* (New York, NY: Riverhead Books, 2009).

are expected to express themselves in their own unique way through coloring, painting, etc. Yet, as children grow older, the flexibility becomes less, and the strain becomes greater.[5]

Aside from reading the Torah and learning about the Yamim Tovim, each one of the Yamim Tovim has something that serves a visual reminder to connect to Hashem:

- Rosh Hashanah has the shofar and *simanim*.
- On Yom Kippur, we wear a *kittel* and shoes that aren't made from leather.
- Sukkos has the sukkah, lulav, and esrog.
- Chanukah has the menorah.
- Purim has costumes, *mishlo'ach manos*, and the *Megillah*.
- Pesach has the *ke'arah*, matzah, and four cups.
- On Shavuos, we decorate our houses and shuls with flowers.
- On Tishah B'Av, we read *Eichah* and *Kinnos*, sit on the floor, and wear shoes not made from leather.

כי הא דיתיב רבן גמליאל וקא דריש: עתידה אשה שתלד בכל יום, שנאמר "הרה ויולדת יחדיו". לגלג עליו אותו תלמיד, אמר: "אין כל חדש תחת השמש"! אמר ליה: בא ואראך דוגמתן בעולם הזה. נפק אחוי ליה תרנגולת.[6]

As in the case where Rabban Gamliel was sitting and he expounded: In the future, [in the World to Come], a woman will give birth every day, as it says: "She will conceive and give birth together." A certain student scorned at him and said: That cannot be, as it has already been stated: "There is nothing new under the sun." Rabban Gamliel said to him: Come and I will show you an example of this in this world. He took him outside and showed him a chicken that lays eggs every day.

---

5   I am not saying learning different subjects are not important. Students should have knowledge in all areas. However, education shouldn't be lectures, but rather classes should be more interactive where students feel like a part of the class instead of a byproduct. With this, they will love to learn and make it their own.

6   *Shabbos* 30b.

Rabban Gamliel could have simply told the student that chickens lay eggs every day; however, he recognized the importance and impact of hands-on learning.

When children come home clean, i.e., the way they went to school, it may indicate something wrong. When our children come home messy and full of dirt, paint, and who knows what else, we know that they had a fun day.

Research shows that "students cheat less frequently on assignments they consider valuable to their learning and that have personal meaning…than assignments completed for the primary purpose of receiving a good grade, pleasing parents, or protecting school related sport/ activity eligibility."[7]

I often tell my students that if they're not having fun, then they're not really learning. They may be memorizing information and spitting it back to do well on an exam, but *"v'lo ha'midrash hu ha'ikar, ela ha'maaseh*—the essence of learning is application."[8] Doing well on a written test doesn't make someone a better person. Doing well on the test of life does.

We see how important it is to teach hands-on in order to engage and involve our students in a meaningful and applicable way.

To Summarize

It's very common to hear someone reflect on the good times they've experienced because they want to relive those moments. Learning in school can also be known as the "good times." Unfortunately, in many schools, the learning turns into a burden as children get older. When we love our work, it becomes easier, even if it is a larger amount. Learning hands-on and demonstrating how the information is applicable to the student are ways to instill a love for what one is learning.

---

7   T.B. Murdock, A. Miller, J. Kohlhardt, "Effects of classroom context variables on high school students' judgments of the acceptability and likelihood of cheating," *Journal of Educational Psychology*, 96 (2004), 765–77.

8   *Avos* 1:17.

Points to Ponder

- Do I enjoy learning? If not, how can I make it more enjoyable?
- How do I learn best?
- Who is one teacher that had a positive impact on my life?

Begin with the End in Mind

I n *Avos* our Sages teach, "Know from where you come and to where
you are going."[1] The second habit of Stephen Covey's *The 7 Habits of
Highly Effective People* is called "begin with the end in mind." Covey
explains: "To begin with the end in mind means to start with a clear understanding of your destination. It means to know where you're going
to better understand where you are now and so that the steps you take
are always in the right direction."[2]

I have found this method very successful when it comes to writing
my children's mitzvah notes. I ask them in the morning before school
what I should write on their mitzvah note for the following day. In order
for me to use that mitzvah note, they would have had to do what the
mitzvah note says. Of course, spontaneous mitzvah notes are also en-
couraged; however, mitzvah notes with a "begin with the end in mind"
mindset will set goals for children.

When children see that they have goals and are accomplishing them,
it gives them a sense of satisfaction. It will also remind them to act
properly and to refrain from doing wrong. This will, God willing, guide
them to act properly because it is the right thing and not just because
they will get a mitzvah note.

---

1   *Avos* 3:1.
2   *The 7 Habits*, p. 55.

וכדרב יהודה דאמר רב יהודה אמר רב לעולם יעסוק אדם בתורה ומצות
אף על פי שלא לשמה שמתוך שלא לשמה בא לשמה.[3]

*As Rav Yehudah said in the name of Rav, a person should
always be involved in Torah and mitzvos, even though it is not
for their own sake; through [performing mitzvos] not for their
sake, he comes to [perform them] for their sake.*[4]

כל ישראל יש להם חלק לעולם הבא...[5]

All of Yisrael have a portion in the World to Come...

רבי חנניא בן עקשיא אומר, רצה הקדוש ברוך הוא לזכות את ישראל,
לפיכך הרבה להם תורה ומצות...[6]

*Rabbi Chananya ben Akashia says, Hakadosh Baruch Hu
wanted to [give] merit [to] Yisrael; therefore, He gave them
Torah and mitzvos in abundance...*

In every printing of *Pirkei Avos*, a Mishnah from *Sanhedrin* is brought
preceding it, which states, "All of Yisrael has a portion in *Olam Haba*."
Then, to conclude each *perek*, a Mishnah from *Makkos* is referenced,
"Rabbi Chananya ben Akashia said, Hashem wants to give merit to
Yisrael, therefore He gives them many mitzvos..."

What is the reasoning for this?

I believe that Chazal are teaching us that if we are going to find ourselves in a difficult situation, think of the future. Hashem wants to give
us merit so that we can enhance our portion in *Olam Haba*. We have to
think long-term, as the Mishnah says:

---

3   *Pesachim* 50b.
4   *Tosafos* (s.v. *V'kan*) explains that although the Gemara in *Berachos* (17a) teaches that it would
    be better for one not to have been created if they perform a mitzvah not for the sake of
    the mitzvah (*she'lo lishmah*), that is referring to one that uses Torah and mitzvos to harm
    others. However, with regards to our Gemara, the one performing the mitzvah *she'lo lishmah*
    is doing it because of a lack in character and not through evil.
5   *Sanhedrin* 90a.
6   *Makkos* 3:16.

וֶהֱוֵי מְחַשֵּׁב הֶפְסֵד מִצְוָה כְּנֶגֶד שְׂכָרָהּ, וּשְׂכַר עֲבֵרָה כְּנֶגֶד הֶפְסֵדָהּ.[7]

One should calculate the loss of a mitzvah against its reward and the 'reward' of a sin against the loss.

Before we act, we should consider what the ramifications may be. Every action has a consequence. Is it really worth sinning to gain a bit of pleasure in this world than to refrain from sin and have infinite pleasure in the World to Come?

Interestingly, in Stephen Covey's introduction to Habit 2, he writes:

> *Picture yourself driving to the funeral parlor or chapel, parking the car, and getting out. As you walk inside the building, you notice the flowers, the soft organ music. You see the faces of friends and family you pass along the way. You feel the shared sorrow of losing, the joy you have known, that radiates from the hearts of the people there.*
>
> *As you walk down to the front of the room and look inside the casket, you suddenly come face to face with yourself. This is your funeral, three years from today. All these people have come to honor you, to express feelings of love and appreciation for your life.*
>
> *As you take a seat and wait for the services to begin, you look at the program in your hand. There are to be four speakers. The first is from your family...The second speaker is one of your friends...The third speaker is from your work or profession...And the fourth is from...some community organization where you've been involved in service.*
>
> *Now think deeply. What would you like each of these speakers to say about you and your life? What kind of husband, wife, father would you like their words to reflect? What character would you like them to have seen in you?...*[8]

---

7   *Avos* 2:1.
8   *The 7 Habits*, pp. 103–4.

Similarly, when the Mishnah tells us to "know where we come from and where we are going," it concludes that we are all going to give an accounting and reckoning before the King of all kings, Hakadosh Baruch Hu.

What impression do we want to leave behind? Will we leave a legacy of favorable memories and impressions that made a difference? When we find ourselves in a dilemma, think of the future.

אמר רבי לוי בר חמא, אמר רבי שמעון בן לקיש: לעולם ירגיז אדם יצר טוב על יצר הרע.[9]

Rabbi Levi bar Chama said in the name of Rabbi Shimon ben Lakish: One should always encourage his good inclination over his evil inclination.

The Gemara teaches that one should always place his *yetzer tov* over his *yetzer hara*. If one is able to do so, then great, but if one isn't capable of doing so, he should learn Torah. If learning Torah helps him subdue his *yetzer hara*, then great, but if not, then he should recite *Shema*. If this helps place his *yetzer tov* over his *yetzer hara*, then amazing, but if not, then one should think of the day of death.

Here, too, Chazal teach us to begin with the end in mind. Think of how you want to be remembered and how you plan to create the legacy you want to leave behind. For example, in order to be remembered as a good parent, you have to act in a way that your children are going to appreciate, and teach them correct values. Understandably, there are many tests in life that don't compare to preparing a mitzvah note in advance; however, it is the same concept. Even if we do something *lo lishmah*, if we work on ourselves to be the best that we can, we will be *zocheh* to learn Torah and perform mitzvos *lishmah*.

To Summarize

Having goals can definitely help an individual achieve many accomplishments in one's lifetime. However, one must strategize as to how he will

---

9   *Berachos* 5a.

succeed in fulfilling his goals. Knowing your strengths and weaknesses, from where you are coming and where you're headed, will be the map to help navigate your journey. When one constantly has his objective in mind, he will be able to guide his actions toward completing his task.

Points to Ponder

- How do I want to be remembered?
- What are some accomplishments I'd like to be remembered for?
- What steps will I take to achieve those goals and be remembered the way I want?

Connection

Throughout Jewish history, we find that there are many students who have had such strong relationships with their *rebbi* or leader that they later on became leaders themselves. Two prominent examples are:

- Yehoshua bin Nun, who attached himself to Moshe Rabbeinu and led the Jewish nation into Eretz Yisrael.
- Elisha HaNavi, who connected himself to Eliyahu HaNavi and became greater in prophecy than Eliyahu was.

No wonder the Sages instruct us, "Make for yourself a *rav*/mentor."[1]

When I learned this Mishnah, I began thinking of one parent-teacher conference we had with Daniel's *morah*. *Baruch Hashem*, she had only wonderful things to tell us. One thing that stuck out was how she described Daniel's tendency to stay close to her so that if he has any questions, he could ask her right away. Daniel loves to learn, and he doesn't want to miss out on anything that his *morah* teaches.

יוֹסֵי בֶן יוֹעֶזֶר אִישׁ צְרֵדָה אוֹמֵר, יְהִי בֵיתְךָ בֵית וַעַד לַחֲכָמִים, וֶהֱוֵי מִתְאַבֵּק בַּעֲפַר רַגְלֵיהֶם, וֶהֱוֵי שׁוֹתֶה בְצָמָא אֶת דִּבְרֵיהֶם.[2]

---

1   *Avos* 1:6.
2   Ibid. 1:4.

Yosi ben Yoezer of Tzereida says, let your house be a place of
meeting for chachamim, sit in the dust of their feet, and drink
their words thirstily.

We learn to become dirty by the feet of the wise and to drink their
words thirstily.

Through learning *Pirkei Avos*, one can see how every Mishnah
connects from *rebbi* to *talmid*. The first Mishnah begins with Moshe
passing the Torah down to his *talmid*, Yehoshua, who passes it down to
the Elders, and so on. Each Mishnah follows by relating that the Tanna
received it from his *rebbi*.

I have always found it beautiful when grandchildren have a nice relationship with their grandparents. The *pasuk* tells us, "עֲטֶרֶת זְקֵנִים בְּנֵי בָנִים—
The crown of the elders is grandchildren."[3] It is bringing many generations together. The *pasuk* tells us, "שְׁאַל אָבִיךָ וְיַגֵּדְךָ זְקֵנֶיךָ וְיֹאמְרוּ לָךְ—Ask
your father, he will inform you; ask your grandfather, and he will
tell you."[4]

The more connected one is, the closer it brings them back to standing in front of Har Sinai and the greater their relationship will be
with Hashem.

אמר ר' פרנך אמר ר' יוחנן כל שהוא תלמיד חכם ובנו תלמיד חכם ובן בנו
תלמיד חכם שוב אין תורה פוסקת מזרעו לעולם שנאמר ואני זאת בריתי
וגו' לא ימושו מפיך ומפי זרעך ומפי זרע זרעך אמר ה' מעתה ועד עולם.[5]

Rabbi Parnach says in the name of Rabbi Yochanan: Anyone
who is a Torah scholar, and whose son is a Torah scholar, and
whose grandson is a Torah scholar, the Torah will never again
cease from his descendants, as it is stated: "And as for Me, this
is My covenant...shall not depart out of your mouth, nor out
of the mouth of your seed, nor out of the mouth of your seed's
seed, says Hashem, from now and forever."

---

3   *Mishlei* 17:6.

4   *Devarim* 32:7.

5   *Bava Metzia* 85a.

The Gemara teaches, "Anyone who is a *talmid chacham* and his son is a *talmid chacham* and his grandson is a *talmid chacham*, the Torah will never cease from his descendants." We see a special connection that isn't just between a parent and child, but includes a grandchild as well.

וְעַתָּה שְׁנֵי בָנֶיךָ הַנּוֹלָדִים לְךָ בְּאֶרֶץ מִצְרַיִם עַד בֹּאִי אֵלֶיךָ מִצְרַיְמָה לִי הֵם אֶפְרַיִם וּמְנַשֶּׁה כִּרְאוּבֵן וְשִׁמְעוֹן יִהְיוּ לִי...הַמַּלְאָךְ הַגֹּאֵל אֹתִי מִכָּל רָע יְבָרֵךְ אֶת הַנְּעָרִים וְיִקָּרֵא בָהֶם שְׁמִי וְשֵׁם אֲבֹתַי אַבְרָהָם וְיִצְחָק וְיִדְגּוּ לָרֹב בְּקֶרֶב הָאָרֶץ...וַיְמָאֵן אָבִיו וַיֹּאמֶר יָדַעְתִּי בְנִי יָדַעְתִּי גַּם הוּא יִהְיֶה לְעָם וְגַם הוּא יִגְדָּל וְאוּלָם אָחִיו הַקָּטֹן יִגְדַּל מִמֶּנּוּ וְזַרְעוֹ יִהְיֶה מְלֹא הַגּוֹיִם...וַיְבָרֲכֵם בַּיּוֹם הַהוּא לֵאמוֹר בְּךָ יְבָרֵךְ יִשְׂרָאֵל לֵאמֹר יְשִׂמְךָ אֱלֹקִים כְּאֶפְרַיִם וְכִמְנַשֶּׁה.⁶

Now, your two sons, who were born to you in the land of Egypt before I came to you in Egypt, shall be mine; Ephraim and Menasheh shall be equal to Reuven and Shimon...The Angel who has redeemed me from all harm—bless the lads. In them may my name be recalled, and the names of my fathers, Avraham and Yitzchak, and may they be abounding multitudes upon the earth...But his father objected, saying, "I know, my son, I know. He too shall become a people, and he too shall be great. Yet, his younger brother shall be greater than he, and his offspring shall be plentiful enough for nations." So he blessed them that day, saying, "By you shall Yisrael invoke blessings, saying: 'God make you like Ephraim and Menasheh.'"

An example of this is Yaakov Avinu and his grandchildren, Menasheh and Ephraim. When Yaakov Avinu was on his deathbed, he called his grandchildren over and gave them a *berachah* that they should be part of the *shevatim* just like his own children. He continued by placing his hands on Ephraim and Menasheh, and he gave a *berachah* to Yosef relating back to his father, Yitzchak, and grandfather, Avraham. Yaakov continued by saying the famous *berachah* of *Hamalach Hagoel*, where he says, "In them may my name be recalled and the names of my fathers,

---

6   *Bereishis* 48:5, 16, 19–20.

Avraham and Yitzchak." A couple of *pesukim* later, Yaakov tells Yosef that his children are going to have descendants who will be great. Not only that, but in the following *pasuk*, Yaakov says that Yisrael should bless their children to be like Ephraim and Menasheh.

I would venture to say that Yaakov is telling Yosef that because his children were able to stay righteous in a corrupt land, they have the *zechus*, as the Gemara teaches, that the Torah won't leave their descendants. I would also say that Yaakov is somewhat comparing himself to his grandchildren by bringing up Avraham and Yitzchak.

דבר אחר: גרתי בגימטריא תרי"ג, כלומר, עם לבן גרתי ותרי"ג מצות שמרתי ולא למדתי ממעשיו הרעים.[7]

Another explanation: The word "garti" has the numerical value of 613—taryag; this means to say, "Though I have sojourned with Lavan, the wicked, I have observed the 613 Divine Commandments, and I have not learned of his evil ways."

Yaakov was sent to his uncle Lavan's house, and *Rashi* teaches that Yaakov kept all 613 mitzvos. Since Yaakov remained righteous in Lavan's house, he was the first in history to be the third consecutive generation to be righteous.

רַבִּי שִׁמְעוֹן אוֹמֵר, שְׁלֹשָׁה כְתָרִים הֵם, כֶּתֶר תּוֹרָה וְכֶתֶר כְּהֻנָּה וְכֶתֶר מַלְכוּת.[8]

Rabbi Shimon says, there are three crowns: the crown of Torah, the crown of priesthood, and the crown of kingship.

I believe that Yaakov was also alluding to the Mishnah that teaches that there are three crowns—Torah, *kehunah*, and *malchus*. The crowns of *kehunah* and *malchus* are given to one automatically through blood. However, the crown of Torah is not automatic, even if one's previous generations were *talmidei chachamim*.

7   Ibid. 32:5, *Rashi*, s.v. *Garti* (תרי"ג = 613 = גרתי).
8   *Avos* 4:13.

וַיַּרְא יִשְׂרָאֵל אֶת בְּנֵי יוֹסֵף וַיֹּאמֶר מִי אֵלֶּה.[9]

And Yisrael saw the children of Yosef and said, "Who are these?"

בקש לברכם ונסתלקה שכינה ממנו, לפי שעתיד ירבעם ואחאב לצאת מאפרים ויהוא ובניו ממנשה.[10]

He wished to bless them, but the Divine Presence departed from him because he saw that from Ephraim would be born the wicked kings Yeravam and Achav, and from Menasheh [would be born] Yehu and his sons.

When Menasheh and Ephraim came into the room, Yaakov asked, "*Who are these?*" *Rashi* teaches that Yaakov wanted to bless them, but he lost his *ruach hakodesh* since he saw that wicked people would come from them. Although they were righteous, Yaakov was teaching them that it takes work to keep Torah in the family.

The *pasuk* says, "תִּתֵּן אֱמֶת לְיַעֲקֹב—Give truth to Yaakov."[11] Yaakov was the link that connected the previous two generations of the Avos to the following two generations—Menasheh and Ephraim.[12]

To Summarize

Having a close connection with a *rav* and mentor, as well as one's parents and, if the case, one's children, is very important. These relationships not only connect one to the past, but it creates a link to the future. Bridging older generations to younger generations brings a certain unity that is everlasting.

---

9   *Bereishis* 48:8.

10   Ibid., *Rashi*, s.v. *Vayar Yisrael.*

11   *Michah* 7:20.

12   The Gemara (*Shabbos* 104a) teaches that אמת is composed of the letters א, מ, ת—the first, middle, and last letters of the *aleph-beis*. אמת—truth is always withstanding and will survive the test of time.

Points to Ponder

- Do I have a *rav* or mentor that I can learn from and contact when I need guidance?
- What are some ways I can connect to others?
- How can I connect more to the truth?

Love of Learning

One of the most extraordinary lessons I have learned from my children is from their passion to learn. The Mishnah says to "love work," which I understood to be referring to what we involve ourselves in, including our occupation. One should love what one does, whether one is an adult or child. A child's occupation is school, and he should love going.

My children are constantly asking questions in order to learn new ideas and concepts. School is a place where they have a whole world at their fingertips. They learn new things every day, such as new letters, math, science, and even social skills.

The best way for children to learn and retain the knowledge is through application:

לֹא הַמִּדְרָשׁ הוּא הָעִקָּר אֶלָּא הַמַּעֲשֶׂה.[1]

It is not the study that is essential [but] rather the action.

The love of learning continues to grow when my children come home and apply what they learn to their daily lives. In *Birchos HaTorah*, we ask:

והערב נא ה' אלקינו את דברי תורתך בפינו ובפיות עמך בית ישראל.

---

1   *Avos* 1:17.

Make it sweet, please Hashem, the words of Your Torah on our
mouths and on the mouths of the House of Yisrael.

To be successful in something, one needs consistency. It is very difficult to be consistent in something that one doesn't find sweet and enjoyable. Mistaking sugar for salt will ruin a recipe and make it extremely
distasteful. This applies to learning as well.

Doug Lemov, author of *Teach Like a Champion 2.0*, calls Technique #62
the "Joy Factor." He writes, "It turns out that finding joy in the work of
learning—the Joy Factor—is a key driver of not just a happy classroom
but a high-achieving classroom. People work harder when they enjoy
working on something..."[2]

The terminology the Gemara uses when searching for a reason is "*Mai
ta'ama*—What is the reason?" The word *ta'am* literally means "taste" or
"flavor."[3] It is used in the Gemara because the more we learn and delve
into Torah, the sweeter it becomes.

The Gemara tells a story of Abaye going to the house of Mari.

אמר אביי כי נפקי מבי מר הוה מר שבענא כי מטאי להתם קריבו לי שיתין צעי
דשיתין מיני קדירה ואכלי בהו שיתין פלוגי ובישולא בתרייתא הוו קרו ליה
צלי קדר ובעאי למיכס צעא אבתרה אמר אביי היינו דאמרי אינשי כפין
עניא ולא ידע אי נמי רווחא לבסימא שכיח.[4]

Abaye said, "When I left the house of Rabbah, I thought I was
full. But, when I arrived at the house of Mari, they brought
me sixty plates with sixty types of cooked food, and I ate sixty
pieces, one of each of them. The last dish they offered was called
pot roast. After eating it, I wanted to eat the plate." Abaye
said about this incident, "This is what people say, 'A poor man
doesn't know when he's hungry and room can always be found
for dessert.'"

---

2   D. Lemov, *Teach Like a Champion 2.0: 62 Techniques That Put Students on the Path to College*
     (San Francisco: Jossey-Bass, 2015), p. 442.

3   מאי טעמא.

4   *Megillah* 7b.

The *Chasam Sofer* explains that the Gemara compares eating food to learning Torah. Abaye thought that when he left Rabbah's house, he was full of Torah. When he arrived at Mari's house, they served him sixty dishes. Each one of the sixty dishes was a *mesechta* in *Shas*. Abaye "tasted," meaning that he learned various *sugyos*. The last *sugya* he learned was about the *Korban Pesach*, hence "pot roast."[5] Abaye enjoyed the *sugya* so much that he wanted to "eat the plate," or finish the *mesechta*. The more he learned, the more he wanted to learn. Abaye stated that room can always be found for sweets. The *Chasam Sofer* explains this statement to mean that the Torah is of endless depth and it is always possible to reach a deeper explanation.

The Mishnah tells us:

בֶּן בַּג בַּג אוֹמֵר, הֲפֹךְ בָּהּ וַהֲפֹךְ בָּהּ, דְּכֹלָּא בָהּ שֶׁאֵין לְךָ מִדָּה טוֹבָה הֵימֶנָּה.[6]

Delve and delve again into the Torah because everything is in it, and there is nothing better than the Torah.

The Mishnah is teaching us to delve twice since once is not enough. The Torah is something that can be learned over and over again, and it gets sweeter each time.

When a boy turns three, it is customary to give him an *upsherin*. Part of the *upsherin* ceremony consists of putting honey onto the letters of the *aleph-beis* and having the child lick the honey after saying each letter. The reason for this is to teach the sweetness of learning to our children, even from a young age.

To Summarize

One acquires a love of learning when the learning is made sweet for them. There are many analogies between food and Torah since they have much in common in terms of connecting to people. People get a sense of joy, bliss, and comfort when eating certain foods. These feelings are

---

5   The *Korban Pesach* had to be roasted.

6   *Avos* 5:21.

felt when one learns as well. Like a tasty dish, when one has a sweet love for learning, they will line up for seconds.

Points to Ponder

- Is Torah sweet for me?
- How can I find joy in my learning?
- How can I make reviewing what I learned sweet?

Chapter Four

LESSONS
FROM CAMP

Snack Time

In today's day and age, we can get anything in an instant with a simple click of a button. Even instant coffee isn't considered instant anymore! Now people can order a coffee from their phones and have it waiting for them as soon as they get to the store. One can order a car to pick them up with a click of a button. I believe that it is possible for someone to live their entire life indoors and have everything they need delivered to them with a voice command to "Alexa"! One can even attend elementary school through college online. We are so caught up in the mindset of instant gratification; everything we want, we want it now.

As Daniel was getting ready for camp, I told him that I was putting a special Rosh Chodesh treat into his knapsack for snack time. The moment he heard the word "treat," he wanted it. I tried to explain that it was his snack for camp, and if he ate it now, he wouldn't have it for later. Luckily for me, he understood and saved the treat for camp.

Chazal teach us that *"Mi she'tarach b'Erev Shabbos yochel b'Shabbos*—those who prepare on Erev Shabbos are able to eat on Shabbos."[1] There are many interpretations as to what this saying teaches us. One lesson I learned is that sometimes it is better not to have instant gratification and to wait things out. Take a look at what happened with Yaakov and Eisav.

---

1   *Avodah Zarah* 3a.

וַיָּזֶד יַעֲקֹב נָזִיד וַיָּבֹא עֵשָׂו מִן הַשָּׂדֶה וְהוּא עָיֵף: וַיֹּאמֶר עֵשָׂו אֶל יַעֲקֹב הַלְעִיטֵנִי
נָא מִן הָאָדֹם הָאָדֹם הַזֶּה כִּי עָיֵף אָנֹכִי עַל כֵּן קָרָא שְׁמוֹ אֱדוֹם: וַיֹּאמֶר יַעֲקֹב
מִכְרָה כַיּוֹם אֶת בְּכֹרָתְךָ לִי: וַיֹּאמֶר עֵשָׂו הִנֵּה אָנֹכִי הוֹלֵךְ לָמוּת וְלָמָּה זֶּה לִי
בְּכֹרָה: וַיֹּאמֶר יַעֲקֹב הִשָּׁבְעָה לִי כַּיּוֹם וַיִּשָּׁבַע לוֹ וַיִּמְכֹּר אֶת בְּכֹרָתוֹ לְיַעֲקֹב:
וְיַעֲקֹב נָתַן לְעֵשָׂו לֶחֶם וּנְזִיד עֲדָשִׁים וַיֹּאכַל וַיֵּשְׁתְּ וַיָּקָם וַיֵּלַךְ וַיִּבֶז עֵשָׂו אֶת
הַבְּכֹרָה:[2]

*[Once when] Yaakov was cooking a stew, Eisav came in from
the field, famished. And Eisav said to Yaakov, "Give me some
of that red stuff to gulp down, for I am famished"—which
is why he was named Edom. Yaakov said, "First sell me your
birthright." And Eisav said, "I am at the point of death, so of
what use is my birthright to me?" But Yaakov said, "Swear to
me first." So he swore to him and sold his birthright to Yaakov.
Yaakov then gave Eisav bread and lentil stew; he ate and
drank, and he got up and went away. Thus did Eisav belittle
the birthright.*

Eisav gave up all of his rights to the *bechor* in order to gulp down the
lentil soup that wasn't even ready! Although Eisav was famished and it
was necessary for him to eat immediately, based on his choice of words,
we can see that his character embodied impulsivity.

Instant gratification can block one from seeing the bigger picture.

Rashi comments that *Olam Hazeh*—this world—is referred to as Erev
Shabbos.[3] As we sing in the Friday night *zemiros*, "*Me'ein olam haba yom
Shabbos menuchah.*"[4] Shabbos is compared to *Olam Haba*—the World to
Come. When one gets caught up with mundane things before Shabbos,
he is focusing on this world; however, when one prepares for Shabbos,
he is looking toward the World to Come.

I've had students come to me in their senior year of high school and
tell me that because they didn't take a class seriously during freshman
year, they have a lower average than expected. During ninth grade,

---

2   *Bereishis* 25:29–34.

3   *Avodah Zarah* 3a; *Rashi, s.v. B'Erev Shabbos.*

4   *Zemiros leil Shabbos, Mah Yedidus Menuchaseich.*

these students wanted to play around and focus on "the now" without putting much thought into the future.

Shlomo HaMelech says:

עָרֵב לָאִישׁ לֶחֶם שָׁקֶר וְאַחַר יִמָּלֵא פִיהוּ חָצָץ.[5]

Deceitful bread may taste sweet, but later on his mouth will be full of gravel.

וְעַל זֶה אָמַר שלמה ערב לאיש לחם שקר ואחר ימלא פיהו חצץ. הטבע מבקש השמחה והשחוק.[6]

And on this Shlomo says, "Bread gained by deceit may be tasty; but later his mouth will be filled with gravel." Nature, [i.e., the body] desires happiness and laughter.

Rabbeinu Bachya elaborates on this *pasuk* and explains that the "deceitful bread" refers to *aveiros* performed because of instant gratification.

Some people act on a whim without thinking of the future. They base their decisions on their emotions instead of on logic. If only we recognized how much we are giving up to gain for the moment. My brother, who is a personal trainer, constantly tells his clients, "What you eat in private shows in public."

רַבִּי יוֹחָנָן בֶּן בְּרוֹקָא אוֹמֵר, כָּל הַמְחַלֵּל שֵׁם שָׁמַיִם בַּסֵּתֶר, נִפְרָעִין מִמֶּנּוּ בַּגָּלוּי.[7]

Rabbi Yochanan ben Berokah says, anyone who desecrates the name of Shamayim in private will be punished in public.

Control yourself in the moment, and you will enjoy yourself in the future.

---

5   *Mishlei* 20:17.

6   Rabbeinu Bachya, *Shemos* 35:1.

7   *Avos* 4:4.

To Summarize

Instant gratification is very common nowadays, especially with more advanced technology coming out. Having a strong will can benefit you when it comes to self-control. Many times, people will become caught up in the moment and act on impulse, only to later regret their words or actions. Having full control is a constant internal struggle, and once one thinks they have mastered it, a stronger challenge will come their way. Similar to how one studies in advance when getting ready for a test, the way to help overcome these challenges is to practice and prepare beforehand.

Points to Ponder

- Do I act in haste or am I able to have patience?
- How am I preparing for my future?
- What is one step I can take to take control over my desires?

Just Ask

Daniel came home from camp one day and told me about the amazing day he had—except for one thing. He didn't get an ice pop when everyone else did. I told him not to worry, and I gave him an ice pop from our freezer at home. I asked him why he didn't get one, and he said that his *morah* hadn't given him one. I called his *morah* and asked why Daniel didn't get an ice pop that day, and she was a bit shocked; she thought that he had gotten one. She explained that the ice pops were given out while everyone was playing in the playground, and she had called out to see if anyone else wanted one. It turns out that Daniel was busy playing and never asked for one in the first place. I therefore explained to Daniel that if he wants something, he has to ask for it, and that he can't just expect it to come to him.

Then it hit me: How often do we expect things to just come to us? We expect to wake up healthy every morning, have money to put food on the table, and have an easy life that's full of joy. These are all great, but do we make sure to ask for what we want? We daven to Hashem to build a connection. The closer our connection is with Hashem, the more likely we will get what we ask for. But we have to ask. If you don't ask, you don't get.

רב אסי רמי כתיב (בראשית א, יב) ותוצא הארץ דשא בתלת בשבתא
וכתיב (בראשית ב, ה) וכל שיח השדה טרם יהיה בארץ במעלי שבתא
מלמד שיצאו דשאים ועמדו על פתח קרקע עד שבא אדם הראשון ובקש

עליהם רחמים וירדו גשמים וצמחו וללמדך שהקב"ה מתאוה לתפלתן של צדיקים.[1]

Rav Asi raises a contradiction: It is written: "And the earth brought forth grass"[2] on the third day of the week of Creation. And it is also written: "No plant of the field was yet on the earth"[3] on Erev Shabbos. Rav Asi explains: This teaches that the grasses emerged and stood at the opening of the ground until Adam HaRishon came and prayed for mercy upon them, and rain came, and they sprouted. To teach you that Hakadosh Baruch Hu desires the prayers of the righteous.

The Gemara teaches us that when the world was created, the grass was ready to sprout on the third day but didn't until the sixth day after Adam davened for rain. Once he davened for rain, Hashem let the vegetation sprout. This is to teach us that Hashem wants to hear our *tefillos*.

Many times, we rely on our *gedolim* to daven for us and to give us *berachos* for success or whatever we need. We ourselves, though, need to daven. Those *berachos* are just like adding wood to the fire, while our *tefillos* are the flames.

There is a Chinese proverb that states, "He who asks may seem like a fool for five minutes; he who doesn't ask remains a fool for life." The Mishnah teaches that one who is embarrassed won't learn.[4] The Bartenura explains:

שהמתבייש לשאל שמא ילעיגו עליו, ישאר תמיד בספקותיו.[5]

Since one who is embarrassed to ask, because others might make fun, will be left with his questions unanswered.

---

1   *Chullin* 60b.
2   *Bereishis* 1:12.
3   Ibid. 2:5.
4   *Avos* 2:5.
5   *Bartenura, Avos* 2:5.

I heard in the name of the Chida, who applies this Mishnah to the *she'eino yodei'a lishol* on Pesach, that the reason the *she'eino yodei'a lishol* doesn't ask is because he is embarrassed of looking foolish.

I find it interesting regarding the four sons on Pesach that although the way we respond may be different, the answer we give to the *rasha* and to the *she'eino yodei'a lishol* is the same.

For both sons, we say, "בַּעֲבוּר זֶה עָשָׂה ה׳ לִי בְּצֵאתִי מִמִּצְרָיִם—For the sake of this Hashem did for me when leaving Mitzrayim."[6]

I would venture to say that both the *rasha* and the *she'eino yodei'a lishol* are excluding themselves. The *rasha* says, "מָה הָעֲבֹדָה הַזֹּאת לָכֶם—What is this service that you are doing?" and the *she'eino yodei'a lishol*, as his name suggests, excludes himself by not asking.

When one asks, one gets answers. When children are young, they seem to ask about everything! When you answer them, they continue to ask more questions on your answers! But this is a good thing. Asking is usually a sign of interest. If someone isn't interested in something, then one wouldn't ask. Interest leads to learning, which hopefully leads to application. On Pesach, we see the importance of asking.

ואם לאו הוא שואל לעצמו ואפילו שני תלמידי חכמים שיודעין בהלכות הפסח שואלין זה לזה.[7]

And if there is no one else, he should ask himself, and even two scholars that know the laws of Pesach should ask each other.

The Gemara teaches that even if one is having the Seder alone, he should ask himself the questions, and even two *talmidei chachamim* who are knowledgeable in the halachos of Pesach must ask one another.

When it comes to education, the first thing an educator has to do is get the students' attention. If the students don't give the educator their attention, the educator won't be able to teach.

When it comes to building any relationship, it is very unlikely it will last without asking each other questions.

---

6   *Shemos* 13:8.
7   *Pesachim* 116a.

וּבְנֵיהֶם אֲשֶׁר לֹא יָדְעוּ יִשְׁמְעוּ וְלָמְדוּ לְיִרְאָה אֶת ה' אֱלֹקֵיכֶם כָּל הַיָּמִים אֲשֶׁר
אַתֶּם חַיִּים עַל הָאֲדָמָה אֲשֶׁר אַתֶּם עֹבְרִים אֶת הַיַּרְדֵּן שָׁמָּה לְרִשְׁתָּהּ.[8]

Their children, who have not had the knowledge, shall hear and learn to revere Hashem your God as long as they live in the land that you are about to cross the Yarden to inherit.

ישאלו בגדולים וילמדו מן המבינים.[9]

They will ask adults and learn from people who do understand.

Before Moshe Rabbeinu passed away, he instructed B'nei Yisrael to teach the Torah and pass it down to future generations. On this, the *Seforno* and others comment that children will ask, and they will listen to those who understand. Not only is it OK to ask, but it's important too.

To Summarize

Asking for assistance may be viewed as a weakness, yet in reality it shows one's strength. Asking a question sharpens one's mind, even if he is asking himself! Asking helps one learn and understand. It is important to take our children's questions seriously and encourage them to continue asking questions so they will learn and continue to be intrigued.

Points to Ponder

- What are some things I can ask from Hashem?
- What are some questions I have that I am embarrassed to ask?
- How can I encourage others to ask questions?

---

8 *Devarim* 31:13.
9 *Seforno, Devarim* ibid.

Smile

One summer, there was a child from Israel in Daniel's bunk who did not understand English well and had difficulty communicating with the other children. Daniel went over to say hi and smiled. The boy's eyes lit up as he smiled back and gave Daniel a hug. It was inspiring to witness.

There is a saying, "A smile is understood in every language." It is amazing that a smile is universally understood. A smile is contagious. A smile has the power to bridge two hearts together. It not only connects others and helps them in stressful times, but it helps the individual smile as well. Studies show that smiling helps reduce stress levels and actually benefits those who smile, emotionally and physically. "These findings show that smiling during brief stressors can help to reduce the intensity of the body's stress response, regardless of whether a person actually feels happy."[1]

When we greet others or even when we are alone, we should aim to be "*b'sever panim yafos*—with a cheerful face."[2] The *Ramak* writes in the second characteristic, "emulating the ways of Hashem," in his *Tomer Devorah*:

---

1   See https://bit.ly/2QQdin7.
2   *Avos* 1:15.

> *One's face should always be shining, and he should greet every person with a cheerful face. Just like the Crown of the Almighty, as it is written in Mishlei, "The light on the face of the Eternal King,"[3] there is no redness or judgment that enters there at all. The light of his face should not change, and anyone who sees him should only find happiness and pleasantness. Nothing should burden him from this at all.[4]*

The Gemara teaches that it is better to smile at one's friend than to give him a glass of milk.[5] It says in *Koheles*, "I know that there is nothing better than being happy and doing good in one's lifetime."[6]

I once took a course on the science of happiness. There was a recurring theme that flowed throughout the course on what true happiness consists of and how to obtain it. Overall, the scientific studies showed that there are two elements that bring happiness: kindness toward others and gratitude. I believe that these work hand-in-hand. People are kind when they appreciate what they have. People who are kind to others are happier people. The *pasuk* tells us, "וְאָהַבְתָּ לְרֵעֲךָ כָּמוֹךָ—Love your neighbor like yourself,"[7] and *Rashi* quotes Rabbi Akiva, who says that this is a *"klal gadol baTorah*—it is the fundamental principle of the Torah."

I believe that in order to follow the *pasuk* of "עִבְדוּ אֶת ה' בְּשִׂמְחָה בֹּאוּ לְפָנָיו בִּרְנָנָה—Serve Hashem with joy, come before Him in song,"[8] one must first fulfill the *pasuk* of וְאָהַבְתָּ לְרֵעֲךָ כָּמוֹךָ. The reason for this is because in order to serve Hashem with *simchah*, one must obtain *simchah* by giving to and loving others.

The *pasuk* tells us that when Yosef sent Yaakov chariots, it revived the spirit of Yaakov.[9] *Rashi* teaches that the *Shechinah* returned to Yaakov.[10]

---

3   *Mishlei* 16:15.
4   *Tomer Devorah* 2:1.
5   *Kesubos* 111b.
6   *Koheles* 3:12.
7   *Vayikra* 19:18.
8   *Tehillim* 100:2.
9   *Bereishis* 45:27.
10   Ibid. 45:27, *Rashi* s.v. *Vatechi ruach Yaakov*.

The *Radak* and others explain that he recovered from a state of worry.[11] It is implied from here that the *Shechinah* will dwell with one who is happy. In order to serve Hashem with *simchah*, one must be kind to others. Without this fundamental principle, it would be impossible for the world to exist. The Mishnah teaches that the world stands on three things: Torah, *avodah*, and *gemilus chassadim*.[12] Based on the above, without *gemilus chassadim*, there is no way one can fulfill the other two pillars properly.

According to this, it was essential that Avraham Avinu embody the *middah* of *chessed* before Yitzchak, who embodied *gevurah/avodah*, would come along.

The Chumash uses the name *Elokim* to describe Hashem during the creation of the world. Only after creation do we see the name Hashem (Y-K-V-K).[13] Rabbeinu Bachya elaborates on this, saying that originally Hashem created the world with *middas ha'din*, and only after Hashem created people, Hashem saw that the world needed *middas ha'rachamim*.

Also on this *pasuk*, Rabbeinu Bachya teaches that the word "*b'hibar'am*" is a reference to Avraham.[14] He quotes the midrash as saying that the world was created for the sake of Avraham, as the *pasuk* says, "*Olam chessed yibaneh*—The world is built on kindness."[15]

On Rosh Hashanah, the day that the world was created,[16] we blow the shofar. Before *tekias shofar*, we say, "עָלָה אֱלֹקִים בִּתְרוּעָה ה' בְּקוֹל שׁוֹפָר—Rise, *Elokim*, with *teruah* blasts; Hashem with the call of the shofar."[17] We ask that Hashem transfer the judgment of *din* into *rachamim*.

As we discussed in the first chapter, Hashem gave us mitzvos to give us benefit.

---

11   *Bereishis* 45:27.

12   *Avos* 1:1.

13   *Bereishis* 2:4.

14   Spelled *beis, hei, beis, reish, aleph, mem*—בהבראם.

15   *Tehillim* 89:3.

16   *Rosh Hashanah* 10b; also, we say "*ha'yom haras olam*—today is the day the world was created" on Rosh Hashanah.

17   *Tehillim* 47:6.

There is a well-known story of a rav who worked in a slaughter-house. Every morning and evening, the rav made an effort to greet the security guard. The owner of the slaughterhouse was always the last to leave, and the guard would lock the gates behind him. One evening, the owner walked out past the security guard and noticed that the guard wasn't locking the door behind him. When the owner asked why, the guard told him that there was still someone in the building. The owner asked how the guard could be so sure, to which the guard responded that when he opens the doors in the morning, he looks forward to the smile and "good morning" from the rav, and every evening he looks forward to the rav's warm smile and "good evening." Out of the hundreds of employees that worked here, the rav was the only one who made sure to greet him with a smile every single day. That morning, the rav had greeted him, but since he hadn't yet said "good evening," the guard knew that he couldn't have left for the night.

At that moment, the owner and guard went around looking for the rav. Finally, after looking all over the facility, they found him locked inside the walk-in freezer with all of the meat. The rav was huddled in the corner, saying Tehillim with tears frozen to his cheeks. Baruch Hashem, they found the rav before it was too late!

We see from this story how a simple smile and "hello" can go a long way. Who knows the effect one can have by simply smiling? The man from the postal service who drops off the mail every day can be going through a rough time and needs a simple "hello" to feel like a person again. The teller at the bank could be on probation and is worried about losing her job, and a simple smile and "thank you" can restore her confidence.

There is a man named Kevin Hines who failed at his attempt of suicide and told his life story. On the way to jump off of the Golden Gate Bridge, he was waiting for someone to show empathy and care.

Hines leaped over a rail on the Golden Gate Bridge in September of 2000 and began a freefall that would reach 75 miles per hour on impact. The moment his fingers left the railing, he felt instant regret...Hines fell about 240 feet in just four seconds. He crashed feet first into the waters below, crushing spinal vertebrae and breaking an ankle. But he survived. "When I resurfaced, I was trying to stay afloat, thinking, 'I am going to drown.' As I was bobbing up and down in the water, I was saying, 'I don't want to die, God, I made a mistake.'"

A sea lion, Hines says, kept pushing him above the water's surface until the Coast Guard rescued him...Hines hopes that each time he tells his story, the hope he conveys to the suffering will enable them to open up, to realize, "I can help myself today," Hines says.

He urges anyone who sees someone suffering and upset, like he was that day on the Golden Gate Bridge...to reach out.[18]

All he needed was a simple "Hey, how are you?"

The next time you smile at someone, for all you know, you could be saving a life.

To Summarize

Did you know that something so effortless could save a life? *Tzedakah tatzil mi'maves*—charity saves from death" doesn't only apply to giving money. A simple smile or "hello" can go a long way.

Points to Ponder

- How can I work on smiling more?
- What are some kind things I can do to help build the world through kindness?
- How can I show appreciation for the kind things others do for me?

---

18   See https://www.psycom.net/kevin-hines-survived-golden-gate-bridge-suicide.

The Little Things

Children get very excited over little things. Once, Ayelet got so excited over a piece of cheese! I was amazed at how excited she was over something so small. I then recognized the reason for her excitement was because she valued the cheese. That was her focus, and nothing else mattered at the moment.

Sometimes, we get too caught up looking at things we wish we could have; we forget about the little things that are important. We appreciate the big things that occur in our lives and disregard the "small" things. If we appreciate the small things in life, we will realize and recognize how great we have it.

In the *parashah* of *bikkurim*, the *pasuk* says, "And you should be happy with all of the good that Hashem your God has given you."[1] The way to be happy is through having *hakaras ha'tov*, recognizing all of the good that Hashem does for you. One way to do this is by focusing on the little things in life that may not always be on your mind. Imagine your everyday life without one of the little things you take for granted. Imagine not having hot water or color everywhere. Unfortunately, people only begin to appreciate something once they lose it. Those who are great take care of and appreciate the little things.

---

1   *Devarim* 26:11.

In the midst of Yaakov preparing for war against his brother, Eisav, he separates from his family to return across the river in order to retrieve some small jugs.[2] What was so significant about these simple little jugs that Yaakov delayed his preparation, separated from his family, and risked his life? The *Megaleh Amukos* answers that Yaakov went back because these jugs were full of oil.[3] One of these jugs never emptied, and it resurfaced many times throughout Jewish history. It was the same jug of oil found in the Chanukah miracle. When Yaakov Avinu realized that he slept in the place of the Beis Hamikdash, he used this jug to pour oil onto a rock to anoint a *mizbei'ach*. Eliyahu HaNavi used this oil when he told the woman to make bread so she and her child could have food.[4] Elisha HaNavi used it, too, when he told the widow to fill as many pots and to sell the oil so her sons wouldn't be captured and sold as slaves.[5]

Yaakov Avinu was able to see the significance of little things and all of the tremendous miracles that would come from them.

The Gemara states that "one who delights in Shabbos will be saved from the oppression of *galus*."[6] Rav Chiya bar Ashi said in the name of Rav that even if one prepares something small, especially for Shabbos, it is considered a delight. Rav Pappa says that this is referring to small fried fish. Something so simple can lead to something so great.

Although at the moment it may be difficult for us to see the importance of the little things, many times in the future we are able to connect the dots and recognize how great those little things really are. One of the little things that people often take for granted is time. Take a moment and reflect back on the time you spent on mundane activity. Think about how much of that time you could have spent learning something new, spending it with family, or becoming a better person. Every moment we have in this world is an opportunity. Don't let those precious moments slip away from you. Those who truly value their

2   *Bereishis* 32:25; *Rashi*, s.v. *Vayivaser Yaakov.*
3   *Sifsei Chein Chanukah—Ohr HaGanuz.*
4   *Melachim I* 17:14.
5   *Melachim II* 4:2.
6   *Shabbos* 118b.

time will use it properly. Let's not wait until the time is taken to fully appreciate the opportunities that we left on the side.

There are many "paying it forward" videos that demonstrate the tremendous effect one can have from a simple action. If we can take positivity and apply those videos to our everyday life, the world will be a much greater place. As the saying goes, "Enjoy the little things in life, for one day you will look back and realize that they were big things."

To Summarize

Little things go a long way. A small gesture, a tiny gift, or a simple favor are a few little things that can make a big difference. Time is one of those little things that we don't recognize how valuable it is until it's about to run out. When we recognize all of the little things we have, we will see how fortunate we really are.

Points to Ponder

- How do I show that the little things in life make a big difference?
- Do I value what I have?
- What do I do to cherish the small moments?

Stepping on Shoes

As a division head at summer camp, things can get very busy very fast, especially by dismissal time. I am very fortunate to have my children attend the same camp that I work at. It is nice seeing them play with their friends and watching them in action. They are in the younger division and get dismissed an hour before we begin our dismissal. Sometimes they run around to find me, and even though it's busy, I love when they come.

One day at dismissal, Daniel came running over, gave me a hug, and hung out right next to me. I was so focused on directing campers to their buses that I bumped into Daniel and stepped on his shoe, causing him to stumble.

I apologized, but Daniel said that it was OK because he'd also tripped, and when I stepped on his shoe, it stopped him from falling.

It was just after Tishah B'Av, and I thought about how the Jewish People were in a dark time. As we discuss on Pesach, *"she'b'chol dor va'dor omdim aleinu l'chaloseinu*—there are people and nations that want to destroy us in every generation." Although they have come close at times, we are still here.

When the Ponevezher Rav was traveling, collecting money for his *yeshiva*, he stopped at the Arch of Titus and said, "Titus, Titus! What has become of you? You tried to destroy Klal Yisrael, and nothing is left of you other than this arch, while we remain here standing."

We must recognize that when events happen in the world, Hashem is sending us a message. Although it is impossible for us to fully comprehend and see the full picture, we must believe that there is rhyme and reason to everything. Many times, the good comes from within what seems to be bad. The *pasuk* says, "וַיְהִי עֶרֶב וַיְהִי בֹקֶר—It was evening and it was morning."[1] First came the darkness, and then came the light. When things look down, recognize that the light is coming from within the darkness. Take a look at the events of Yosef's life. Yosef was sold by his brothers and ended up in Mitzrayim, where he landed in prison. He was in Mitzrayim, which was the lowest country, and in the prison that housed the lowest of the low. Can we imagine what could be going through Yosef's head?! But guess who else was in there with him? The chief butler and chief baker from the house of Pharaoh. All of these events led to Yosef becoming the ruler in Mitzrayim and setting up the next phase of history—the promise Hashem made to Avraham,[2] which eventually led to Klal Yisrael becoming a nation and entering Eretz Yisrael.

When I stepped on Daniel's foot, I thought that I hurt him. Yet I actually saved him from falling. Hashem works in mysterious ways. We may view things as bad things happening, but in reality, Hashem is all good, and everything He does is good.

זימנא חדא בעו לשדורי ישראל דורון לבי קיסר אמרו מאן ייזיל ייזיל
נחום איש גם זו דמלומד בניסין הוא שדרו בידיה מלא סיפטא דאבנים
טובות ומרגליות אזל בת בההוא דירה בליליא קמו הנך דיוראי ושקלינהו
לסיפטיה ומלונהו עפרא (למחר כי חזנהו אמר גם זו לטובה) כי מטא התם
[שרינהו לסיפטא חזנהו דמלו עפרא] בעא מלכא למקטלינהו לכולהו אמר
קא מחייכו בי יהודאי [אמר גם זו לטובה] אתא אליהו אדמי ליה כחד
מינייהו א״ל דלמא הא עפרא מעפרא דאברהם אבוהון הוא דכי הוה שדי
עפרא הוו סייפיה גילי הוו גירי דכתיב (ישעיהו מא, ב) יתן כעפר חרבו כקש
נדף קשתו הויא חדא מדינתא דלא מצו למיכבשה בדקו מיניה וכבשוה
עיילו לבי גנזיה ומלוהו לסיפטיה אבנים טובות ומרגליות ושדרוהו ביקרא

---

1   *Bereishis* 1:5.
2   *Daas Zekeinim, Bereishis* 39:1.

רבה כי אתו ביתו בההוא דיורא אמרו ליה מאי אייתית בהדך דעבדי לך
יקרא כולי האי אמר להו מאי דשקלי מהכא אמטי להתם סתרו לדירייהו
ואמטינהו לבי מלכא אמרו ליה האי עפרא דאייתי הכא מדידן הוא בדקוה
ולא אשכחוה וקטלינהו להנך דיוראי.[3]

Once, the Jews wished to send a gift to the house of the
emperor. They said: "Who should go? Let Nachum Ish Gam
Zu go, as he is accustomed to miracles." They sent with him
a chest full of jewels and pearls, and he went and spent the
night in a certain inn. During the night, the residents took all
of the precious jewels and pearls from the chest and filled it
with earth. The next day, when he saw what had happened,
Nachum Ish Gam Zu said: "This too is for the good." When he
arrived there, they opened the chest and saw that it was filled
with earth. The king wished to put all the Jewish emissaries to
death. He said: "The Jews are mocking me." Nachum Ish Gam
Zu said: "This too is for the good." Eliyahu HaNavi came and
appeared before the ruler as one of his ministers. He said to
the ruler: "Perhaps this earth is from the earth of their father
Avraham. As when he threw earth, it turned into swords, and
when he threw straw, it turned into arrows, as it is written in
a prophecy that the Sages interpreted this verse as a reference
to Avraham: 'His sword makes them as the dust, his bow as
the driven stubble.'"[4] There was one province that the Romans
were unable to conquer. They took some of this earth, tested it
by throwing it at their enemies, and conquered that province.
When the ruler saw that this earth indeed had miraculous powers, his servants entered his treasury and filled Nachum Ish
Gam Zu's chest with precious jewels and pearls and sent him
off with great honor. When Nachum Ish Gam Zu came to spend
the night at that same inn, the residents said to him: "What did
you bring with you to the emperor that he bestowed upon you

---

3   *Taanis* 21a.
4   *Yeshayahu* 41:2.

such great honor?" He said to them: "That which I took from here, I brought there." They tore down their inn and brought the soil underneath to the king's palace. They said to him: "That earth that was brought here was from our property." The miracle had been performed only in the merit of Nachum Ish Gam Zu. The emperor tested the inn's soil in battle, and it was not found to have miraculous powers, and he had those residents of the inn put to death.

During the coronavirus pandemic, we went camping in our backyard. We put up a tent and made a bonfire to roast marshmallows and make s'mores. Each child got one marshmallow and a piece of chocolate. As Ayelet was taking her chocolate, it fell on the ground, but *baruch Hashem* we had one last piece that she could have. Then as Ayelet's marshmallow was roasting, the stick broke and the marshmallow fell into the fire. *Baruch Hashem*, we had one more extra! But, unfortunately while roasting, that stick broke as well, causing the marshmallow to fall into the fire. Ayelet felt a bit down, but at least she had her chocolate. Ayelet sandwiched her chocolate between her matzah and headed for the swings. Well, wouldn't you know, but she fell off of the swing, scraping her hands, and her marshmallow-less s'more fell on the floor.

After shedding a few tears and brushing herself off, Ayelet looked up at me, gave me a smile, and started to sing, "*Gam zu l'tovah*—This is also for the best!" We were so amazed! (*Baruch Hashem*, we were able to get more marshmallows and chocolate, and Ayelet had many s'mores!)

About a week and a half later, while Ayelet was riding on her brand-new scooter, she fell off and scraped both of her knees. As she was crying, she began to sing, "*Gam zu l'tovah*—This is also for the best!"

Sometimes, things look like they are taking a turn for the worst, but we cannot give up hope. We have to realize that Hashem is our father, and a father would never want to harm his child. Sometimes we have to deal with negative consequences from our actions, but it comes from Hashem Who is only Good. We don't always see the full picture, and that's why we must have faith that the good comes from within the "bad."

To Summarize

"*Gam zu l'tovah*—this is also for the best" is a phrase that changes one's paradigm on life. When we recognize that we are merely pieces to a puzzle, we also acknowledge that many things are out of our control. All Hashem does is for the good, even if it seems to us that it is not so. When something that seems negative occurs, we only admit that Hashem is good when we say that "this too is for the good."

Points to Ponder

- When was a time I thought things were going very bad but later recognized that without those moments, all the good that followed wouldn't have happened?
- How can I remind myself to say "*Gam zu l'tovah*" more often?
- What is something I can do today to work on my *emunah* and see that everything comes from Hashem?

Magic

One day at camp, we had a magician come and perform. It was very exciting, and the kids loved it. After the show, all of the campers were trying to perform their own magic tricks, as if they were ready to put on a performance.

Fast forward to the end of the day. Ayelet was trying to perform a magic trick. She had a bead in one hand, and with the other hand open, she asked, "Where is the bead?"

Many times in life, we try to outsmart Hashem by justifying that what we are doing is OK or that we weren't fully aware of the consequences. We try to make something obvious into something complex to vindicate our actions.

Ayelet really thought that she was doing magic, but to everyone else it was obvious which hand the bead was in. Many times, we try to use sleight of hand to perform the actions we want; however, one is only fooling oneself because Hashem knows good and well what our intentions are.

The *pasuk* says:

רַבּוֹת מַחֲשָׁבוֹת בְּלֶב אִישׁ וַעֲצַת ה' הִיא תָקוּם.[1]

There are many thoughts in a man's heart, but the council of Hashem will prevail.

---

1   *Mishlei* 19:21.

וּכְעִסַתָּה צָרָתָהּ גַּם כַּעַס בַּעֲבוּר הַרְעִמָהּ כִּי סָגַר ה' בְּעַד רַחְמָהּ.[2]

Moreover, her rival, to make her miserable, would taunt her that Hashem had closed her womb.

שְׂבֵעִים בַּלֶּחֶם נִשְׂכָּרוּ וּרְעֵבִים חָדֵלּוּ עַד עֲקָרָה יָלְדָה שִׁבְעָה וְרַבַּת בָּנִים אֻמְלָלָה.[3]

Men once sated must hire out for bread; men once hungry hunger no more. While the barren woman bears seven, the mother of many is depressed.

There is a saying: "Bad decisions made with good intentions are still bad decisions." Peninah would mock Chanah and cause her pain with the intention that Chanah should daven with much more concentration to Hashem. However, it was the wrong way to go about it. For this reason, Peninah was punished and lost most of her own children.[4]

וַיְהִי בִּשְׁכֹּן יִשְׂרָאֵל בָּאָרֶץ הַהִוא וַיֵּלֶךְ רְאוּבֵן וַיִּשְׁכַּב אֶת בִּלְהָה פִּילֶגֶשׁ אָבִיו וַיִּשְׁמַע יִשְׂרָאֵל...[5]

While Yisrael stayed in that land, Reuven went and lay with Bilhah, his father's concubine; and Yisrael found out...

פַּחַז כַּמַּיִם אַל תּוֹתַר כִּי עָלִיתָ מִשְׁכְּבֵי אָבִיךָ אָז חִלַּלְתָּ יְצוּעִי עָלָה.[6]

Reckless as water, you shall excel no longer; for when you mounted your father's bed, you brought disgrace—my couch he ascended.

Reuven had good intentions when he moved his father's bed out of the tent of Bilhah to his mother Leah's tent. Yet, we find that he was rebuked by Yaakov later on when Yaakov called his children together

---

2   *Shmuel I* 1:6; see *Rashi*.
3   Ibid. 2:5; see *Rashi*.
4   See *Rashi* on *Shmuel I* 2:5.
5   *Bereishis* 35:22.
6   Ibid. 49:4.

before his death. Yaakov compares Reuven to waters that are rushing recklessly. Rushing waters are moving fast with one goal—to get downstream. When someone acts with haste, they may not think about others. Yaakov is telling Reuven to slow down and take other people into consideration before acting. What happens when one acts rapidly without considering the full picture is that they may think their intentions are good, but looking back, it may not be the way of the Torah. This will cause a *chillul Hashem.* Yaakov tells Reuven, "אָז חִלַּלְתָּ—Then you brought desecration." You acted out of haste and did what was right in your mind, but in the end, it brought disgrace.

I used to wonder how pilots and captains of ships know how to reach their destinations when there are no landmarks at sea or in the sky. However, I came to understand that the more one flies or sails, the better one is able to navigate through a place that doesn't seem to have direction.

The same applies to those who learn Torah. In a world that seems to have no direction, those who study and apply Torah have clarity and guidance to reach their destination. Those who don't follow the ways of the Torah lack in guidance and can easily get lost. Ultimately, this leads to justifying why one is living the life one chooses. "One who interprets Torah not according to halachah…does not have a share in *Olam Haba.*"[7] Hashem gave us the Torah because it is the best thing for us. Let's not fall for our own illusions.

To Summarize

Imagine trying to outsmart your GPS to beat traffic or building a house while circumventing the blueprints. This is what we're doing when we live life based on our feelings and not on the words of the Torah. Torah is our guidebook that directs us and gives us clarity in life; without it, we'd be lost.

---

7   *Avos* 3:11.

Points to Ponder

- How often in my daily routine do I justify that I'm doing the right thing when in reality I know I'm wrong?
- How can I make sure that my good intentions aren't really harming others and are truly to benefit the other person?
- What can I do to ensure I follow the Torah k'halachah?

Water

t was raining on the way home from camp one summer day. As we were driving, we began speaking about water. Daniel asked, "What color is water?"

"That's a great question," I responded. "Water is clear."

Right then, I thought of the Gemara that said, "*Ein mayim ela Torah*—There is no water except for Torah."[1] Chazal compare water to Torah. Just like one can't live without water, so too, one cannot live without Torah.

תנו רבנן: פעם אחת גזרה מלכות הרשעה שלא יעסקו ישראל בתורה.
בא פפוס בן יהודה ומצאו לרבי עקיבא שהיה מקהיל קהלות ברבים ועוסק
בתורה. אמר לו: עקיבא אי אתה מתירא מפני מלכות? אמר לו: אמשול
לך משל, למה הדבר דומה—לשועל שהיה מהלך על גב הנהר, וראה דגים
שהיו מתקבצים ממקום למקום. אמר להם: מפני מה אתם בורחים? אמרו
לו: מפני רשתות שמביאין עלינו בני אדם. אמר להם: רצונכם שתעלו
ליבשה, ונדור אני ואתם, כשם שדרו אבותי עם אבותיכם? אמרו לו: אתה
הוא שאומרים עליך פקח שבחיות?! לא פקח אתה, אלא טפש אתה! ומה
במקום חיותנו, אנו מתיראין, במקום מיתתנו—על אחת כמה וכמה. אף
אנחנו עכשיו שאנו יושבים ועוסקים בתורה, שכתוב בה: "כי הוא חייך וארך
ימיך", כך, אם אנו הולכים ומבטלים ממנו—על אחת כמה וכמה!‏[2]

---

1   *Bava Kama* 82a.

2   *Berachos* 61b.

The Rabbanan taught: One time, the evil empire of Rome decreed that Israel may not engage in Torah. Pappus ben Yehudah came and found Rabbi Akiva, who was convening assemblies in public and engaging in Torah. Pappus said to him: "Akiva, are you not afraid of the empire?" Rabbi Akiva answered him: "I will relate a parable. To what can this be compared? To a fox walking along a riverbank, when he sees fish gathering and fleeing from place to place. The fox said to them: 'From what are you fleeing?' They said to him: 'We are fleeing from the nets that people cast upon us.' He said to them: 'Do you wish to come up onto dry land, and we will reside together just as my ancestors resided with your ancestors?' The fish said to him: 'You are the one of whom they say, "He is the cleverest of animals"? You are not clever; you are a fool. If we are afraid in the water, our habitat that gives us life, then in a habitat that causes our death, all the more so.' So too, we Jews, now that we sit and engage in Torah study, about which it is written: 'For that is your life, and the length of your days,'[3] we fear the empire to this extent; if we proceed to sit idle from its study, as its abandonment is the habitat that causes our death, all the more so will we fear the empire."

The Mishnah teaches that we should drink the words of the wise thirstily.[4] Chazal teach that this is referring to learning Torah from the *chachamim.*

The *Zohar* teaches that there are *"shiv'im panim la'Torah*—seventy faces of Torah."[5] Anyone can learn Torah, no matter how old or young, simple or wise he is. Water is clear; it doesn't have a color. However, if one adds color to water, the water will turn that color. I believe the same is true with Torah. Torah is "clear," and we are the colors. Water also takes the shape of whatever vessel it is placed into; the way we view

---

3   *Devarim* 30:20.
4   *Avos* 1:4.
5   *Zohar* 3:20.

the Torah is how it will appear. Water is always pulled to the lowest of places. So too, Torah can be found in the lowest of people. There is always a spark within that the Torah ignites.

וַיַּסַּע מֹשֶׁה אֶת יִשְׂרָאֵל מִיַּם סוּף וַיֵּצְאוּ אֶל מִדְבַּר שׁוּר וַיֵּלְכוּ שְׁלֹשֶׁת יָמִים בַּמִּדְבָּר וְלֹא מָצְאוּ מָיִם וַיָּבֹאוּ מָרָתָה וְלֹא יָכְלוּ לִשְׁתֹּת מַיִם מִמָּרָה כִּי מָרִים הֵם עַל כֵּן קָרָא שְׁמָהּ מָרָה וַיִּלֹּנוּ הָעָם עַל מֹשֶׁה לֵּאמֹר מַה נִּשְׁתֶּה וַיִּצְעַק אֶל ה' וַיּוֹרֵהוּ ה' עֵץ וַיַּשְׁלֵךְ אֶל הַמַּיִם וַיִּמְתְּקוּ הַמָּיִם שָׁם שָׂם לוֹ חֹק וּמִשְׁפָּט וְשָׁם נִסָּהוּ וַיֹּאמֶר אִם שָׁמוֹעַ תִּשְׁמַע לְקוֹל ה' אֱלֹקֶיךָ וְהַיָּשָׁר בְּעֵינָיו תַּעֲשֶׂה וְהַאֲזַנְתָּ לְמִצְוֹתָיו וְשָׁמַרְתָּ כָּל חֻקָּיו כָּל הַמַּחֲלָה אֲשֶׁר שַׂמְתִּי בְמִצְרַיִם לֹא אָשִׂים עָלֶיךָ כִּי אֲנִי ה' רֹפְאֶךָ וַיָּבֹאוּ אֵילִמָה וְשָׁם שְׁתֵּים עֶשְׂרֵה עֵינֹת מַיִם וְשִׁבְעִים תְּמָרִים וַיַּחֲנוּ שָׁם עַל הַמָּיִם.[6]

Then Moshe caused Yisrael to set out from the Yam Suf. They went on into the wilderness of Shur; they traveled three days in the wilderness and found no water. They came to Marah, but they could not drink the water of Marah because it was bitter; that is why it was named Marah. And the people grumbled against Moshe, saying, "What shall we drink?" So he cried out to Hashem, and Hashem showed him a piece of wood; he threw it into the water, and the water became sweet. There He made for them a fixed rule, and there He put them to the test. He said, "If you will obey Hashem your God diligently, doing what is upright in His eyes, listening to His commandments and observing all His laws, then I will not bring upon you any of the diseases that I brought upon the Egyptians, for I Hashem am your healer." And they came to Eilim, where there were twelve springs of water and seventy palm trees; and they encamped there beside the water.

The *pesukim* teach us that B'nei Yisrael traveled for three days and did not find any water. They then came to a place called Marah but couldn't drink from the water since it was bitter. So the people asked Moshe for something to drink. Moshe cried out to Hashem and was shown a piece

---

6   *Shemos* 15:22–27.

of wood. Moshe took the wood and threw it into the water, making the water sweet so B'nei Yisrael were able to drink. Moshe proceeds to tell them that if they follow the ways of Hashem, they will not endure the sicknesses that the *Mitzrim* went through, for "Hashem is your healer." Moshe then leads B'nei Yisrael to Eilim, where there were twelve springs of water and seventy palm trees. This is where they encamped beside the water.

This episode seems very interesting. Let's attempt to break it down for further understanding:

- First, is there significance to the three days without water?
- Second, how did the wooden stick that Moshe threw into the water make it sweet?
- Third, why is now the time to tell B'nei Yisrael to follow the mitzvos so that they won't become afflicted like the Egyptians?
- Last, of what significance were the twelve springs and seventy palm trees in Eilim?

...אין מים אלא תורה שנאמר (ישעיהו נה, א) הוי כל צמא לכו למים כיון שהלכו שלשת ימים בלא תורה נלאו עמדו נביאים שביניהם ותיקנו להם שיהו קורין בשבת ומפסיקין באחד וקורין בשני ומפסיקין שלישי ורביעי וקורין בחמישי ומפסיקין ערב שבת כדי שלא ילינו ג׳ ימים בלא תורה.[7]

...Water here is referring to nothing other than Torah, as it is stated "Ho, everyone who thirsts, come for water."[8] Since the Jews traveled for three days without Torah, they became weary, and therefore the prophets among them arose and instituted for them that they should read from the Torah each Shabbos, and pause on Sunday, and read again on Monday, and pause on Tuesday and Wednesday, and read again on Thursday, and pause on Shabbos eve, so they would not remain three days without hearing the Torah.

---

7   *Bava Kama* 82a.
8   *Yeshayahu* 55:1.

Based on this *pasuk*, the Gemara teaches that the *nevi'im* among B'nei Yisrael instituted to read the Torah on Monday, Thursday, and Shabbos so that we wouldn't go three days without Torah since B'nei Yisrael were weakened when they went three days in the desert without Torah.[9] From here, we see that water is compared to Torah.

My father told me that the piece of wood Moshe threw in to the bitter waters represented the *eitz chaim*—tree of life. The *pasuk* says, "עֵץ חַיִּים הִיא לַמַּחֲזִיקִים בָּהּ—It is a tree of life to those who hold on to it."[10] The way to make the water sweet is by throwing a wooden stick into it. The way to make the Torah sweet is by connecting it to the *eitz chaim*. Those who learn Torah simply for intellectual stimulation will never appreciate the sweetness of Torah.

That is why it was the time to tell B'nei Yisrael that if they follow the Torah they won't get the sicknesses that the Egyptians got. If they are connected to the *eitz chaim*, they won't need to worry about getting sick because grabbing ahold of Torah is attaching oneself to Hashem, and "Hashem is your healer."

Rashi explains that the twelve springs represent the twelve *shevatim*.[11] The *Chizkuni* on *Shemos* says that the *pasuk* tells us that they encamped beside the water to learn the laws of Torah. I believe that the seventy palm trees correspond to the *shivim panim la'Torah*—seventy faces of Torah. Just as Devorah HaNeviah would judge under a palm tree,[12] that is where B'nei Yisrael learned the laws of the Torah and connected to the *eitz chaim*. And like the *pasuk* says, "צַדִּיק כַּתָּמָר יִפְרָח—The righteous shall flourish like a palm tree."[13]

We can perceive the mitzvos and commandments of the Torah as many chances and opportunities to receive merit and reward.

---

9   See *Maharsha* and *Ramban* (*Shemos* 15:25) for further explanation on why the establishment of Torah reading every three days was necessary.
10   *Mishlei* 3:18.
11   *Shemos* 15:27; *Rashi*, s.v. *Shteim esrei aynos mayim*.
12   *Shoftim* 4:5.
13   *Tehillim* 92:13.

ר׳ חנניא בן עקשיא אומר רצה הקב״ה לזכות את ישראל לפיכך הרבה
להם תורה ומצות.[14]

*Rabbi Chanina ben Akashia says, Hakadosh Baruch Hu
wanted to give merit to Yisrael; therefore, He gave them Torah
and mitzvos in abundance.*

We learn that Hashem wants us to have great merit, and that is why
He gives us the gifts of the Torah and mitzvos. All we have to do is
grab hold.

וְלָקַחְתָּ מִמֵּימֵי הַיְאֹר וְשָׁפַכְתָּ הַיַּבָּשָׁה וְהָיוּ הַמַּיִם אֲשֶׁר תִּקַּח מִן הַיְאֹר וְהָיוּ
לְדָם בַּיַּבָּשֶׁת.[15]

*Take some water from the Nile and pour it on the dry ground,
and it—the water that you take from the Nile—will turn to
blood on the dry ground.*

I heard a beautiful *d'var Torah* from my father explaining the *pasuk* of
when Hashem tells Moshe to spill water on the ground and it turns to
blood. Hashem tells Moshe that with this sign, "The people will believe
that you were sent by Me." The question is, if the people didn't believe
the first two miracles, why would they believe the third one? The answer is that water dispels *kishuf*—black magic, and therefore the people
would know his trick was real and not *kishuf.*"

The Gemara relates a story demonstrating the falsehood of Mitzrayim
and the power of water.

זעירי איקלע לאלכסנדריא של מצרים זבן חמרא כי מטא לאשקוייה מיא
פשר וקם גמלא דוסקניתא אמרו ליה אי לאו זעירי את לא הוה מהדרין
לך מי איכא דזבין מידי הכא ולא בדיק ליה אמיא.[16]

*Zeiri happened to come to Alexandria of Egypt. He bought
a donkey. When he was about to give it to drink, [the donkey]
disappeared and it turned into the plank of a bridge. They said*

---

14   *Makkos* 23b.
15   *Shemos* 4:9.
16   *Sanhedrin* 67b.

to him: "If you were not Zeiri, we would not refund you. Is there anyone who buys an item here and does not examine it first with water?"

We see that Torah is compared to water. We live in a world that shows us one thing when it's really another. This world is full of *sheker*, but Torah is the *emes*. The truth will always withstand time and pierce through any distortion. That is why the only way to test the *kishuf* is with water. Torah has withstood the test of time and will be everlasting, unlike the policies that other nations have tried to instill and force upon us. It is vital that we remain TC (Torah Correct) and not PC (Politically Correct).

To Summarize

Torah, like water, is fluid. It takes the shape of the vessel that contains it. It is on the highest of levels, yet it trickles down to the lowest of places. Torah and water are the sources that bring other things to life and continuously sustain them.

Points to Ponder

- Do I have a set time to learn Torah every day?
- What parts of Torah do I enjoy learning?
- Do I show humility like water and try to help those in low places?

Spreading Fire

We had an amazing talent show in camp one summer. One contestant was juggling a few torches lit with fire. Toward the end of his performance, he held two lit torches in one hand and blew the fire out of one torch in the other hand. The contestant then switched the torch that was blown out with one of the lit torches. He began to blow the fire out of the second torch, acting as if he didn't realize that the first torch was relit, since it touched the final torch that was still lit. He repeated this several times, making everyone laugh—my children especially.

As I was watching my children laugh, it occurred to me that fire and laughter are very similar. Both can be spread without losing from the source. When we light a candle, the fire does not diminish from its source, and so too, one who causes others to laugh does not take away the humor. If anything, it is just the opposite—it becomes greater! A simple match can light a massive Lag Ba'Omer bonfire, and a simple joke can fill an entire stadium with laughter!

On Chanukah, we light the *menorah* by our front door, window, or in public in order to publicize the great miracle Hashem has done for us.[1] "נֵר ה׳ נִשְׁמַת אָדָם—the light of Hashem is the soul of man"[2] is represented

---

1   *Shabbos* 21b; *Rashi, s.v. Mi'bachutz.*
2   *Mishlei* 20:27.

by the *menorah*. The light of Hashem—the *menorah*—represents one's *neshamah*. By looking at the *ner Chanukah*, one adds to the spark within, just as when one teaches Torah; they only add, and it doesn't decrease.

It is so simple to make a baby laugh. One way to get Eliana to laugh is by making funny sounds and voices or just simply smiling at her! The *pasuk* tells us, "עִבְדוּ אֶת ה' בְּשִׂמְחָה—Serve Hashem with joy."[3] Many people wonder why they can't achieve great heights in their Torah and Judaism. One major reason is because they aren't truly happy. One who is truly happy can reach these great heights.

ללמדך שאין שכינה שורה לא מתוך עצבות...אלא מתוך דבר שמחה של מצוה.[4]

To teach you that the Divine Presence doesn't rest on one in the midst of sadness...but rather on one who is involved in the joy of a mitzvah.

שרתה עליו שכינה שפרשה ממנו.[5]

The Shechinah that had departed from him rested again upon him.

כ"ב שנה משפרש ממנו עד שירד יעקב למצרים...[6]

Twenty-two years from the time he left him until Yaakov went down to Egypt...

The Gemara teaches us that the *Shechinah* rests on one who is happy. We see this by Yaakov, who became saddened when he believed his son, Yosef, had died. *Rashi* says that this sadness lasted for twenty-two years—the entire time he was separated from Yosef. When he found out that Yosef was actually still alive, the verse says that he returned to his state of happiness and achieved *ruach hakodesh* again.

---

3   *Tehillim* 100:2.
4   *Shabbos* 30b.
5   *Bereishis* 45:27; *Rashi*, s.v. *Vatechi ruach Yaakov*.
6   Ibid. 37:34; *Rashi*, s.v. *Yamim rabim*.

"*Mi'she'nichnas Adar marbim b'simchah*—When the month of Adar comes, we increase our happiness."[7] Purim, which is in the month of Adar, is the only Jewish holiday in which every mitzvah of the day is centered on gathering others closer and spreading joy.[8] Interestingly, Purim is also the only holiday where we don't light candles at its onset. I believe that lighting candles reminds us of spreading the light and connecting to Hashem through *simchah*. On Purim, we don't need this reminder because the entire day is about spreading joy through serving Hashem.

וֶהֱוֵי מִתְחַמֵּם כְּנֶגֶד אוּרָן שֶׁל חֲכָמִים, וֶהֱוֵי זָהִיר בְּגַחַלְתָּן שֶׁלֹּא תִכָּוֶה...וְכָל דִּבְרֵיהֶם כְּגַחֲלֵי אֵשׁ.[9]

And you should warm yourself before the fire of the wise, but beware of being singed by their glowing coals...and all their words are like coals of fire.

Fire and laughter can be used for both positive and negative. The Mishnah teaches, "One should warm oneself near the fire of the *chachamim*, yet be careful of their radiant coal so that one should not get burned." One can use fire to gain warmth if it is in a controlled environment, or one can destroy with fire. This, too, applies with laughter. They say that laughter is the best medicine; however, it is only the case when it is used properly. Laughing at someone else can be like a fire that destroys, transferring something with life and potential to mere ashes that give nothing.

וַיֵּרָא מַלְאַךְ ה' אֵלָיו בְּלַבַּת אֵשׁ מִתּוֹךְ הַסְּנֶה וַיַּרְא וְהִנֵּה הַסְּנֶה בֹּעֵר בָּאֵשׁ וְהַסְּנֶה אֵינֶנּוּ אֻכָּל.[10]

An angel of Hashem appeared to him in a blazing fire from within a bush. He gazed, and there was a bush all aflame, yet the bush was not consumed.

---

7   *Taanis* 29a.
8   See earlier, "Teamwork Makes the Dreamwork."
9   *Avos* 2:10.
10   *Shemos* 3:2.

וַיֹּאמֶר אַל תִּקְרַב הֲלֹם שַׁל נְעָלֶיךָ מֵעַל רַגְלֶיךָ כִּי הַמָּקוֹם אֲשֶׁר אַתָּה עוֹמֵד
עָלָיו אַדְמַת קֹדֶשׁ הוּא.[11]

*And He said, "Do not come closer. Remove your sandals from
your feet, for the place on which you stand is holy ground."*

When Hashem introduced himself to Moshe, it was through fire.
However, as the *pasuk* teaches, "The bush was on fire, yet it was not
being consumed." Hashem then tells Moshe to remove his shoes because it is holy ground that he is standing on. When we use laughter as
a positive way to connect with others, not only does it benefit everyone,
but it makes one holy. However, if someone were to use laughter to put
others down and embarrass someone, it is like a fire of destruction. Let
us light up the world by spreading joy and laughter.

To Summarize

Laughter, like fire, spreads without diminishing from the source; in
fact, it strengthens it. Fire is a physical element that embodies a spiritual entity. It can be used for positive or negative—to warm or destroy.
This holds true with laughter as well.

Points to Ponder

- How can I spread spirituality to others?
- Do I laugh enough?
- What is something small I can do to help spread joy to others?

---

11   Ibid., v. 5.

Jumpshot

One day after camp, I was playing basketball with Daniel. He was three at the time, and it was difficult for him to shoot the ball into the hoop. I taught him how to shoot, how to stand properly, and how to position his hands and body. Then I showed him how to bend his knees in order to jump. I explained that the more he bends his knees, the higher he will be able to jump.

While reflecting on this lesson, I thought about how sometimes in life we have to descend in order to ascend, as it discusses in the Gemara when comparing the Jewish nation to the moon. Just like the moon waxes and wanes, so too, we learn the concept of *yeridah l'tzorech aliyah*.[1]

When Yosef was sent down to *Mitzrayim*, the *pasuk* says, "הוּרַד מִצְרָיְמָה—He was sent down to Egypt."[2] Later, when Yosef reveals himself to his brothers, he tells them, "מַהֲרוּ וַעֲלוּ אֶל אָבִי—Quickly go up to my father."[3] *Rashi* comments that Yosef specifically told the brothers to go up because "*Eretz Yisrael gavohah mikol ha'artzos*—Eretz Yisrael is higher than all other lands."[4] Two questions come to my mind:

---

1   *Sanhedrin* 42a.
2   *Bereishis* 39:1.
3   Ibid. 45:9.
4   Ibid., *Rashi*, s.v. *Va'alu el avi*.

- First, don't the brothers know that they came down to Mitzrayim, and that in order to get their father they would have to go up? So why does Yosef feel the need to tell them to "go up" to his father?
- Second, why doesn't *Rashi* comment about the topography when Yosef was sold and went down to *Mitzrayim*? Why is it only significant regarding going up?

I believe that *Rashi* is alluding what Yosef was hinting to the brothers. Yosef tells his brothers not to worry because everything was from Hashem, and he would not take any vengeance on them. Yosef recognized that Hashem was in control of everything and that there was a purpose that he landed in Mitzrayim. But even more than that, Yosef recognized that in order for B'nei Yisrael to become a great nation, they would first have to descend. They would first go down in order to go up. *Rashi* isn't just telling us that Eretz Yisrael is above other lands; we can look at a map to discover that. *Rashi* is teaching us that in order to reach great heights, we will have to go through some lows.

וַיִּקְרָא אֱלֹקִים לָאוֹר יוֹם וְלַחֹשֶׁךְ קָרָא לָיְלָה וַיְהִי עֶרֶב וַיְהִי בֹקֶר יוֹם אֶחָד.[5]

And God called the light Day, and the darkness He called Night.
And there was evening and there was morning, a first day.

Only after the creation of day and night was the day completed. The Torah is teaching us that a complete day consists of both night and day. So too, a complete person has their times of light as well as their times of darkness. But in order to appreciate the light, darkness has to come first.

נשמה שהיא חיה לעולם ואינה מתה במות הגוף.[6]

"An eternal soul," surviving the death of the body it inhabits.

Every Jew has a *neshamah* that comes from Hashem. The *Chizkuni* on *Bereishis* teaches that the breath that Hashem breathed into man is the *neshamah*, an everlasting soul that does not die with the body.

---

5   Ibid. 1:5.
6   Ibid. 2:7; *Chizkuni*, s.v. *Nishmas chaim*.

Mankind was placed in the world to fix it for Hashem's honor, as we say in the *tefillah* of *Aleinu*: "*L'saken olam b'malchus Sha-dai*—to perfect the universe through the Almighty's sovereignty." Why couldn't Hashem keep the *neshamah* by Him? In order for a *neshamah* to be complete, it has to come down into this world first, and only then can it go back up. Someone who is born wealthy will not appreciate money as much as one who has to save up or go through turbulent times in order to sustain an income and a means to live. For one to value something, there is usually a fear of losing it. As the Swiss psychiatrist Carl Jung once said, "The word 'happy' would lose its meaning if not balanced with sadness."

Many times, we come to appreciate what we have when we lose it. When students come to me and tell me how things aren't going their way, or that they messed up in something, I explain to them that life is like a rubber band. Stretching a rubber band causes it to contract and have resistance. This is like our lows in life. However, once the rubber band is released, it flies across the room. When it lacks the resistance, the rubber band will just stay in its place without the ability to shoot its way across the room. We must realize that when we feel that life is pulling us down, it is only so that we can launch ourselves even further. Sometimes bending our knees can help us reach great heights.

To Summarize

In order to fully appreciate light, one must experience darkness. We all have ups and downs in life. One could stay down, but that wouldn't help accomplish anything. One who uses their downs as momentum to boost himself upward recognizes that the down was only a stepping stone to reach a higher level.

Points to Ponder

- How do I bounce back stronger after a "failure"?
- How can I remember that my downs are only to help me grow?
- How can I use what pulls me down to launch me forward?

LESSON 10

Just Keep Swimming

Swimming is one of those activities that can be very nerve-wracking when one is beginning to learn. Some children dive right in, while others take their time to get their feet wet. My children are among the latter group. They would take their time getting used to the water, and only eventually, if we had enough time, would they even descend down the steps. Every time we would go swimming, it was the same routine. I found this odd, yet interesting.

Now they are quite comfortable jumping in without the whole process of getting their feet wet. I wondered what took them so long to finally jump right in. In her book, *Motivated Minds*, Dr. Deborah Stipek writes that "…kids gravitate toward…the 'just-right' challenge that will boost their competence to the next level."[1] Children will stay on something until they have mastered it, lose interest, and move on.

וַיֹּאמֶר עֵשָׂו אֶל יַעֲקֹב הַלְעִיטֵנִי נָא מִן הָאָדֹם הָאָדֹם הַזֶּה כִּי עָיֵף אָנֹכִי...[2]

And Eisav said to Yaakov, "Give me some of that very red stuff, for I am famished…"

---

1   D. Stipek and K. Seal, *Motivated Minds: Raising Children to Love Learning* (New York: H. Holt and Company, 2001), p. 45.
2   *Bereishis* 25:30.

I find that as time goes on, people feel the urge to cut corners and rush things in order to move on. We live in a time that everything must be ready in an instant. This is the mentality of Eisav. We know that when cooked, red lentils change to a yellow/green color. Yet Eisav wanted the soup raw—before it was even cooked.

אֶרֶךְ אַפַּיִם רַב תְּבוּנָה וּקְצַר רוּחַ מֵרִים אִוֶּלֶת.[3]

Patience shows much understanding, impatience elevates foolishness.

תנו רבנן: לעולם יהא אדם ענוותן כהלל...מעשה בשני בני אדם שהמרו זה את זה, אמרו: כל מי שילך ויקניט את הלל יטול ארבע מאות זוז. אמר אחד מהם: אני אקניטנו. אותו היום ערב שבת היה, והלל חפף את ראשו. הלך ועבר על פתח ביתו, אמר: מי כאן הלל, מי כאן הלל? נתעטף ויצא לקראתו. אמר לו: בני, מה אתה מבקש? אמר לו: שאלה יש לי לשאול. אמר לו: שאל בני. שאל...לימים נזדווגו שלשתן למקום אחד, אמרו ענוותנותו של הלל קרבתנו תחת כנפי השכינה.[4]

The Sages taught: A person should always be patient like Hillel...There was an incident involving two people who made a bet with each other and said: "Anyone who will go and aggravate Hillel will win four-hundred zuz." One of them said: "I will provoke him." That day was Erev Shabbos, and Hillel was washing his head. He went and passed the entrance to Hillel's house and said: "Who here is Hillel, who here is Hillel?" Hillel wrapped himself and went out to greet him. He said to him: "My son, what do you seek?" He said to him: "I have a question to ask." Hillel said to him: "Ask, my son, ask."...Eventually, the three gathered together in one place, and they said: "Hillel's patience brought us beneath the wings of the Divine Presence."

The Gemara teaches that one should be patient like Hillel, and it illustrates the idea with stories displaying the patience of Hillel. One

---

3   *Mishlei* 14:29.

4   *Shabbos* 30b–31a.

example is the first story the Gemara brings. There was a bet between two people that whoever could get Hillel angry would win four hundred *zuz*. On Erev Shabbos, the day that is probably the most hectic for Jews all around the world, one of them came to the house of Hillel a few times, each time asked a seemingly random and pointless question, and yet Hillel kept his cool and answered all of his questions. Hillel even offered to sit with the person and answer any other questions he had. At the conclusion of this Gemara, there is a conversation between the converts of Hillel, who all said that it was Hillel's patience that brought them closer to the *Shechinah*.

Hillel also teaches that *"Lo ha'kapdan melamed*—one who is impatient cannot teach."[5] When it comes to education, we must be patient. Trying to rush a flower to grow won't help it. Pouring more and more water on it will cause it to die. So too, when educating children, be patient.

The Mishnah teaches that the way to acquire Torah is "מַיִם בְּמִשּׂוּרָה תִשְׁתֶּה—by drinking water in small measures,"[6] i.e., a little bit at a time. Patience is vital for success.

כִּי מִיץ חָלָב יוֹצִיא חֶמְאָה וּמִיץ אַף יוֹצִיא דָם וּמִיץ אַפַּיִם יוֹצִיא רִיב.[7]

When milk is under pressure it produces butter, when a nose is pressured it produces blood, when patience is pressured it produces strife.

My children learned the lesson of patience from an incident that happened just after Pesach. We'd finished packing all the Pesach accessories at Bubby and Zaidy's house, but wanting something other than *matzah brei*, we ordered pizza. When the pizza arrived, it was still very hot, yet some of us were hungrier than others and a bit impatient. While Daniel was one of the patient ones, Ayelet, who didn't know better, was not. She put a piece of pizza in her mouth, quickly spat it out, and began to cry. Even though she was too young to speak, it was obvious that she'd

---

5   *Avos* 2:6.

6   Ibid. 6:4.

7   *Mishlei* 30:33.

burnt her tongue. In trying to comfort her, Daniel told Ayelet that she had to wait and blow on her food to cool it off.

Whether it is a slice of pizza or a hot cup of coffee, I am sure that this happens many times throughout one's lifetime. Sometimes, we are just too impatient and tend to "burn" ourselves. As a result, we then have to suffer the discomfort all day and sometimes even longer. If we would wait, think things through, and be a bit more patient, we would have much happier and healthier lives.

The lesson here is to "Keep calm and carry on." Don't always rush, because when we rush into things, we may regret our decisions and miss great opportunities. If it's meant to be, it'll be. A major key to success is to be patient. If we rush too often in life, we just may end up eating tasteless pizza.

To Summarize

It is very easy to lose one's cool and want to move things forward when they're moving slow. There are times that jumping the gun can be harmful for an individual or group of people. One who loses patience shows that they are not in control. Having patience is no simple task, especially when we are waiting for others. However, it is a very important characteristic to obtain. Patience may seem bitter, but its fruits are sweet.

Points to Ponder

- What are some of my "just-right" challenges?
- How can I work on my patience when under pressure?
- What are some strategies to help me just "keep swimming" when faced with many obstacles?

LESSONS FROM THE GRANDPARENTS' HOME

A World of Instruction

When Grandma and Zaidy got Daniel a new trampoline, he was so eager to play with it that he decided to put it together all by himself. However, at two years old, he found it difficult to do. It is very difficult to build something without instruction; it is actually nearly impossible to be 100% successful without any guidelines or instructions. The Mishnah teaches, "*Aseh lecha rav*"[1]—that one should always have a mentor to reach out to for guidance.

Nowadays, almost everything comes with a little paper called "the instructions." So too, Hashem created this world with a set of instructions called "the Torah." Indeed, the word *Torah* comes from the word "*hora'ah*," which means guidance. The *pasuk* says, "שְׁמַע בְּנִי מוּסַר אָבִיךָ וְאַל תִּטֹּשׁ תּוֹרַת אִמֶּךָ—Listen, my son, to the rebuke of your father, and don't forsake the guidance of your mother.[2]

ב' פעמים כתיב במשלי אל תטוש תורת אמך תורה שבכתב ותורה שבעל פה.[3]

Two times in Mishlei it is written, "Do not forsake the guidance of your mother"; [the two times correspond to] the Written Torah and the Oral Torah.

---

1   *Avos* 1:6.
2   *Mishlei* 1:8.
3   *Sefer Chassidim* 970.

The *Sefer Chassidim* comments on this *pasuk*, saying that the two times in *Mishlei* that it says, "וְאַל תִּטֹּשׁ תּוֹרַת אִמֶּךָ" are referring to the *Torah She'bichsav* and the *Torah She'baal Peh.*

The *Targum* translates the end of this *pasuk* as "Do not stray from the manners of your mother."

Even if we don't fully understand what our parents tell us, we should follow their words and guidance.

People may wonder why the Torah tells us how to do basic things, such as how to wake up in the morning or cutting our nails. The answer is because the Torah is a guidebook. A guidebook of instructions doesn't start from step fifteen! It begins with step one!

I once did an activity with my class where I handed out a sentence written in Morse code, and I instructed my students to decode the sentence into proper English. After about five minutes of trying to figure out one of the letters, my students were ready to give up. I told them not to worry, as I then handed out a second sheet of paper with the key showing each letter represented by the lines and dots. The lesson I was trying to give over to them was that the Torah isn't just a guidebook that we can open and read, but rather it is a guidebook that we need to learn the deeper understanding in order to be truly successful. How can we learn deeper than the surface? Through having a *rav* to learn from and to guide us in the proper direction. The Gemara teaches, "*O chavrusa o misusa*—A companion or death."[4] We need someone to learn with in order to help us stay balanced. If one learns alone, one will not be as challenged as one would be when learning with someone else.

אַרְבַּע עֶשְׂרֵה שָׁנִין דַּהֲוָה בְּבֵית עֵבֶר.[5]

Fourteen years that he was in the house of Ever.

The Gemara tells us that Yaakov Avinu sat and learned for fourteen years before he went to the house of Lavan. The reason he spent these

---

4   *Taanis* 23a.

5   *Megillah* 17a.

years learning was in order to prepare himself for the scandalous environment he was on his way to, the house of Lavan.

וְאֶת יְהוּדָה שָׁלַח לְפָנָיו אֶל יוֹסֵף לְהוֹרֹת לְפָנָיו גֹּשְׁנָה וַיָּבֹאוּ אַרְצָה גֹּשֶׁן.[6]

He had sent Yehudah ahead of him to Yosef, to point the way before him to Goshen, and they came to the land of Goshen.

קדם שיגיע לשם. ומדרש אגדה להורות לפניו—לתקן לו בית תלמוד שמשם תצא הוראה.[7]

"Before he should arrive there." A midrashic comment is l'horos l'fanav—to establish for him a House of Study from which guidance will go forth.

ואת יהודה שלח לפניו...להתקין לו בית ועד שיהא מורה בו דברי תורה ושיהיו השבטים לומדים בו.[8]

He had sent Yehudah ahead of him...to establish for him a meeting place so that there would be guidance in it with words of Torah, and it should be that the shevatim will learn there.

Before the *shevatim* went down to dwell in Mitzrayim, Yehudah was sent down to the land of Goshen to establish a yeshiva in order to have guidance in this new land.

וּגְבוּל יָם וְהָיָה לָכֶם הַיָּם הַגָּדוֹל וּגְבוּל זֶה יִהְיֶה לָכֶם גְּבוּל יָם.[9]

For the western boundary you shall have the coast of the Yam Suf; that shall serve as your western boundary.

When Moshe Rabbeinu established the *arei miklat*, he appointed the Levi'im to live there. We know that *Shevet Levi* was accustomed to

---

6 *Bereishis* 46:28.
7 Ibid., Rashi, s.v. *L'fanav*.
8 *Bereishis Rabbah* 95:3.
9 *Bamidbar* 34:6.

learning Torah since they were involved in learning Torah and did not take part in the back-breaking labor in Mitzrayim.[10]

תנא תלמיד שגלה מגלין רבו עמו...הרב שגלה מגלין ישיבתו עמו.[11]

It was taught in a Beraisa: a student who is exiled, his rav is exiled with him...a rav who is exiled, his yeshiva is exiled with him.

When it comes to *arei miklat*, the Gemara teaches that if a student kills accidentally, his *rebbi* must go with him to the *ir miklat* in order to learn with him. Also, if a *rebbi* kills by accident, the entire yeshiva goes to the *ir miklat* with the *rebbi* so that he could continue teaching Torah.

These are some examples of the importance of a rabbi from whom one can learn from his ways and accept his guidance. We see throughout Jewish history that the first thing Jewish communities would do when settling into a new environment was to build *batei midrashos* and yeshivos to instill a Torah education in their children and give guidance to the community.

וַיִּגְּשׁוּ אֵלָיו וַיֹּאמְרוּ גִּדְרֹת צֹאן נִבְנֶה לְמִקְנֵנוּ פֹּה וְעָרִים לְטַפֵּנוּ...בְּנוּ לָכֶם עָרִים לְטַפְּכֶם וּגְדֵרֹת לְצֹנַאֲכֶם וְהַיֹּצֵא מִפִּיכֶם תַּעֲשׂוּ.[12]

Then they stepped up to him and said, "We will build here sheepfolds for our flocks and towns for our children..." "Build towns for your children and sheepfolds for your flocks, but do what you have promised."

בעבר הירדן תלת בארץ ישראל תלת אמר אביי בגלעד שכיחי רוצחים.[13]

Three [cities designated] on the east bank of the Jordan, [where two-and-a-half tribes resided,] and three [cities designated] in Eretz Yisrael [where more than nine tribes resided]? Abaye

---

10   Rabbeinu Bachya, *Shemos* 5:4.
11   *Makkos* 10a.
12   *Bamidbar* 32:16, 24.
13   *Makkos* 9b.

said: In Gilad, which is located on the east bank of the Jordan, murderers are common.

When B'nei Yisrael were dividing the land, the tribes of Reuven and Gad requested to stay on the other side of the Yarden. They expressed their will to build pens for their flocks and cities for their children—in that order. In Moshe's response, he rebukes them by indicating that they first take care of their children and then their possessions.

The Gemara questions why there were three *arei miklat* designated in Eretz Yisrael, where nine-and-a-half *shevatim* lived, and three *arei miklat* designated on the other side of the Yarden where only two-and-a-half *shevatim* lived. Abaye answered that murder was more common in the lands across the Yarden.

One who goes to the *arei miklat* is one who kills inadvertently, not with intention to kill. If so, why is it that there were so many more people killing unintentionally within these two *shevatim* that they needed three *arei miklat* for themselves? Abaye's answer doesn't seem to resolve the issue, because the presence of murderers doesn't explain why there are *unintended* deaths!

Mikdashei HaLevi elaborates on this point about why murder was more common in the land of Gilad, across the Yarden. He says that when the tribes of Reuven and Gad requested to stay on the other side of the Yarden, their priorities weren't correct. The reason there was more murder by these *shevatim* was because they were more focused on the security of their possessions than the security of their children. Therefore, explains the *Mikdashei HaLevi*, when one is not focused on the upbringing and security/responsibility of their children, it reflects in the lack of *chinuch* by the parents of their children. This ultimately leads to neglect, which then generates a new generation of people who aren't careful with their environment. When people aren't careful with their surroundings, it can lead to murder, even unintentionally, which is why they needed more *arei miklat* designated in their territories.[14]

---

14   *Parashas Masei.*

We have the blueprints that instruct and guide us in the choices we make by prioritizing our *chinuch ha'banim* while finding the proper balance to focus on our livelihood.

To Summarize

Almost everything comes with a manual on how to use it; this applies to life as well. We have the Book of Life—the Torah. Throughout history, B'nei Yisrael made sure that wherever they would sojourn would have an established place of learning. Educating our youth in the proper Torah path will help guide them throughout life's challenges.

Points to Ponder

- How am I connecting myself to a *rav* who can give me direction in life?
- Do I have a *chavrusa* to learn with? If yes, what are some benefits I see when learning with my *chavrusa*?
- How am I leading a life of Torah for future generations?

Peek-a-boo

Many times, when young children are in trouble, they attempt to hide in order to avoid the consequences. There are times that they cover their eyes as if they just transported from the scene, somewhat like an ostrich sticking its head in the ground when sensing danger. Once, we went to visit my grandparents in Eretz Yisrael, and I observed my Bubby playing peek-a-boo with my children. From their reaction, it seemed that they truly believed they had disappeared when they covered their eyes and reappeared when they uncovered them.

Many times, we act the same way. When we are going through difficult times, we believe that Hashem is hiding and has disappeared. We must recognize that there is always an *ayin ro'eh*—an eye that is constantly watching us.

There is so much we can learn from the eyes. All emotion can be found in the eyes.

וְעֵינֵי לֵאָה רַכּוֹת וְרָחֵל הָיְתָה יְפַת תֹּאַר וִיפַת מַרְאֶה.[1]

Leah had delicate eyes; Rachel was comely and shapely.

---

1   *Bereishis* 29:17.

שהיתה סבורה לעלות בגורלו של עשו ובוכה, שהיו הכל אומרים שני בנים
לרבקה ושתי בנות ללבן, הגדולה לגדול והקטנה לקטן.[2]

*She thought she would have to fall to the lot of Eisav, and she
therefore wept continually, because everyone said, "Rivkah has
two sons, Lavan has two daughters—the elder daughter for
the elder son, the younger daughter for the younger son."*

We see an example of this with Leah. The *pasuk* says that her eyes
were tender. *Rashi* informs us that her eyes were tender (from crying)
because she thought she was destined to marry Eisav.

Throughout *Tanach*, we find the terminology of "finding favor in
one's eyes." We also find where the opposite emotion is referred to in
relation to eyes.[3] We see how different emotions are expressed through
one's eyes.

There is a saying that the eyes are the "windows to the soul." Shlomo
HaMelech says:

מְאוֹר עֵינַיִם יְשַׂמַּח לֵב.[4]

What brightens the eye gladdens the heart.

We refer to this in the final paragraph of *Shema* when we say,

וְלֹא תָתוּרוּ אַחֲרֵי לְבַבְכֶם וְאַחֲרֵי עֵינֵיכֶם אֲשֶׁר אַתֶּם זֹנִים אַחֲרֵיהֶם.[5]

And do not go after your heart and after your eyes.

הלב והעינים הם מרגלים לגוף, מסרסרים לו את העברות, העין רואה והלב
חומד והגוף עושה את העברה.[6]

---

2   Ibid., *Rashi*, s.v. *Rakos.*

3   The *Ohr Hachaim* (*Bamidbar* 11:10) correlates the anger of Hashem with eyes. The *pasuk*
    says, "Hashem was extremely angry, and in the eyes of Moshe, it was evil."

4   *Mishlei* 15:30.

5   *Bamidbar* 15:39.

6   Ibid., *Rashi*, s.v. *V'lo sasuru acharei levavchem.*

*The heart and the eyes are the "spies" of the body—they act
as its agents for sinning: the eye sees, the heart lusts, and the
body commits the sin.*

Rashi explains that the eyes see, the heart desires, and the body sins.
This lesson that the verse teaches about the eyes is so important that
guarding the eyes is one of the six constant mitzvos.

והשתדל אחר כך לעצום עיניך וחוש ראותך מהביט אל מה שאיננו צריך
לך או מה שיטריד לבך מחשוב במה שיועילך ופרוש ממותר הראות כפי
יכלתך.[7]

*Afterward, endeavor to shut your eyes and shut your sense of
sight from seeing that which you do not need, or that which will
distract your mind from thinking of what will be of use to you.
Separate yourself as much as you can from superfluous sights,
just like you separate from looking at things that are forbidden
to look at.*

The *Chovos Halevavos* teaches that one should close his eyes in order
to guard himself from sights that can be damaging because the heart
and eyes are the two agents of sin.

הֶחָכָם עֵינָיו בְּרֹאשׁוֹ וְהַכְּסִיל בַּחֹשֶׁךְ הוֹלֵךְ...[8]

*A wise man has his eyes in his head, whereas a fool walks in
darkness...*

בתחלת הדבר, מסתכל מה יהא בסופה.[9]

In the beginning of the matter, he contemplates the end results.

אי כל דא אית בהו, לית דינא למהוי בנקיו, כד מברכין בהו לקודשא
בריך הוא. בגין דבהו, ובדוגמא דלהון, מתברך שמא קדישא. ועל דא

---

7   *Chovos Halevavos, Shaar Ha'prishus,* chap. 5.
8   *Koheles* 2:14.
9   Ibid., *Rashi, s.v. HaChacham einav b'rosho.*

אתון דחכמיתו טובא, היך לא אשגחתון להאי. ולא שמשתון לרבי שמעיה
חסידא, ואיהו אמר, כל טנופא, וכל לכלוכא, סליקו ליה לסטרא אחרא,
דהא סטרא אחרא מהאי טנופא ולכלוכא אתזן. (תרומה קנ״ד ע״ב) ועל דא
מים אחרונים חובה, וחובה אינון.[10]

Shlomo HaMelech teaches that a wise man has eyes in his head and
a fool walks in darkness. On this, *Rashi* and others explain that a wise
person considers the future.

The *Zohar* asks, where else should one's eyes be if not in his head? Why
does Shlomo HaMelech teach that one's eyes are in his head regarding
a wise person? What about every individual? The *Zohar* answers that
the reason one isn't allowed to walk four *amos* without a head covering
is because the *Shechinah* rests on one's head. A wise person, who has
the *Shechinah* on his head, thinks before he speaks and contemplates
the future.

האמר רבא גמירי דאין יצר הרע שולט אלא במה שעיניו רואות.[11]

*Rava said: It is learned as a tradition that the evil inclination
controls only that which a person's eyes see.*

The Gemara teaches that the *yetzer hara* only controls what the eye
sees. A wise person has the foresight to guard his eyes from seeing evil
because the *Shechinah* dwells above him, and thus the *yetzer hara* will
not be able to take control.

The final *dibbur* engraved on the *luchos* is *lo sachmod*—not to covet.[12]

אנשים רבים יתמהו על זאת המצוה. איך יהיה אדם שלא יחמוד דבר יפה
בלבו כל מה שהוא נחמד למראה למראה עיניו...על כן אין ראוי להתעסק בו
בדברי העולם רק ביראת השם לבדו.[13]

*Many people have wondered about this commandment; how
is it that a man not covet in his heart that which is beautiful*

---

10   *Zohar* 3:186:2.

11   *Sotah* 8a.

12   *Shemos* 20:14.

13   *Ibn Ezra, Shemos,* ibid.

[and] all that which appears pleasant in his eyes?...Therefore,
it's not admirable to involve himself with worldly matters, only
with the fear of Hashem.

A wise person will recognize that Hashem is in control. Like it says:

רֵאשִׁית חָכְמָה יִרְאַת ה'.[14]

The beginning of wisdom is the fear of Hashem.

...אמר להון אנא נמי מלכא אנא מיחשב חשיבנא הבו לי מידי יהבו ליה
גולגלתא חדא אתייה תקליה לכוליה דהבא וכספא דידיה בהדיה לא
הוה מתקליה אמר להון לרבנן מאי האי אמרי גולגלתא לעינא דבישרא
ודמא דלא קא שבע אמר להו ממאי דהכי הוא שקלי קלילי עפרא וכסייה
לאלתר תקלא.[15]

He said to them: "I too, I am a king; I am very important.
Give me something." They gave him one eyeball. He brought it
and he weighed all the gold and silver that he had against the
eyeball, and it did not balance. He said to the Sages: "What is
this?" They said: "It is the eyeball of flesh and blood, which is
not satisfied." He said to them: "From where do you know that
this is the reason?" [The Sages answered him:] "Take a small
amount of dirt and cover the eye." He did so, and it was imme-
diately balanced.

There is a fascinating episode involving Alexander the Great teaching
us the importance of humility. When Alexander the Great requested
a souvenir from Gan Eden, he was given a pupil of an eye. Alexander
weighed the pupil against all of his gold and silver, and the pupil outweighed it all. He asked the *chachamim* about this phenomenon, and
they responded, "It is a pupil of a human eye, which is never satisfied
with what it has." Alexander challenged the *chachamim* and asked them
to prove what they were saying was true. The *chachamim* instructed

---

14   *Tehillim* 111:10.
15   *Tamid* 32b.

Alexander to take some dirt and cover the eye so that it can't see and it will be outweighed immediately. When one is humble and isn't always looking at the riches of the world, he will be satisfied with what he has.

אמר רב הונא: מאי דכתיב: "שמח בחור בילדותך ויטיבך לבך בימי בחורותיך והלך בדרכי לבך ובמראה עיניך ודע כי על כל אלה יביאך האלקים במשפט"—עד כאן דברי יצר הרע, מכאן ואילך דברי יצר טוב.[16]

Rav Huna said: What is the meaning of that which is written: "Rejoice young man in your youth, and let your heart cheer you in the days of your youth, and walk in the ways of your heart and in the sight of your eyes; but know that for all these things God will bring you to judgment"? Until here, the words of the evil inclination; from here on, the words of the good inclination.

We cover our eyes when we say *Shema* in order to direct our concentration solely toward Hashem. We remove all distractions that we may see because we recognize that the *Shechinah* is dwelling within us. The eyes are the only part of the body that are never covered; even during the coronavirus, when everyone wore masks, the eyes were revealed. The eyes truly are the window to the soul, and we must make sure not to pull the shades down—blocking the light of our *neshamah* from connecting to Hashem.

אמר רבי שמואל בר נחמני אמר רבי יונתן: מאי דכתיב "לבבתני אחותי כלה לבבתני באחת מעיניך"—בתחילה באחת מעיניך, לכשתעשי—בשתי עיניך.[17]

Rabbi Shmuel bar Nachmani said that Rabbi Yonasan said: What is the meaning of that which is written: "You have captivated my heart, my sister, my bride; you have captivated my heart with one of your eyes"? At first [when you, the Jewish People, merely accepted the Torah upon yourselves it was] with

---

16   *Shabbos* 63b.
17   Ibid. 88b.

*one of your eyes; when you perform [the mitzvos it will be] with
both of your eyes.*

The Gemara explains the *pasuk*, "You have captured My heart, My sister, O bride you have captured My heart with one of your eyes" by saying that initially, when we accepted the Torah, we "attracted" Hashem with one of His eyes. But when we follow and perform the Torah, Hashem says that we attract Him with both eyes.

To Summarize

What the eyes see, the heart desires. A wise person is able to anticipate the future to safeguard himself from viewing things his heart should not desire. All emotion can be seen in the eyes, for they are the windows to the soul. Have a good outlook on life and connect with others. Not only do we connect with others through our eyes, but Hashem connects through His "eyes" as well.

Points to Ponder

- What are some actions I am taking to guard my eyes?
- How am I using my eyes to connect with others?
- How can I work on my *ayin tovah*—good eye?

Goin' Up

When Ayelet began walking and climbing, I remembered the advice the doctor gave us when Daniel was at this stage. The doctor told us that the two bottom bookshelves belonged to the child, and thus not to keep anything of value on them because the children will undoubtedly get to it. What the doctor left out was that, in reality, children will get to anything they really want.

My dear children taught me that there is nothing out of reach. It doesn't matter what shelf it is on; if their eyes are on the prize, it is in their reach. When we moved things to the top shelf, Ayelet would still figure out a way to reach it. She would move a chair or step on a nearby box, and sometimes even use the couch. It didn't really matter how high something was; she figured out a way to reach it. One time, Daniel asked me to hold him, and without me realizing it, he grabbed something off the shelf.

Many times, we see something that we want, whether it is monetary possessions or certain achievements, and we give up on them because they seem out of reach. If we pause for a moment and think of other ways we can achieve our aspirations, we will be unstoppable. We can achieve anything if we put our minds to it. The only one who can stop us is ourselves.

One should have a mindset that they could accomplish anything and be able to continue moving forward.

אֹרַח חַיִּים לְמַעְלָה לְמַשְׂכִּיל לְמַעַן סוּר מִשְּׁאוֹל מָטָּה.[1]

For an intelligent man, the path of life leads upward in order to avoid the Gehinnom below.

האדם נקרא הולך, שצריך לילך תמיד מדרגא לדרגא, ואם לא יעלה למעלה ירד מטה מטה, חס ושלום, כי בלתי אפשר שיעמד בדרגא חדא.[2]

A person is called "going" because he should always go from level to level, and if he is not continuously ascending, he will descend to the depths, Heaven forbid, because it is impossible to stay on the same level.

On the *pasuk* in *Mishlei* that says, "The path of life for the wise leads upward," the *Gra* comments, saying that man is called "going," for if one chooses, he could continue to ascend, and if he *chas v'shalom* chooses not to, he will descend. It is impossible to stay set in place. As my *Zaidy*, *zt"l*, would say, "Life is like going up a greased pole; the moment one stops is the moment they slide down." The moment one feels satisfied with where he is, that's the moment he begins to descend.

Even the nations of the world recognize the importance of continuously moving forward. As Martin Luther King Jr. once said, "If you can't fly, then run; if you can't run, then walk; if you can't walk, then crawl; but whatever you do, you have to keep moving forward."

וטעמא דבית הלל דמעלין בקדש ואין מורידין.[3]

And the reason according to Beis Hillel is because we ascend in sanctity and don't descend.

The Gemara teaches that when we light candles on Chanukah, we follow the reasoning of Beis Hillel, who says that we light from one to eight since we increase the *kedushah* and don't subtract from it. The essence of a Jew is to move up in *kedushah*. In Judaism, and in life as

---

1   *Mishlei* 15:24.
2   Vilna Gaon, *Mishlei* ibid.
3   *Shabbos* 21b.

well, one is either going up and becoming closer to Hashem, or down and creating separation. We must focus on going up.

וּמֹשֶׁה עָלָה אֶל הָאֱלֹקִים...[4]

And Moshe went up to God.

The *pasuk* tells us that Moshe went up when receiving the Torah. So too, we get a spiritual *aliyah* when reading the Torah. When we move forward and follow in the ways of Hashem, improving ourselves, Hashem helps us become successful.

עֲשֵׂה רְצוֹנוֹ כִרְצוֹנְךָ, כְּדֵי שֶׁיַּעֲשֶׂה רְצוֹנְךָ כִרְצוֹנוֹ. בַּטֵּל רְצוֹנְךָ מִפְּנֵי רְצוֹנוֹ, כְּדֵי שֶׁיְּבַטֵּל רְצוֹן אֲחֵרִים מִפְּנֵי רְצוֹנֶךָ.[5]

Make your will like His will, in order that He makes His will like your will. Annul your will for His will in order that He annuls the will of others against your will.

וַיְהִי בִּנְסֹעַ הָאָרֹן וַיֹּאמֶר מֹשֶׁה קוּמָה ה' וְיָפֻצוּ אֹיְבֶיךָ וְיָנֻסוּ מְשַׂנְאֶיךָ מִפָּנֶיךָ.[6]

When the Ark would travel, Moshe would say: "Arise Hashem! Let Your enemies be scattered, and may Your foes flee before You!" And when it rested, he would say: "Return, Hashem, to Yisrael's myriads of thousands!"

פי' אם יתאספו לבא על ישראל יפוצו ולא ימצא בהם שנים ביחד ואם יבאו ינוסו ולא תהיה להם תקומה זו היא תפלת הדרך שלהם.[7]

This is a prayer that if enemies will gather to attack Yisrael, they should be dispersed by God before carrying out their plans. If, for some reason, they had already succeeded in gathering, God should put them to flight.

---

4   *Shemos* 19:3.
5   *Avos* 2:4.
6   *Bamidbar* 10:35.
7   *Daas Zekeinim, Bamidbar* ibid.

The *pasuk* teaches that when B'nei Yisrael would move forward with the *Aron*, not only would Hashem travel with them, but Hashem would scatter any enemies who would try to harm B'nei Yisrael.

> והיה כאשר ירים משה ידו וגבר ישראל וגו', וכי ידיו של משה עושות מלחמה
> או שוברות מלחמה. אלא לומר לך, כל זמן שהיו ישראל מסתכלים כלפי
> מעלה ומשעבדין את לבם לאביהם שבשמים היו מתגברים. ואם לאו, היו
> נופלין. כיוצא בדבר אתה אומר, עשה לך שרף ושים אתו על נס, והיה
> כל הנשוך וראה אתו וחי. וכי נחש ממית, או נחש מחיה. אלא, בזמן
> שישראל מסתכלין כלפי מעלה ומשעבדין את לבם לאביהן שבשמים, היו
> מתרפאים, ואם לאו, היו נמוקים.[8]

> *"And it came to pass, when Moshe held up his hand, Yisrael pre-vailed…"*[9] *Did the hands of Moshe wage war or break [Israel's ability to wage] war? Rather, this teaches that as long as Israel would look upward and subject their hearts to their Father in Heaven, they prevailed, and if not, they fell. Similarly, "Make for yourself a fiery serpent and mount it on a pole. And if any-one who is bitten shall look at it, he shall live."*[10] *Did the serpent kill or did the serpent keep alive? Rather, when Yisrael would look upward and subject their hearts to their Father in Heaven, they were healed, and if not, their [flesh] would melt away.*

The Mishnah teaches that when Moshe raised his hands, B'nei Yisrael prevailed, and when they would look up at the copper snake, they were healed. The Mishnah asked, was it really the hands of Moshe or the snake that caused B'nei Yisrael to overcome or to become healed? The Mishnah answers that rather, when B'nei Yisrael lifted their eyes toward the heavens, they were reminded of their Father in Heaven, and they conquered and were cured.

When we focus on moving forward and keep our heads and eyes raised toward Hashem, we will be successful in what we set out to do. We have to focus on moving up and being the best that we can be.

---

8   *Rosh Hashanah* 3:8.
9   *Shemos* 17:11.
10 *Bamidbar* 21:9.

To Summarize

If there is a will, there's a way. We, as people, have the power to get whatever we want as long as we have enough will. In life, we are either going up or down; there is no middle ground. Without the will to continuously move up, one will naturally go down. The only one who could prevent you from accomplishing your mission is yourself.

Points to Ponder

- What are some dreams or goals I wish to accomplish?
- How am I going to elevate myself to overcome the obstacles in my path?
- What is something small I can take upon myself to work on my connection between me and Hashem?

Fallin' Down

Daniel loves to learn; sometimes he learns from his mistakes. One mistake he (hopefully) learned from was when he was trying to balance on one foot while standing on his booster, which was on a chair. As you may have guessed, he fell. He bumped his head and began crying; however, not out of pain but out of disappointment. Why was he disappointed? Daniel wasn't disappointed that he fell; rather, he was disappointed that I didn't catch him. I was confused; I wondered why he expected me to catch him when I wasn't next to him. After some thought, I came to the conclusion that since I am his father and I am always there for him, he expected me to catch him no matter what.

I realized that people do this all the time. People will do something wrong, make mistakes, and then blame Hashem for not catching them when they fall. Yes, Hashem is our Father and is always watching over us, but we can't blame Him for not catching us!

When people are successful, it may be easier to thank Hashem for all of the good. However, when something that seems bad happens, some may doubt the existence of Hashem. They may say, "Where was Hashem when that happened?" or "If Hashem really exists, then He'll get me out of this situation!"

There is a well-known poem called "Footprints in the Sand," which is a discussion between man and God. The man ascends to Heaven and watches his life playing before him. Afterward, he tells God, "I noticed that whenever things were going well, there were always two sets of footprints. However, when I was going through difficult times, I only noticed one set of footprints. Where were You?" God replied, "When things were going well, I walked beside you, and that's why you saw two sets of footprints. When things weren't going well, I put you on my shoulders and carried you through. That single set of footprints were Mine."[1] Hashem is always guiding us in the direction we seek.

וְאַחַר בָּאוּ מֹשֶׁה וְאַהֲרֹן וַיֹּאמְרוּ אֶל פַּרְעֹה כֹּה אָמַר ה׳ אֱלֹקֵי יִשְׂרָאֵל שַׁלַּח אֶת עַמִּי וְיָחֹגּוּ לִי בַּמִּדְבָּר: וַיֹּאמֶר פַּרְעֹה מִי ה׳ אֲשֶׁר אֶשְׁמַע בְּקֹלוֹ לְשַׁלַּח אֶת יִשְׂרָאֵל לֹא יָדַעְתִּי אֶת ה׳ וְגַם אֶת יִשְׂרָאֵל לֹא אֲשַׁלֵּחַ:...תֶּבֶן אֵין נִתָּן לַעֲבָדֶיךָ וּלְבֵנִים אֹמְרִים לָנוּ עֲשׂוּ וְהִנֵּה עֲבָדֶיךָ מֻכִּים וְחָטָאת עַמֶּךָ:...וַיִּרְאוּ שֹׁטְרֵי בְנֵי יִשְׂרָאֵל אֹתָם בְּרָע לֵאמֹר לֹא תִגְרְעוּ מִלִּבְנֵיכֶם דְּבַר יוֹם בְּיוֹמוֹ:[2]

Afterward, Moshe and Aharon went and said to Pharaoh, "Thus says Hashem, the God of Yisrael: Let My people go that they may celebrate a festival for Me in the wilderness." But Pharaoh said, "Who is Hashem that I should heed Him and let Yisrael go? I do not know Hashem, nor will I let Yisrael go"..."No straw is issued to your servants, yet they demand of us: 'Make bricks!' Thus, your servants are being beaten, when the fault is with your own people."

When Moshe and Aharon first approached Pharaoh to take the nation out for a few days, Pharaoh was cruel, denied Hashem, and increased the labor. Later on, the *pasuk* says, "I [Hashem] will harden Pharaoh's heart."[3] It seems unfair to Pharaoh that he was punished if Hashem was the one that hardened his heart and made him stubborn.

מאחר שהרשיע והתריס כנגדי, וגלוי לפני שאין נחת רוח באומות לתת לב שלם לשוב, טוב שיתקשה לבו, למען הרבות בו אותותי, ותכירו אתם

---

1   P. Burston and C. Burston, *Chicken Soup to Warm the Neshamah: 101 Short Stories, Insights & Sayings Containing Life-Long Lessons* (Monroe, NY: 2012), pp. 64–65.

2   *Shemos* 5:1, 2, 16, 19.

3   Ibid. 7:3.

את גבורתי. וכן מדתו של הקב"ה, מביא פרעניות על האמות כדי שישמעו
ישראל וייראו...[4]

*Since he has wickedly resisted Me, and it is manifest to Me that
the heathen nations find no spiritual satisfaction in setting
their whole heart to return to Me penitently, it is better that
his heart should be hardened in order that My signs may be
multiplied against him so that they may recognize My Divine
power. Such, indeed, is the method of Hakadosh Baruch Hu: He
brings punishment upon the nations so that Yisrael may hear
of it and fear Him.*

However, *Rashi* and others explain that previously Pharaoh was the
one who hardened his own heart and caused his own stubbornness. At
this later point in time, Hashem simply guided him along on the path
he was heading.

If Hashem is going to help someone be stubborn and harden his heart
against His own people, then how much more will Hashem help guide
one who is trying to fulfill His Will!

The Skulener Rebbe was once thrown into solitary confinement, and
he took the opportunity to learn without distraction. He thought about
how *Baruch She'amar* is full of praises that we say to Hashem, but he
couldn't understand the meaning of "*Baruch gozer u'mekayeim*—Blessed
is He, the One who decrees and fulfills." How is it a praise that
Hashem decrees things against us and fulfills them? The Rebbe asked
Hashem that he shouldn't be released until he found an answer. Sure
enough, the Rebbe came up with an answer: the praise we are giving is
"Blessed is Hashem Who decrees and gives us the ability to withstand
those decrees."

אמר רבי יונתן הפשתני הזה כשפשתני לוקה אינו מקיש עליו ביותר מפני
שהיא פוקעת, וכשפשתנו יפה הוא מקיש עליו ביותר, למה שהיא משתבחת
והולכת. כך הקדוש ברוך הוא אינו מנסה את הרשעים, למה שאין יכולין
לעמד...אמר רבי אלעזר לבעל הבית שהיה לו שתי פרות אחת כחה יפה

---

4   Ibid., *Rashi*, s.v. *Va'ani aksheh.*

וְאַחַת כֹּחָהּ רַע, עַל מִי הוּא נוֹתֵן אֶת הָעֹל לֹא עַל אוֹתָהּ שֶׁכֹּחָהּ יָפֶה, כָּךְ אֵין
הַקָּדוֹשׁ בָּרוּךְ הוּא מְנַסֶּה אֶלָּא הַצַּדִּיקִים...[5]

*Rabbi Yonasan said: When a flax worker knows that his flax is
of good quality, the more he beats it, the more it improves and
the more it glistens; but if it is of inferior quality, he cannot
give it one knock without it splitting. Similarly, Hakadosh
Baruch Hu does not test the wicked—why? Because they cannot withstand it...Rabbi Elazar said: When a man possesses
two cows, one strong and the other weak, on which one does
he put the yoke? Surely on the strong one. Similarly, Hakadosh
Baruch Hu tests only the righteous...*

וְאַתָּה תְּצַוֶּה אֶת בְּנֵי יִשְׂרָאֵל וְיִקְחוּ אֵלֶיךָ שֶׁמֶן זַיִת זָךְ כָּתִית לַמָּאוֹר לְהַעֲלֹת
נֵר תָּמִיד.[6]

*You shall further instruct the B'nei Yisrael to bring you pure oil
of beaten olives for lighting, for kindling lamps regularly.*

Rabbi Elimelech Biderman explains the opening *pasuk* in *Parashas
Tetzaveh*, "[A]nd you should take for you olive oil that is pure from
beaten olives for lighting [the *Menorah*]..." The purest oil is oil that is
crushed. That is the oil used by the Kohen Gadol to light the *Menorah*.
The way one becomes a shining light is by being crushed and making
the best out of their situation.

Sometimes we have to fall in order to learn to get back up. We must
learn from our mistakes and recognize that Hashem will always be there
to help us back up.

To Summarize

"If you stumble, make it part of the dance" is a cute quote with a powerful message. We may fall many times, but we could use the decline to

---

5   *Bereishis Rabbah* 55:2.

6   *Shemos* 27:20.

give us momentum to move forward. We have to realize that when we feel ourselves falling, we are still connected to a rope held by Hashem.

Points to Ponder

- Do I recognize that Hashem is with me even in times of distress?
- Do I realize that if I'm going through hardships, it means that Hashem sees me as righteous?
- How can I take my "down moments" and use them to help light the way for others?

As Far as the Eye Can See

It is easier to connect the dots once there are dots to connect. We don't always see the bigger picture until after a string of events take place. There are many *hashgachah pratis* stories that people tell over, and many miracles that we don't take notice of until afterward. Only then do things begin to make sense. There are times when we don't see the picture at all!

One Pesach, when discussing the story of *geulas Mitzrayim*, Daniel turned to Bubby Leah and asked, "Were you and *Zaidy* slaves to Pharaoh in Mitzrayim?"

Now, this may seem a bit disrespectful, but I understood where Daniel's question came from. The oldest people that Daniel knows are my grandparents. In his mind, when he thinks of people from a long time ago, he thinks of them. When we mentioned how our elders were slaves to Pharaoh in Mitzrayim, the first image that popped into his head were the elders he knew.

Hashem is Infinite, and that is why we can't even picture Him. We cannot imagine something that we have never seen before. It is impossible because we are finite and limited beings. We are unable to comprehend why certain things happen until after we put the pieces together and connect the dots. We are like small children whose eyes can't see over the bakery counter. Hashem is our father, and He can see everything—from His height.

My children love doing puzzles and building with Lego. It makes things much easier to complete a puzzle when the box is in front of you since you have an idea of where the pieces go. When one removes the box, it makes it more difficult to complete the puzzle. However, the one that is building the puzzle shouldn't give up and throw the entire puzzle away because he can't see where the pieces go at that moment. After some time, he will figure out where they belong, and even if he doesn't, he still believes that the pieces go somewhere.

We must recognize that we are all pieces to a large puzzle. Hashem has the box in front of Him, so to speak, and is putting the pieces where they belong. We have to believe that each piece is part of the greater picture, even though we don't have the box in front of us.

One of the gifts of Purim is that we get a glimpse of how the pieces align and fit together. From the sin of bowing down to Nevuchadnetzar's idol, attending the party of Achashveirosh, Esther becoming queen, Haman's ascent to power, and all of the details that seemed to "happen," all of them come together when we take a look from afar. It's always easier to connect the dots when the dots are shown.

When someone is invested in a situation, one must take extra caution before acting or accusing someone else. The Gemara teaches us that if one is invested in his testimony, the testimony is invalid.[1] The reason for this is because they are biased and cannot give a fair testimony.

My Great Grandma Helen, *a"h*, would play cards with her friends. I never fully grasped the game, but whenever she would attempt to teach me how to play, she would constantly remind me to look at the whole table and not to focus only on my cards.

When playing basketball, it is important to dribble with your eyes up, looking around at an opportunity to pass or shoot. One who looks down when dribbling will miss out on any open opportunities.

In our own lives, it is important to take a step back and look at a bigger picture. This is a concept in education called "backwards by design," where one begins with the end goal and then sets the steps to reach that

---

1   *Sanhedrin* 23b.

goal. It is important that one steps back once in a while to make sure one is heading in the right direction. If one does not look from afar, one might become too focused on the task at hand, making it the priority. This results in never reaching their goal. Employers who micromanage can become very overwhelming for their employees and could drive themselves crazy if every detail isn't the way they like it.

When planting, the seed first rots and then begins to bud, developing into a beautiful tree. If one were to get upset at the seed for rotting and give up hope, he would lose out on the final product. Although at the moment it seems like all is ruined, recognize that Hashem has a plan and sees the full picture.

בקש להודיעו דרכיו של הקדוש ברוך הוא, ונתן לו, שנאמר: "הודיעני נא
את דרכיך", אמר לפניו: רבונו של עולם! מפני מה יש צדיק וטוב לו, ויש
צדיק ורע לו, יש רשע וטוב לו, ויש רשע ורע לו?...[2]

Moshe requested that the ways in which Hakadosh Baruch Hu conducts the world be revealed to him, and He granted it to him, as it is stated: "Show me Your ways…" Moshe said before Hashem: "Master of the Universe. Why is it that the righteous prosper, the righteous suffer, the wicked prosper, the wicked suffer?"

The Gemara relates that Moshe asked Hashem why the righteous suffer and the wicked prosper. Hashem responds, "You will have a place next to Me,"[3] meaning when you are viewing the world from My perspective, you will see things clearly.

When someone is in traffic, they start getting anxious and wondering if they're going to be on time or where the traffic is coming from. However, the news reporter in the helicopter sees the full picture and has no questions. Someone once told Rav Yaakov Meir Shechter, *shlit"a*, that if you look up at the sky, everything seems to be in order. You have the sun, moon, clouds, and stars in their proper places. However,

---

2   *Berachos* 7a.

3   *Shemos* 33:21.

down here on Earth, it seems like everything is all over the place. Rav Yaakov Meir responded, "It depends where you are looking from. If you are above looking down, everything will seem in order as well." It all depends on the perspective.

Someone once went into the cockpit of a plane and was amazed by all of the buttons. He asked the pilot, "What does this button do?" The pilot questioned, "And you know what all of the other buttons do?"[4] Many times, we question why Hashem does certain things, as if we understand all of the other calculations of Hashem.

We have to recognize that we are pieces to the puzzle, and we must be the best we can be. By doing this, we will be *zocheh* to see and understand why everything happens when Mashiach comes and brings us clarity.

To Summarize

One rule I've learned is that history cannot be viewed in a vacuum. Sometimes in life, one has to take a few steps back and look at the bigger picture. Trying to judge all that goes on in a specific occurrence without a greater understanding is foolish. We sometimes get a glimpse of Divine intervention in different scenarios throughout our lives, yet even with this small glimpse, we still don't have the full image. We have to strengthen our faith in the Artist, i.e., Hashem, Who knows how His picture will look.

Points to Ponder

- Do I recognize that I am a major piece to a grander puzzle?
- Do I realize that my Plan B is really Hashem's Plan A?
- Do I recognize Hashem during the good times as I do during the "bad" ones?

---

4   Heard from Rav Elimelech Biderman, *shlit"a, Parashas Vayakhel* 5779.

Reaching for the Stars

Eliana was sitting in her bouncer, staring at the toys hanging down. I watched her and wondered what her little brain was thinking. All of a sudden, she tried to grab one of the toys! It was very exciting that she was becoming more interactive and aware of herself and her surroundings. She was well short of reaching the toys, but she continued to try and reach them.

Later that day, Eliana was back in her bouncer, staring at the toys again. This time, I knew what she was thinking. She reached her hand out to grab, and missed, but she didn't give up. She tried again and again. Suddenly, she grabbed the toy! It was incredible!

Sometimes we shortchange ourselves by thinking that our goals are out of reach, and we give up on them. You will never regret reaching your goals, but you will regret giving up on them. The Mishnah tells us, *"Lefum tzaara agra—*According to the pain is the reward."[1]

The more you work for something, the greater you will feel when you achieve it.

ורבי יוחנן אמר לך: מאי "רחוק"—שהיה רחוק מדבר עבירה מעיקרא. ומאי "קרוב"—שהיה קרוב לדבר עבירה, ונתרחק ממנו השתא.[2]

---

1   *Avos* 5:23.
2   *Berachos* 34b.

*And Rabbi Yochanan can say to you: What is the meaning of
"he who is far"? This refers to one who was distant from an act
of transgression from the outset. What is meant by "he who is
near"? This refers to one who was close to an act of transgression but has now distanced from it.*

The Gemara teaches that those who sin and do *teshuvah* reside closer
to Hashem in *Olam Haba*. When one works on oneself to be the greatest
he can be, even though he may have fallen, he can become closer to
Hashem than someone who was righteous his entire life. As my Rosh
Yeshiva says, "A negative ten can become a positive ten, and a negative
one can be a positive one."

Hashem created each individual as an individual. If someone tries to
be like someone else, then they are not living the life that is meant for
them. Each person is a different piece in the puzzle, and no two pieces
can fit into the same spot. Reb Zusha of Anipoli said that he isn't afraid
when they ask him in *Shamayim* why he wasn't like Hillel HaZaken,
who learned even without money, or like Rabbi Yehudah Hanassi, who
was very rich, or Yosef HaTzaddik, who was able to control his desires.
Rather, the question he fears is why he wasn't the best Zusha that he
could have been.

Many times, people try to imitate the ways of the *tzaddikim*, but that
isn't the proper way to live one's life. Emulate, don't imitate.

There is a story with a rabbi that had a broom in the room where he
was going to light the *menorah*. Before lighting, the rabbi asked his *gabbai* to please remove the broom before he lit the candles. After the *chassidim* left and the ceremony was over, the *gabbai* asked if the reason for
removing the broom was because of having the proper atmosphere or
for cleanliness. The rabbi said, "No, the reason I didn't want the broom
in the room when I lit was because then the *chassidim* would make sure
to have a broom next to them when they would light *menorah*."

As silly as this story sounds, it's true. People spend their entire lives
trying to be someone they are not. It is sad to witness when people
throw their lives away to try and fit in with others. Something my Rosh
Yeshiva told me, and I repeat to my students, is that the people you

associate with now will not necessarily be with you later on in life, but the decisions you make and the consequences from those actions with those people now will be with you always.

ולהגיד גדלתו של הקדוש ברוך הוא, שאדם טובע כמה מטבעות בחותם אחד וכולן דומין זה לזה, ומלך מלכי המלכים הקדוש ברוך הוא טבע כל אדם בחותמו של אדם הראשון ואין אחד מהן דומה לחברו. לפיכך כל אחד ואחד חיב לומר, בשבילי נברא העולם.³

...When a person stamps a seal on many coins, all of the coins are identical to one another. However, The King of all kings stamped all people with the seal of Adam HaRishon and not one is similar to another. That's why each person is obligated to say, "This world was created for me."

"Be yourself because everyone else is taken." When we recognize who we are, we realize how great we can become and work to be the greatest we can be. Each individual plays a *different* role in society. A team is made up of players playing their own position, but together. One player trying to play the role of another player will ultimately cause the team to fail.

אע״פ שמנאן בחייהם בשמותם, חזר ומנאם במיתתם, להודיע חבתם, שנמשלו לכוכבים, שמוציאם ומכניסם במספר ובשמותם.⁴

Although they were already counted by name while they were living, it again enumerates them when it tells us of their death, thus showing how dear they are—that they are compared to the stars that Hashem brings out and brings in by number and name when they cease to shine.

וַיּוֹצֵא אֹתוֹ הַחוּצָה וַיֹּאמֶר הַבֶּט נָא הַשָּׁמַיְמָה וּסְפֹר הַכּוֹכָבִים אִם תּוּכַל לִסְפֹּר אֹתָם וַיֹּאמֶר לוֹ כֹּה יִהְיֶה זַרְעֶךָ.⁵

---

3   *Sanhedrin* 4:5.

4   *Shemos* 1:1, *Rashi, s.v. V'eileh shemos B'nei Yisrael.*

5   *Bereishis* 15:5.

He took him outside and said, "Look toward heaven and count the stars, if you are able to count them." And He added, "So shall your offspring be."

Every star has its moment to shine. Hashem brings in and out each star by name and number, showing how dear and precious each star is. We are compared to the stars, as Hashem alluded to Avraham. Each one of us will have our moment to shine, as the Mishnah says, "There is no person who does not have his own time."[6] Everyone has their time to shine. It won't always come easy. We have to reach for the stars and be the best that we can be in order to be the star we were meant to be.

To Summarize

There is a major difference in emulating and imitating. One can be the best version of themselves while emulating the ways of others. The world was created for you. Each individual has their personal mission that they are destined to accomplish. Be yourself because everyone else is taken.

Points to Ponder

- What makes me unique?
- How can I find my shine?
- Do I see the shine in others?

---

6   *Avos* 4:3.

Joy of a Mitzvah

Spending time with Zaidy is always so much fun. Before Sukkos, Daniel went with me and Zaidy to buy his very own set of *arba minim*—four species. Daniel was so excited when he saw the *lulavim* and *esrogim* that he ran over to pick one out for himself. After spending much time picking some *esrogim* up and putting some back, he finally found the one! Then it was time to choose his lulav, *hadasim*, and *aravos*! Finally, Daniel had all of his *arba minim*! He was literally jumping for joy!

This gave me so much *nachas*! He was so happy to do a mitzvah! I learned a valuable lesson from that moment. How do we look at mitzvos? Do we have joy when performing mitzvos? Are mitzvos something that we take pride in and look forward to, or do we see them as a burden?

We should take pride in who we are and jump for joy at every opportunity we have to perform mitzvos!

We must take pride in who we are and appreciate the gift we have. When we do, we will be able to have much joy and pleasure within our daily lives. The word עֶנֶג means "joy" or "pleasure." If *chas v'shalom* we don't have joy of mitzvos, we turn the עֶנֶג into a נֶגַע—blemish.[1]

The mitzvos are a gift directly from Hashem. As we say each morning and when we read the Torah, "*Asher bachar banu mi'kol ha'amim v'nasan*

---

1   The letters of עֶנֶג—joy—can be switched to the word נֶגַע—blemish.

lanu es Toraso..." Hashem specifically chose us to receive His special Torah. "עִבְדוּ אֶת ה' בְּשִׂמְחָה בֹּאוּ לְפָנָיו בִּרְנָנָה —Serve Hashem with joy, come before Him in song."[2] We have to serve Hashem with joy.

כשם שמשנכנס אב ממעטין בשמחה כך משנכנס אדר מרבין בשמחה.[3]

Just as when Av begins, one decreases rejoicing, so too, when the month of Adar begins, one increases rejoicing.

The Gemara quotes the Mishnah that teaches that when we enter the month of Av, we decrease our *simchah*, and when we enter the month of Adar, we increase it. Although we reduce our *simchah* in the month of Av, it is important to realize that it does not mean to go into a state of depression. We should continue to be *b'simchah*, but on a lower level.

As mentioned earlier, even when the Gemara discusses serving Hashem with awe, it says to rejoice with trepidation![4] Furthermore, the most serious day of the year, Yom Kippur, should also be joyous—we have the greatest opportunity of *teshuvah* on that day.

As the Gemara teaches:

א"ר שמעון ב"ג לא היו ימים טובים לישראל כחמשה עשר באב וכיוה"כ.[5]

Rabbi Shimon ben Gamliel says that there are no greater days for Yisrael than the fifteenth of Av and Yom Kippur.

אביי בר אבין ור' חנינא בר אבין מחלפי סעודתייהו להדדי.[6]

Abaye bar Avin and Rabbi Chanina bar Avin would exchange their meals with each other.

---

2   *Tehillim* 100:2.
3   *Taanis* 29a.
4   *Berachos* 30b.
5   *Taanis* 30b.
6   *Megillah* 7b.

זה אוכל עם זה בפורים של שנה זו ובשניה סועד חברו עמו.[7]

This one would eat with this one on Purim of this year, and the next [year] his friend would feast with him.

The Gemara relates that Abaye bar Avin and Rabbi Chanina bar Avin would exchange their Purim meals with one another. *Rashi* explains that when the Gemara says "exchange," it means that they would switch off hosting the Purim meal bi-yearly. The significance of this *Rashi* is to teach us that one should have the *seudah* together with others and not alone. Since Purim is a day of joy, having a meal with others increases joy.

One may ask what is so important about doing things with joy. When we have joy in our life, we have less stress, less anxiety, and less worries. We can see things with clarity and recognize that there is a bigger picture. The little things don't bother us, and we can develop into the best we can be. We are redeemed from certain things that others may feel pressured by.

In her book, *The How of Happiness*, Sonja Lyubomirsky explains and elaborates on scientific evidence for why one should be happy and live a life of joy.

> *In becoming happier, we not only boost experiences of joy, contentment, love, pride, and awe, but also improve other aspects of our lives: our energy levels, our immune systems, our engagement with work and with other people, and our physical and mental health. In becoming happier, we bolster as well our feelings of self-confidence and self-esteem; we come to believe that we are worthy human beings, deserving of respect. A final and perhaps least appreciated plus is that if we become happier, we benefit not only ourselves but also our partners, families, communities, and even society at large.[8]*

---

7   Ibid., s.v. *Machlefei seudasaihu.*

8   Sonja Lyubomirsky, *The How of Happiness: A Scientific Approach to Getting the Life You Want* (Penguin Press, 2007), p. 26.

On a similar note, the girls have been singing "dip the apple in the honey" for well over two weeks after Rosh Hashanah with the same enthusiasm they had the first time they sang it (maybe even with a little more). When doing something with joy, it keeps it fresh and new. It's like a rejuvenation. When we do a mitzvah several times, such as tefillin or Shabbos, does it become "dry," or do we do it with more enthusiasm each time? We should learn about the mitzvos we do and not make it a routine. Just as one has so much joy performing a mitzvah for the first time, we must recognize that every day is the first day of the rest of our lives; every day we are renewed. Like the first time a boy dons tefillin or when a girl lights Shabbos candles, we should have the joy and excitement of the youth radiate from within us.

To Summarize

Having routine and structure is important in one's life; however, it is necessary to change things every so often. When one introduces something new into their everyday schedule, it makes the day unordinary. Having delight in something familiar brings that sense of renewal and joy into one's daily routine.

Points to Ponder

- How can I add joy to my daily life?
- Do I learn about the mitzvos I do?
- How can I achieve a sense of fulfillment each time I perform a mitzvah?

Routine

On the topic of doing things out of routine, I recall a time when Daniel was learning about making *berachos*. When we were at Bubby and Zaidy's house for dinner, I reminded Daniel to make a *berachah* on his food. Daniel made a beautiful *berachah*, and we all answered *Amen*! Daniel then asked why I didn't make a *berachah*. I took a minute to think about what he meant because I clearly remembered making a *berachah*. I then realized what he meant and explained to him that I did make a *berachah* but said it quietly. That's why he didn't hear me make a *berachah*.

As we continued to eat, I thought about Daniel's question and came to the realization that many times I am focused on the food I'm about to eat rather than on the *berachah* I am saying or on others answering *Amen*. I decided to take upon myself to stop for a couple of seconds before eating and focus on the meaning and sanctity of the *berachah* as I say it.

Sadly, many times when we daven or say *berachos*, it is out of habit or routine. One could be davening *Shemoneh Esreh* and only realize that he's reached *Modim* because he finds himself bowing down!

There is a story told in the name of the Kotzker Rebbe, who was once observing one of his students davening *Minchah*. The student was *shukeling* back and forth and seemed very involved in his *tefillah*. When the student finished, the Rebbe said to him, "Welcome back."

The student asked in wonder, "I've been here the whole time, why is the Rebbe welcoming me back?" The Rebbe replied, "Yes, physically you were here, but your mind was traveling all over the world." The student was *shukeling* out of habit and wasn't focusing on the words of his *tefillah*. Davening had become a routine. We have to recognize that each time we daven, learn, or perform a mitzvah, it is never a repeat of something we've done before. Rather, each time we are reaching a new level. Just as when playing a video game one has excitement for unlocking a new achievement, so too, when performing mitzvos, we reach greater heights and unlock new rankings.

One of the main mitzvos of Pesach is "וְהִגַּדְתָּ לְבִנְךָ בַּיּוֹם הַהוּא—you should tell over to your children on that day."[1] One thing I learned from experience is that when you tell a story to children, they have loads of questions.

מזגו לו כוס שני וכאן הבן שואל אביו ואם אין דעת בבן אביו מלמדו.[2]

We pour the second cup, and here the son asks his father. And if the son does not have the intelligence to ask, his father teaches him.

The Mishnah discusses the four questions on Seder night that one must ask. Why must one ask questions if one already knows the story? Since, as we learn, "*V'lo ha'bayshan lomed*—An embarrassed person doesn't learn."[3] When one is afraid to ask, it means that one is afraid of change. Since when one asks one may receive an answer one isn't fond of, one feels better off not asking. Also, when one does receive an answer one doesn't like, that means one has to change something about oneself. Without change, one lives a mechanical life. It is merely surviving. A heartbeat has constant change, but when a monitor flatlines, it means that there is no life at all.

---

1   *Shemos* 13:8.
2   *Pesachim* 116a.
3   *Avos* 2:5.

There are four categories of nature: an inanimate object, plant, animal, and humanity.[4] The inanimate object, called in Hebrew a *domeim*, is something still with no life, such as a rock. The fourth son on Seder night, the *she'eino yodei'a lishol*, is the son who doesn't ask anything and simply sits there like a lifeless object.

When one lives out of routine, it is passive. There is no life to the things he does.

The *pasuk* teaches that when it comes to following the Torah and mitzvos, "וָחַי בָּהֶם—live with them!"[5] You must be alive and living to perform the mitzvos of Hashem!

To Summarize

Thinking before one acts not only helps one control oneself, but it can give meaning to the action one is about to perform. Recognize that everything we do in Judaism has meaning; nothing is done without reason. A routine is essential for success; however, living a life programmed like a robot isn't much of a life. Take a moment to think about the meaning of your actions before you act.

Points to Ponder

- Is most of my day done out of habit or routine? If so, why?
- What is one part of my day that I can focus on and enhance?
- How can I find purpose in the little things I do so they don't become a burden?

---

4   דומם וצומח וחי ומדבר, see *Tomer Devorah*, chap. 3.
5   *Vayikra* 18:5.

Goals

One day, while we were eating lunch at Bubby's house, Daniel wanted to play with the playdough. However, we don't allow playdough by the table during a meal because children will likely end up eating the playdough with their food! I told Daniel that he could play with the playdough after he finishes his lunch. He wasn't too happy hearing that, and so he decided that he wasn't going to eat. Meanwhile, I finished what was on my plate and began to *bentch*. As soon as I finished *bentching*, Daniel came over to me with a big smile and said, "Daddy! You ate all of your food! You get a prize! You can play with the playdough!" He ended up eating his lunch, and when he finished, we played with the playdough together.

This taught me the person giving "gets" more than the person receiving. Sometimes we think that when we give our time, money, or possessions to others, we are losing. However, we are really gaining. Research shows that those who give and are kind to others are actually happier people.[1]

כִּי תִשָּׂא אֶת רֹאשׁ בְּנֵי יִשְׂרָאֵל לִפְקֻדֵיהֶם וְנָתְנוּ אִישׁ כֹּפֶר נַפְשׁוֹ לַה׳ בִּפְקֹד אֹתָם...[2]

---

1   E. Dunn and M. Norton, "How Money Actually Buys Happiness," accessed August 7, 2014. See https://hbr.org/2013/06/how-money-actually-buys-happiness.

2   *Shemos* 30:12.

When you take a census of the B'nei Yisrael according to their enrollment, each shall pay Hashem a compensation for himself on being enlisted.

When the Jews gave the half-shekel, the *pasuk* uses the word *v'nasnu*—and to give. The *Baal HaTurim* points out that the word *v'nasnu* is a palindrome[3] because when one gives, they receive as well.

We see this when the *pasuk* says, "וְיִקְחוּ לִי תְּרוּמָה—And you shall take for Me *terumah*."[4] Why does it say "And you shall take" if everyone is supposed to give? It isn't grammatically correct. The answer is that Hashem is teaching us that giving is really receiving.

The *Kli Yakar* teaches that not only does one not lose by giving *tzedakah*, but one gains so much more.[5]

וּצְדָקָה תַּצִּיל מִמָּוֶת.[6]

And charity saves from death.

רבי יהושע בן לוי אמר כל הרגיל לעשות צדקה זוכה והויין לו בנים בעלי חכמה בעלי עושר בעלי אגדה.[7]

Rabbi Yehoshua ben Levi says: Anyone who is accustomed to performing acts of charity merits blessing; he will have sons who are masters of wisdom, masters of wealth, and masters of Aggadah.

שאל טורנוסרופוס הרשע את ר״ע אם אלקיכם אוהב עניים הוא, מפני מה אינו מפרנסם אמר לו כדי שניצול אנו בהן מדינה של גיהנם...תניא רבי יהודה אומר גדולה צדקה שמקרבת את הגאולה...[8]

---

3   A word, phrase, or sequence that reads the same backward as forward (e.g., ונתן).
4   *Shemos* 25:2.
5   *Kli Yakar*, *Shemos* 25:2.
6   *Mishlei* 10:2.
7   *Bava Basra* 9b.
8   Ibid., 10a.

The wicked Turnus Rufus asked Rabbi Akiva: "If your God loves the poor, why does He not support them?" Rabbi Akiva said to him: "So that through them we will be saved from the judgment of Gehinom..." It is taught in a Beraisa that Rabbi Yehudah says: Great is charity in that it advances the redemption.

Some benefits of tzedakah are as follows: it saves from death, it destroys any evil decrees,[9] one merits to have intelligent children, it saves one from *Gehinom*, and it speeds up the redemption.

לעולם אין אדם מעני מן הצדקה ולא דבר רע ולא היזק מתגלגל על ידה
שנאמר והיה מעשה הצדקה שלום.[10]

No man is ever impoverished from giving charity, nor is evil or harm ever caused by it; as it is written, "And the work of righteousness shall be peace."

The *Shulchan Aruch* mentions other benefits for giving tzedakah, such as not becoming poor and nothing bad coming from it, and whoever has mercy on the poor, Hashem will have mercy on him.

Someone who is truly selfish will care about others since he views them as serving his own needs. When a selfish person understands that giving tzedakah will benefit himself, then there is no question that he will give. The Gemara teaches:

כל המבקש רחמים על חבירו והוא צריך לאותו דבר הוא נענה
תחילה...ויתפלל אברהם אל האלקים וירפא אלקים את אבימלך ואת
אשתו ואמהותיו וכתיב וה׳ פקד את שרה כאשר אמר וגו׳ כאשר אמר
אברהם אל אבימלך.[11]

Anyone who davens on behalf of another concerning the same matter will be answered first..."And Avraham davened for Avimelech and his wife, and they had children." Later, it says

---

9   As we say on Rosh Hashanah and Yom Kippur: "*Teshuvah, tefillah, u'tzedakah maavirin es ro'a ha'gezeirah.*"

10   *Shulchan Aruch, Yoreh De'ah* 247:2.

11   *Bava Kama* 92a.

that Hashem remembered Sarah "as Avraham said with regard
to Avimelech"...

In the merit of Avraham's *tefillah* for Avimelech, Avraham was *zocheh*
to have a child.

כל המרחם על הבריות מרחמין עליו מן השמים וכל שאינו מרחם על
הבריות אין מרחמין עליו מן השמים.[12]

*Anyone who has compassion for Hashem's creatures will re-
ceive compassion from Heaven, and anyone who does not have
compassion for Hashem's creatures will not receive compassion
from Heaven.*

The Gemara teaches that anyone who is kind to the creations of
Hashem, Hashem will be kind to him. Everything Hashem does is *middah k'neged middah.*

נָתוֹן תִּתֵּן לוֹ וְלֹא יֵרַע לְבָבְךָ בְּתִתְּךָ לוֹ כִּי בִּגְלַל הַדָּבָר הַזֶּה יְבָרֶכְךָ ה' אֱלֹקֶיךָ
בְּכָל מַעֲשֶׂךָ וּבְכֹל מִשְׁלַח יָדֶךָ.[13]

*Give to him readily and have no regrets when you do so, for in
return, Hashem your God will bless you in all your efforts and
in all that you do.*

שתתן לו בטובת עין. וגם הוא יברך אותך וזה פועל הרבה כדאיתא
במדרש רות דיותר משהעשיר עושה עם העני העני עושה עם העשיר היינו
שמברכו...[14]

*That you give generously, and as a result the poor person will
bless you, which has a great effect, as explained in Midrash
Rus, that more than the rich person gives to the poor, the poor
does for the rich, meaning that he blesses him.*

---

12 *Shabbos* 151b.
13 *Devarim* 15:10.
14 *Haamek Davar, Devarim* ibid.

The *pasuk* teaches that one shouldn't have any regrets for giving tzedakah because Hashem will bless you for all of your efforts and all that you gave. The *Haamek Davar* comments on this *pasuk*, saying that in reality the poor person does more for the rich person than the rich does for the poor; when giving tzedakah, he will give you a blessing.

וְאַל תַּחְשֹׁב שֶׁיִּהְיֶה לְךָ בִּדְבַר חֶסְרוֹן מָמוֹנְךָ, כִּי בִּגְלַל הַדָּבָר הַהוּא יְבָרֶכְךָ הַשֵּׁם וְיָפֶה לְךָ בִּרְכָתוֹ רֶגַע קָטָן מִכַּמָּה אוֹצָרוֹת שֶׁל זָהָב וָכָסֶף...[15]

And do not think that there will be a lack in your money, "as because of [this] thing, Hashem will bless you." And his blessing for one small instant is better for you than several storehouses of gold and silver.

The *Sefer Hachinuch* says that the *berachah* from giving to a pauper for even a small moment is worth more than several storage houses of gold and silver.

We should view ourselves as investors with all of the good we receive from our Employer. Hashem doesn't just give us what *we* need to live, but He gives us enough to support others. I once heard a beautiful understanding of how B'nei Yisrael were able to perform the mitzvah of tzedakah in the desert, even though Hashem satiated everyone with the *man*. It would seem that there was no need for tzedakah. However, as we know the world needs *chessed* in order to exist, so there must have been some giving, even in the desert. It existed in the form of those who had been wealthy in the past, and thus had the pleasure of tasting fine delicacies, who would explain the flavors and tastes to others who hadn't had those experiences. Giving tzedakah isn't just monetary, rather it can be given in many forms.

Winston Churchill once said, "We make a living by what we get. We make a life by what we give."

---

15   *Sefer Hachinuch* 478.

To Summarize

The happiest kind of people are those who do for others. The reason for this is because when one gives, they receive more in return. Think of the phrase, "Tzedakah saves from death." A simple smile is considered charity and that could save a person's life!

Points to Ponder

- How often am I giving others time, money, or anything else they may need?
- How can I set my goal to give more to others?
- When are some times that I saw giving to others actually benefited me?

Hashem Is Here, There, and Everywhere

Who is better at reading a bedtime story than Grandma? During bedtime one night, Grandma came by to give goodnight kisses. Daniel asked for Grandma to lie next to him and tell him a story to help him fall asleep. "No problem," Grandma said, and she went to Daniel's bed to lie down. Shortly after, Ayelet also wanted to hear a story. So, Grandma finished the story next to Daniel and then headed to Ayelet's room. A couple of minutes later, Daniel wanted to hear another story, but he had to wait until Grandma finished telling the story to Ayelet. This back-and-forth went on for about a half hour.

It occurred to me how fortunate we are that we have a Father and a King who is always there for us—even while dealing with others. Yes, Grandma is amazing, but she can only be in one place at one time. Hashem, though, is here, there, and everywhere—all at the same exact moment.

Obviously, we don't have to bring any sources or proofs that Hashem is everywhere since we know that He is Infinite and there is no way for us finite beings to begin to comprehend what it means to be infinite. However, we can understand that wherever we turn, we can see the greatness of Hashem.

Everything in this world can be used as a tool to bring us closer to Hashem:

- When the train was invented, *tzaddikim* said that it teaches the value of a moment. If someone comes a moment late, one will miss the train.
- When the telegram was invented, *tzaddikim* said that it teaches us the value of each word, since each word costs more money.
- The Chafetz Chaim, *zt"l*, taught that the telephone teaches belief in *tefillah*, because people could be on the other side of the world and hear one another.[1]

I was once teaching the Mishnah that says there is always an eye that sees, an ear that hears, and everything is written on record,[2] and one student couldn't understand the Mishnah. I took out my cell phone and showed him how the camera was like an eye that sees, the recording was like an ear that hears, and the notes are where everything is written down on record. I went a step further and showed how a video contains all three.

Unfortunately, often people only recognize Hashem when they see open miracles or hear wonderful stories of *hashgachah pratis*. There is a story told that once the Noam Elimelech was giving a *shiur* on *emunah* and *bitachon*. He mentioned how everything has Divine intervention—from the greatest of things to a piece of manure. One student was skeptical and said that Hashem wouldn't bother with such lowly things. Sure enough, when this student left the *shiur*, he slipped on ice and was sliding to the edge of the mountain when suddenly there was something that he bumped into, preventing his fall. The student looked down to see what potentially saved his life. Much to his surprise, it was a pile of horse manure! We must recognize that everything in this world is controlled by Hashem.

If we take a look at nature, we will recognize the tremendous wonders that Hashem created. I love going to the zoo and aquarium with my

---

1   Based on Rabbi Elimelech Biderman's *Torah Wellsprings, Parashas Ki Sisa*.
2   *Avos* 2:1.

children because, aside from seeing animals and fish we wouldn't see in our backyard, we discuss the amazing ways Hashem created them. We discuss the way the animals are shaped and how it benefits them, what each animal eats, and how they protect themselves from predators. Even fruits and vegetables can be the subject of conversation.

In truth, we don't have to go to zoos, aquariums, gardens, or even look outside to witness the miracles of nature. If we look at ourselves, we can see miraculous things. In *Shemoneh Esreh* we say *Modim*, in which we recognize the miracles and wonders Hashem does for us every moment of every day. We say *Asher Yatzar*, where we describe the wonders of the body and conclude the *berachah* with "*u'mafli la'asos*—Who performs wondrous things."[3] Regarding the eye, the pupil becomes smaller in the light and dilates in the dark. The reason for this adjustment is so that the eye can see properly. The pupil adjusts automatically.

Recognizing that Hashem created and is in control of everything will change one's entire perspective on life. One will recognize that everything has rhyme and reason, even if one doesn't witness it instantly. There are those who believe that everything is just science. What scientists find doesn't necessarily contradict anything in the Torah; however, those who believe there is nothing more to science are living empty lives because Hashem is the one who controls science.

There is a well-known question asked by the *Beis Yosef* as to why we light the *menorah* on Chanukah for eight nights instead of seven. If there was enough oil to last one day and it lasted for seven additional days, it would seem that Chanukah should be seven days, not eight.

There are hundreds of answers to this question. One answer is that the extra day is for the miracle that oil burns. One may think that it's natural for oil to burn, which is correct, but we have to recognize that even that which is natural comes from Hashem, rendering it supernatural.

Someone once asked the Kotzker Rebbe where Hashem is, and the Rebbe replied, "Wherever you let Him in." Even when we think that the

---

3   *Berachos* 60b.

world is taking its natural course and things seem to be working out as we planned, we must recognize that Hashem is within nature.

To Summarize

Everything in this world has Hashem within it or else it wouldn't exist. This means that in reality, everything is supernatural—even what we call "natural." People in essence are supernatural since we have a *neshamah*. Everything in this world can strengthen our relationship with Hashem. Try to take the mundane and view it as supernatural.

Points to Ponder

- Do I recognize that everything comes from Hashem?
- Is Hashem constantly on my mind?
- Do I try to make sure my actions are *l'shem Shamayim*?

Daniel's Thoughts

- "Hashem is like a bee. There are times that people are not nice to others and don't follow the ways of Hashem. These people get punished from Hashem like a sting. When people are nice to others and follow the ways of Hashem, Hashem makes it sweet like honey.

  "Hashem also gave us Torah, which is sweet like honey. Even the sting at the end will be sweet like honey. We can always do *teshuvah*."

- "A person is like Hashem. Just like we cannot see Hashem but we know He is there (through His creations), when a person is *tzanu'a*, people cannot see our *neshamah*. However, people see us through our actions."

- "When we are happy and do mitzvos, Hashem is also happy and makes our enemies go away. When we are unhappy and don't do mitzvos, Hashem is unhappy and sends the *goyim* to harm us. If they harm us before we daven to Hashem to save us, then they will win the war. If we daven and do *teshuvah* beforehand, Hashem will make our enemies go away."

- One Motza'ei Shabbos at *Avos U'banim*, we had a raffle. There were the exact number of prizes as there were children. Daniel waited excitedly for his ticket number to be called. We waited and waited until it got to a point where Daniel was either going to win something small or the grand prize! The child who didn't win the grand prize would get a smaller prize so that everyone could be a winner. Even though Daniel did not get the grand prize, he was content with what he got. All of a sudden, the boy who won the grand prize asked Daniel to switch prizes with him because he'd wanted the smaller prize (a football) all along. When Daniel realized that this boy really wanted to trade with him, he said yes! It is amazing how Hashem runs this world! Daniel's ticket was never called for the grand prize, and yet he still ended up with the prize he wanted! Hashem helps every single Jew—even if we don't see the full picture.

- As Daniel was eating his French toast with syrup, he noticed that when he made a line in his syrup with his fork, the syrup closed the gap by unifying again. Daniel then said that this must be how it was when Moshe Rabbeinu split the Yam Suf and how Yehoshua bin Nun split the Yarden

  I cannot stress the impact hands-on learning has on children. Giving them a visual of the lesson cannot be duplicated. As referenced in the Gemara, "לא תהא שמיעה גדולה מראייה,"[1] merely hearing something cannot be compared to seeing it.

- On the second Shabbos after Pesach, *Parashas Tazria-Metzora*, we were learning *Pirkei Avos* together. The Mishnah teaches about the relationship one should have with his rabbi. The Mishnah states, "Warm yourself next to the fire of the *chachamim*, but be careful not to be burned by their coals."[2] We discussed how coals have the ability to warm a person, but if one uses them the wrong way, they could burn him. So too, a rabbi whom one learns from can warm one's soul, but if he were to act or speak disrespectfully to his *rabbi*, it will burn him, and he'll be cursed. Getting angry is a huge *aveirah*, and it's like lighting a fire. As alluded to from the Mishnah, fire that is uncontrolled is very dangerous. Daniel then connected this idea to one who speaks

---

1   *Rosh Hashanah* 25b.
2   *Avos* 2:10.

lashon hara out of anger. One who speaks *lashon hara* out of anger is like someone who is spreading a dangerous fire that kills. The Gemara teaches, "Speaking *lashon hara* kills three people: the one who speaks it, the one who accepts it, and the one who it is said about."[3]

One must be careful to have self-control and be patient. This will help prevent many unnecessary wildfires.

- "Don't just be thankful for what you have; also be thankful for things you don't have and what others have."

---

3   *Arachin* 15b.

Conclusion

There's a *mashal* of a boy who was walking with his father when they came across a man who was sweating and looked beaten down, as he was *schlepping* a large sack over his shoulder. The boy asked the man what he was carrying. The man replied that the steps in front of his house broke, and he needed to get more bricks to fix them. As the father and son continued on their way, they came across another man holding a large sack over his shoulder, but this man didn't look worn and beaten down. On the contrary, he looked uplifted and full of life! The boy asked him what he was carrying. The man replied that he was digging in the valley and came across a great treasure! The father explained to his son that both men were carrying a heavy package; one man had bricks, which was a burden to him, and so the package was heavy, while the other had treasures, and although it may have been heavy, carrying it was not a burden.

People may see raising children as a burden, what with their constant nagging, questioning, etc. One way to ease the burden and recognize the treasures one is carrying is to look at what children do as learning experiences; it can change one's view and bring *menuchas ha'nefesh*.

In discussing loving learning through play,[1] Dr. Stipek mentions research done by Swiss psychologist Jean Piaget. "Remember when

---

1   Stipek and Seal, *Motivated Minds.*

your baby kept throwing his bottle or his teddy bear out of the crib, and you kept picking them up and telling him, 'No, no, don't throw!' What may have seemed like stubbornness was really your baby's serious scientific study of the laws of gravity." I remember the amazement on Daniel's face of how the spoon looked bent and bigger when he put it into his cup of water. Instead of getting upset at children for acting like children and learning new things (their behavior and questions), we should embrace it and treat it as an experiment.

Children learn so much from the way we act. When our response to their experimenting is positive, it will encourage learning. Yes, not every time is right to experiment and boundaries should be set; however, when the answer is constantly "no," it only discourages learning new things. Instead of getting upset when a drink spills, use that moment as a teaching moment of how we don't get angry. "Oh! Your drink spilled, that's OK, mistakes happen. Let me help you." Or "I wonder what we should do to clean it up. We'll just make sure to be more careful next time." You can then discuss different ways to be more careful. When a child hears this, they learn that not only is it OK to make mistakes but that we can actually learn from those mistakes.

Focusing on the positive changes one's paradigm of life.

In the *berachah* of *Al Ha'tzaddikim*, we mention "*V'sein sachar tov l'chol ha'botchim b'shimcha b'emes*—and give great reward to all of those who truly believe in Your Name." My Rosh Yeshiva, Rabbi Ahron Kaufman, taught me that the greatest reward is children. Children are the greatest reward one can have. May Hashem always let us see the value of our precious gems!

Afterword

B'chasdei Hashem, we were blessed with two more children as I worked on this book. I began thinking that lessons don't only have to be learned from children who are already born but also from a child who is not yet born.

One lesson we can learn is the locked potential that this child has. Who knows what this child will accomplish and how much the child will change the world? There's a saying that I teach my students before Rosh Hashanah: "One can count the number of seeds in an apple, but it's impossible to count the number of apples in a seed." With the help of Hashem, a tiny apple seed turns into a massive tree that produces tons of apples. So too with people!

Another lesson to be learned is that as long as we are connected to the source, we will always be satisfied. Just as the baby gets all of its nutrition through the umbilical cord, so too, we must connect to our spiritual umbilical cord. As we learn from Shlomo HaMelech, "[Torah] is the tree of life for those who grab onto it, and those who hold on are happy."[1] Torah is our spiritual umbilical cord. By connecting to it, we receive our nutrition. The closer one is to a cell tower, the better service one has. The same is true with the connection to Torah.

---

1   Mishlei 3:18.

When we daven, we are constantly mentioning the Avos to show that although they may have lived a long time ago, we are still connected to them. This is similar to someone who has a long rope from the heavens to the earth and shakes it from one side; the other side will shake as well since it is connected. The stronger your connection, the greater your source of nutrition. As long as a leaf is connected to the tree, it will receive its nourishment. The moment it takes leave of the tree, i.e., its source of nourishment, it begins to lose nutrition and shrivel up (eventually to end up in children's arts and crafts projects).

My Mashgiach, Rabbi Farkas, once told me that on Pesach we are like a baby, and thus we are careful with what we put into our mouths. Just as we are careful that a baby doesn't put anything dangerous into its mouth, so too, we are careful not to eat *chametz*. After Pesach, we are able to recognize what *chametz* represents, and we are no longer like a baby. We can begin to eat *chametz* because we are like an older child and not as cautious with what goes into our mouths.

I'd like to add to this idea of comparing oneself to a baby during Pesach. Pesach is also known as the "Rosh Hashanah of *emunah*." A child doesn't ask or worry where their nutrition is coming from since they are connected to the source. When one is connected to the source, there is no need to worry.

Appendix

A Parent's Prayer from the Shelah HaKadosh
תפילת השל"ה הקדוש לאבות על בניהם

This special *tefillah* was composed by the Shelah HaKadosh to express the prayers of parents on behalf of their children. The Shelah HaKadosh said that the optimal time for parents to recite this *tefillah* is on Erev Rosh Chodesh Sivan, since that is the month Hashem gave us the Torah and when we began to be called His children; however, it may be recited anytime.

אַתָּה הוּא ה' אֱלֹקֵינוּ עַד שֶׁלֹּא בָרָאתָ הָעוֹלָם, וְאַתָּה הוּא אֱלֹקֵינוּ מִשֶּׁבָּרֵאתָ הָעוֹלָם, וּמֵעוֹלָם וְעַד עוֹלָם אַתָּה קֵל. וּבָרָאתָ עוֹלָמְךָ בְּגִין לְאִשְׁתְּמוֹדָע אֱלָקוּתֶךָ בְּאֶמְצָעוּת תּוֹרָתְךָ הַקְּדוֹשָׁה, כְּמוֹ שֶׁאָמְרוּ רַבּוֹתֵינוּ זִכְרוֹנָם לִבְרָכָה בְּרֵאשִׁית בִּשְׁבִיל תּוֹרָה, וּבִשְׁבִיל יִשְׂרָאֵל, כִּי הֵם עַמְּךָ וְנַחֲלָתְךָ אֲשֶׁר בָּחַרְתָּ בָּהֶם מִכָּל הָאֻמּוֹת וְנָתַתָּ לָהֶם תּוֹרָתְךָ הַקְּדוֹשָׁה וְקֵרַבְתָּם לְשִׁמְךָ הַגָּדוֹל. וְעַל קִיּוּם הַתּוֹרָה בָּא לָנוּ מִמְּךָ ה' אֱלֹקֵינוּ שְׁנֵי צִוּוּיִים: כָּתַבְתָּ בְּתוֹרָתְךָ פְּרוּ וּרְבוּ, וְכָתַבְתָּ בְּתוֹרָתְךָ וְלִמַּדְתֶּם אוֹתָם אֶת בְּנֵיכֶם. וְהַכַּוָּנָה בִּשְׁתֵּיהֶן אַחַת, כִּי לֹא לְתֹהוּ בְּרָאתָ כִּי אִם לָשֶׁבֶת, וְלִכְבוֹדְךָ בָּרָאתָ יָצַרְתָּ אַף עָשִׂיתָ, כְּדֵי שֶׁנִּהְיֶה אֲנַחְנוּ וְצֶאֱצָאֵי כָּל עַמְּךָ בֵּית יִשְׂרָאֵל יוֹדְעֵי שְׁמֶךָ וְלוֹמְדֵי תוֹרָתֶךָ:

וּבְכֵן אָבוֹא אֵלֶיךָ ה' מֶלֶךְ מַלְכֵי הַמְּלָכִים וְאַפִּיל תְּחִנָּתִי וְעֵינַי לְךָ תְלוּיוֹת עַד שֶׁתְּחָנֵּנִי וְתִשְׁמַע תְּפִלָּתִי לְהַזְמִין לִי בָּנִים וּבָנוֹת, וְגַם הֵם יִפְרוּ וְיִרְבּוּ הֵם

264

וּבְנֵיהֶם וּבְנֵי בְנֵיהֶם עַד סוֹף כָּל הַדּוֹרוֹת, לְתַכְלִית שֶׁהֵם וַאֲנִי וַאֲנַחְנוּ כֻּלָּנוּ
יַעַסְקוּ בְּתוֹרָתְךָ הַקְּדוֹשָׁה לִלְמֹד וּלְלַמֵּד לִשְׁמֹר וְלַעֲשׂוֹת וּלְקַיֵּם אֶת כָּל דִּבְרֵי
תַלְמוּד תּוֹרָתֶךָ בְּאַהֲבָה. וְהָאֵר עֵינֵינוּ בְּתוֹרָתֶךָ וְדַבֵּק לִבֵּנוּ בְּמִצְוֹתֶיךָ לְאַהֲבָה
וּלְיִרְאָה אֶת שְׁמֶךָ:

אָבִינוּ אָב הָרַחֲמָן, תֵּן לְכֻלָּנוּ חַיִּים אֲרֻכִּים וּבְרוּכִים. מִי כָּמוֹךָ אַב הָרַחֲמִים
זוֹכֵר יְצוּרָיו לְחַיִּים בְּרַחֲמִים. זָכְרֵנוּ לְחַיִּים נִצְחִיִּים כְּמוֹ שֶׁהִתְפַּלֵּל אַבְרָהָם
אָבִינוּ "לוּ יִחְיֶה לְפָנֶיךָ" וּפֵרְשׁוּ רַבּוֹתֵינוּ זִכְרוֹנָם לִבְרָכָה, בְּיִרְאָתֶךָ:

כִּי עַל כֵּן בָּאתִי לְבַקֵּשׁ וּלְחַנֵּן מִלְּפָנֶיךָ, שֶׁיְּהֵא זַרְעִי וְזֶרַע זַרְעִי זֶרַע כָּשֵׁר, וְאַל
תִּמָּצֵא בְּזַרְעִי וּבְזֶרַע זַרְעִי עַד עוֹלָם שׁוּם פְּסוּל וָשֶׁמֶץ, אַךְ שָׁלוֹם וֶאֱמֶת וְטוֹב
וְיָשָׁר בְּעֵינֵי אֱלֹקִים וּבְעֵינֵי אָדָם, וְיִהְיוּ בַּעֲלֵי תוֹרָה, מָאֲרֵי מִקְרָא, מָאֲרֵי
מִשְׁנָה, מָאֲרֵי תַלְמוּד, מָאֲרֵי רָזָא, מָאֲרֵי מִצְוָה, מָאֲרֵי גוֹמְלֵי חֲסָדִים, מָאֲרֵי
מִדּוֹת תְּרוּמִיּוֹת, וְיַעַבְדוּךְ בְּאַהֲבָה וּבְיִרְאָה פְּנִימִית וְלֹא יִרְאָה חִיצוֹנִית. וְתֵן
לְכָל גְּוִיָּה מֵהֶם דֵּי מַחְסוֹרָהּ בְּכָבוֹד, וְתֵן לָהֶם בְּרִיאוּת וְכָבוֹד וְכֹחַ, וְתֵן לָהֶם
קוֹמָה וְיוֹפִי וְחֵן וָחֶסֶד. וְיִהְיֶה אַהֲבָה וְאַחֲוָה וְשָׁלוֹם בֵּינֵיהֶם. וְתַזְמִין לָהֶם זִוּוּגִים
הֲגוּנִים מִזֶּרַע תַּלְמִידֵי חֲכָמִים מִזֶּרַע צַדִּיקִים. וְגַם הֵם זִוּוּגָם יִהְיֶה כְּמוֹתָם כְּכָל
אֲשֶׁר הִתְפַּלַּלְתִּי עֲלֵיהֶם, כִּי זִכְרוֹן אֶחָד עוֹלֶה לְכָאן וּלְכָאן:

אַתָּה יְיָ יוֹדֵעַ כָּל תַּעֲלוּמוֹת, וּלְפָנֶיךָ נִגְלוּ מַצְפּוּנֵי לִבִּי, כִּי כַוָּנָתִי בְּכָל אֵלֶּה
לְמַעַן שִׁמְךָ הַגָּדוֹל וְהַקָּדוֹשׁ וּלְמַעַן תּוֹרָתְךָ הַקְּדוֹשָׁה. עַל כֵּן עֲנֵנִי ה' עֲנֵנִי
בַּעֲבוּר הָאָבוֹת הַקְּדוֹשִׁים אַבְרָהָם יִצְחָק וְיַעֲקֹב, וּבִגְלַל אָבוֹת תּוֹשִׁיעַ בָּנִים
לִהְיוֹת הָעֲנָפִים דּוֹמִים לְשָׁרְשָׁם בַּעֲבוּר דָּוִד עַבְדְּךָ רֶגֶל רְבִיעִי בַּמֶּרְכָּבָה
הַמְשׁוֹרֵר בְּרוּחַ קָדְשֶׁךָ:

שִׁיר הַמַּעֲלוֹת, אַשְׁרֵי כָּל יְרֵא ה' הַהֹלֵךְ בִּדְרָכָיו: יְגִיעַ כַּפֶּיךָ כִּי תֹאכֵל אַשְׁרֶיךָ
וְטוֹב לָךְ: אֶשְׁתְּךָ כְּגֶפֶן פֹּרִיָּה בְּיַרְכְּתֵי בֵיתֶךָ, בָּנֶיךָ כִּשְׁתִלֵי זֵיתִים סָבִיב
לְשֻׁלְחָנֶךָ: הִנֵּה כִי כֵן יְבֹרַךְ גָּבֶר יְרֵא ה': יְבָרֶכְךָ ה' מִצִּיּוֹן וּרְאֵה בְּטוּב יְרוּשָׁלָיִם,
כֹּל יְמֵי חַיֶּיךָ: וּרְאֵה בָנִים לְבָנֶיךָ, שָׁלוֹם עַל יִשְׂרָאֵל:

אָנָּא ה' שׁוֹמֵעַ תְּפִלָּה, יְקֻיַּם בִּי הַפָּסוּק, וַאֲנִי זֹאת בְּרִיתִי אוֹתָם אָמַר ה' רוּחִי
אֲשֶׁר עָלֶיךָ וּדְבָרַי אֲשֶׁר שַׂמְתִּי בְּפִיךָ לֹא יָמוּשׁוּ מִפִּיךָ וּמִפִּי זַרְעֲךָ וּמִפִּי זֶרַע
זַרְעֲךָ אָמַר ה' מֵעַתָּה וְעַד עוֹלָם: יִהְיוּ לְרָצוֹן אִמְרֵי פִי וְהֶגְיוֹן לִבִּי לְפָנֶיךָ ה'
צוּרִי וְגוֹאֲלִי:

*You have been Hashem, our G-d, before You created the world,
and You are Hashem, our G-d, since You have created the world,
and forever You are Almighty. And You created Your world to
make known Your Divinity through Your holy Torah. As our*

Sages of blessed memory explained "In the beginning"—for Torah and for Yisrael, for they are Your nation and Your chosen portion whom You have selected from among all nations and You have given them Your holy Torah and brought them toward Your great Name. To guarantee the continuance of the Torah, we received from You, Hashem our G-d, two commandments: You wrote in Your Torah, "Be fruitful and multiply," and You wrote in Your Torah, "You shall teach them to your children." The intention of both of them is one, because You did not create the world to be unoccupied, rather to be settled; and that it is for Your honor that You created, fashioned, and made it, so that we, our offspring, and all the offspring of your people Yisrael will know Your Name and study Your Torah.

And therefore, I come before You, Hashem, King of all kings, and I cast my supplication. My eyes are set upon You until You favor me and hear my prayer, to provide me with sons and daughters. They too should be fruitful and multiply; they and their children and their children's children until the end of all generations, in order that they, and I, and we all engage in Your holy Torah, to learn and to teach, to observe and to perform, and to fulfill all the words of Your Torah's teaching with love. Enlighten our eyes with Your Torah and connect our hearts to Your commandments to love and fear Your Name.

Our Father, compassionate Father, bestow upon us all a long and blessed life. Who is like You, compassionate Father, Who remembers His creations for life with mercy. Remember us for eternal life, as Avraham our father prayed, "If only [Yishmael] would live before You," which the Sages interpreted as "live in awe of You."

For this I have come to beseech and appeal before You, that my offspring and my offspring's offspring be proper, and do not find, in my offspring and my offspring's offspring, inadequacy or imperfection. Only peace and truth and goodness, and integrity in the eyes of our G-d and in the eyes of man. They shall be masters of Torah, masters in Scriptures, masters in Mishnah, masters in Talmud, masters in Kabbalah, masters in mitzvos, masters in kindness, and masters in worthy characteristics. They serve you with an inner love and reverence, not merely outward fear. Provide the needs of every one of them with honor, and grant them health and honor and strength, and grant them prominence and presence, grace and kindness. Grant them that there shall be love and companionship and tranquility between them. Provide them with suitable marriage partners of scholarly and righteous descent. Their mates, too, shall be blessed with all that I have asked for my offspring since one remembrance affects many.

You, Hashem, know everything that is hidden, and before You all my heart's secrets are revealed. For my intention in all of these [requests] is for the sake of Your great and holy Name and for the sake of the holy Torah. Therefore, answer me, Hashem, answer me in the sake of our holy forefathers, Avraham, Yitzchak, and Yaakov, because the fathers save the children, so the branches will be like the roots. For the sake of Dovid Your servant, who is the fourth leg of Your Chariot, who sings with Divine inspiration.

A song of ascents, fortunate is everyone who fears Hashem, who walks in His ways. When you eat of the work of your hands, you are fortunate, and good will be yours. Your wife is like a fruitful vine in the inner chambers of your home; your children are like olive shoots around your table. Behold! So is blessed the man who fears Hashem. May Hashem bless you from Zion, and may you see the good of Yerushalayim, all the days of your life. And you will see your children's children, peace upon Yisrael.

Please, Hashem, Who listens to prayer, may the verse be fulfilled through me: "And for Me, My covenant with them," says Hashem, "My spirit, which rests upon you, and My words, which I have placed in your mouth, shall not depart from your mouth and from the mouths of your children, and from the mouths of your children's children," said Hashem, "from now until Eternity." The words of my mouth and the thoughts of my heart should be accepted favorably before You, Hashem, my Rock and my Redeemer.

Glossary

The following glossary provides a partial explanation of some of the Hebrew, Yiddish (Y.) and Aramaic (A.) words and phrases used in this book. The spellings and explanations reflect the way the specific word is used herein. Often, there are alternate spellings and meanings for the words.

a"h: an acronym for *alav ha'shalom*; peace be upon him.

Acher: lit., other.

Adar: sixth month of the Hebrew calendar.

aleph-beis: Hebrew alphabet.

aliyah: elevating; getting called up to the Torah.

Amalek: the nation of Amalek was the first to fight with the Jewish nation upon their exodus from Egypt. The Jews are commanded to wipe out the entire nation of Amalek. We are not able to fulfill this till Mashiach comes.

Amen: truth or faith; said at the conclusion of a blessing.

Anshei K'nesses HaGedolah: Men of the Great Assembly.

arba minim: four species used on Sukkos.

arei miklat: cities of refuge.

Aron: (the Holy) Ark.

Av: eleventh month of the Hebrew calendar.

Avinu: our father.

avodah: service, worship, work.

avodah zarah: idol worship.

avodas Hashem: serving Hashem.

Avos: fathers; forefathers.

Avos U'banim: lit., fathers and sons; name of learning program for fathers and sons.

ayin hara: evil eye.

b'chasdei Hashem: with the kindness of Hashem.

b'karov mamash: very soon.

b'nei Torah: lit., children of Torah; those who lead their life in the way of Torah.

B'nei Yisrael: children of Israel; Jewish nation.

Beis Yaakov: Jewish schools for girls.

bar: (A.) son of.

baruch Hashem: blessed is Hashem.

Beis Hamikdash: the Holy Temple.

beis midrash (pl.–batei midrashos): house of study.

bentch: (Y.) recite the blessings after meals.

berachah (pl.–berachos): blessing.

Beraisa: (A.) teachings during the times of the Mishnah that were left out of the inclusion of the six orders of Mishnah.

bikkurim: first fruits of the season that were brought to the Holy Temple.

Birchos Ha'shachar: morning blessings.

Birchos HaTorah: blessings on the Torah.

bitachon: trust.

Bubby: (Y.) grandmother.

chachamim: wise men, sages.

chametz: leavened foods, such as bread; food forbidden on Pesach.

chanoch: educate.

Chanukah: Festival of Lights.

charoses: one of the two dips we have during the Seder on Pesach; this dip is sweet with a mixture of fruits, nuts, and wine.

chas v'shalom: Heaven forbid.

Chassidim: righteous people.

Chazal: acronym for *chachameinu zichronam li'verachah*; our Sages of blessed memory.

chelbenah: foul-smelling spice included in the *ketores* offering.

cheshbon ha'nefesh: calculation of the soul.

chiddushim: new insights.

chochmah: wisdom.

daven: (Y.) pray.

Dayan Ha'emes: the True Judge.

derech eretz kadmah laTorah: proper mannerisms precede Torah.

d'var halachah: words of Jewish law.

eishes chayil: woman of valor; the expression is derived from the prayer said on Friday nights.

eitz ha'daas: the tree of knowledge.

emes: truth; trustworthy.

emunah: faith.

Erev Yom Kippur: Yom Kippur eve.

esrog (pl.–esrogim): citron; one of the four species used on Sukkos.

gabbai: assistant who helps in a shul; assistant to a rabbi.

gadol ha'dor: leader of the generation.

Gan Eden: Garden of Eden.

gedolim: great ones; great Jewish sages.

Gemara: (A.) Talmud.

gematria: numerical value.

gemilus chassadim: giving of loving-kindness.

geulah: redemption.

geulas Mitzrayim: redemption from Egypt.

gevurah: strength.

Goshen: name of land where Jews sojourned during exile in Egypt.

goyim: nations of the world.

Haggadah (pl.–Haggados): Jewish book that guides us through the order of the Seder of Pesach; includes the texts and prayers we recite.

Hakadosh Baruch Hu: the Holy One, blessed be He.

hakaras ha'tov: recognizing the good.

Hakhel: gathering of the Jewish nation that occurred every seven years during Sukkos.

halachah: Jewish law.

Hamalach Hagoel: lit., angel that redeems; a prayer one says during the nighttime *Shema*, derived from the blessing Yaakov gave to his grandchildren Menasheh and Ephraim.

Har Sinai: Mount Sinai.

HaRishon: the first.

Hashem: lit., the Name; refers to God.

hashgachah pratis: Divine providence.

Ha'tov V'Ha'meitiv: the Good and the One who does good.

HaTzaddik: the righteous.

Ha'yom Yom…L'Shabbos: Today is the day…of the week.

HaZaken: the elder.

hekdesh: sanctified for the Temple.

Imeinu: our mother; refers to the Matriarchs.

ir miklat: city of refuge; one would flee to one of these six cities if he accidentally killed another.

ke'arah: Seder plate.

kabbalah: lit., reception or tradition; self-improvement.

karpas: a vegetable we eat on the first night of pesach, some people use celery, or potato, or a radish. We dip it into salt-water.

kavanah: intention.

kedushah: holiness or sanctity.

kehunah: priesthood.

ketores: incense offering.

kishuf: black magic.

klal gadol baTorah: general rule of the Torah.

Klal Yisrael: Jewish nation.

Kodesh HaKodashim: the Holy of Holies; only the Kohen Gadol (High Priest) was granted access to this room on Yom Kippur.

Koheles: Ecclesiastes; written by King Solomon.

Kohen: priest.

korban: sacrifice.

Korban Pesach: Pesach offering.

kulo tov: all is good.

l'havdil: to separate.

l'tovah: for the best.

lashon: language; tongue.

lashon hara: lit., evil language; slander or gossip.

lev tov: good heart.

lishmah: for the sake of.

lulav (pl.–lulavim): palm branch; one of the four species used on Sukkos.

Makas Choshech: Plague of Darkness.

maaser: tithe.

machlokes: argument, disagreement.

maggid: storyteller.

malachim: angels.

malchus: kingship.

maror: bitter herb we eat on Pesach.

mashal: analogy.

Mashgiach: lit., one who guides; dean of a yeshiva.

Matan Torah: the giving and acceptance of the Torah.

matanos l'evyonim: gifts to the poor.

matzah: unleavened bread; eaten during the festival of Pesach.

matzah brei: matzah mixed with egg omelet, often eaten on Pesach.

Mechaber: lit., author; compiler; Rav Yosef Karo, author of the *Shulchan Aruch*.

Megillah: scroll.

Menorah: seven-branched candelabrum used in the Holy Temple; eight-branched candelabrum used on Chanukah.

menuchas ha'nefesh: relaxation of the soul.

mezuzah (pl.–mezuzos): lit., doorpost; refers to a scroll containing certain *pesukim* placed on one's doorposts.

midbar: desert.

middah k'neged middah: measure for measure.

middos: plural for *middah*; lit., measures; character traits.

midrash: studies on Jewish Scripture.

minhag: custom; tradition.

Mishkan: Tabernacle.

Mishlei: Proverbs.

mishlo'ach manos: to send gifts; a mitzvah on the holiday of Purim.

Mishnah: teaching composed by Rabbi Yehudah HaNasi during the time period of the Tanna'im.

mishteh: festive meal.

Mitzrayim: Egypt.

mitzvah (pl.–mitzvos): commandment; deed.

mitzvah notes: notes many parents send to their child's teachers describing good deeds the child performed.

mizbei'ach: altar.

Modeh Ani: a prayer of thanks one says immediately when they wake up in the morning; we thank Hashem for returning our soul and giving us life.

moros: female teachers.

Mashiach: Messiah.

Mashiach Tzidkeinu: the Righteous Messiah.

Motza'ei Shabbos: the going out of Shabbos; Saturday night.

mussar: positive reinforcement.

nachas: joy.

Navi: prophet or prophets, when referring to Scripture.

negel vasser: (Y.) *netilas yadayim*; washing hands.

ner Chanukah (pl.–neiros Chanukah): Chanukah candle, light.

neshamah: soul.

netilas yadayim: washing hands.

olam chessed yibaneh: the world was built on kindness.

Olam Haba: World to Come.

olam katan: small world.

parnasah: livelihood.

parashah: (Torah) portion.

pasuk (pl.–pesukim): verse.

Pesach: holiday of Passover.

Pharaoh: king of Egypt.

pikuach nefesh: saving a life.

Pirkei Avos: Ethics of the Fathers.

Pisom and Ramses: storage cities built for Pharaoh by the Jews when we were slaves in Egypt.

Purim: joyous holiday when the Jews were saved from annihilation while exiled under the Persian Empire.

rasha: wicked person; also refers to the wicked son of the Pesach Seder.

Rebbe: Chassidic leader.

rebbi (pl.–rebbeim): Torah teacher.

Rosh Yeshiva: dean or spiritual leader of a yeshiva.

ruach ha'kodesh: Divine spirit.

Sodom: Canaanite city located near the Dead Sea.

schlepping: (Y.) carrying a burden.

Seder (pl.–Sedarim): lit., order; the meal on the night of Pesach.

Sefer Torah: Torah scroll.

Sefiras Ha'omer: counting the forty-nine days between Pesach and Shavuos.

segulos: remedies; protections.

seudah: meal.

Shabbos: Saturday.

Shabbos Abba: lit., Shabbos father; common among Jewish preschools when acting out a "Shabbos party."

shalom bayis: peaceful home.

Shavuos: holiday on the sixth of Sivan when we commemorate receiving the Torah.

she'eino yodei'a lishol: the fourth son on Seder night; the son who doesn't know how to ask.

she'lo lishmah: not for the sake of (usually the mitzvah).

Shechinah: Divine presence.

sheker: false; a lie.

Shema: text derived from three *parshiyos* in the Torah; an affirmation of our faith in Hashem.

Shemoneh Esreh: the silent prayer said thrice daily.

shevet (pl.–shevatim): tribe.

shiur: class, lecture; measurement.

Shivah Asar B'Tamuz: the seventeenth of Tamuz; the day Nevuchadnetzar breached the walls of Jerusalem.

shukeling: (Y.) shaking.

Shulchan Aruch: four volumes of Jewish law, written by Rav Yosef Karo.

shul: (Y.) synagogue.

siman (pl.–simanim): sign; omen.

simchah: happiness.

sukkah: a temporary hut used on the holiday of Sukkos to eat, drink, sleep, and live in.

Sukkos: Jewish holiday commemorating the shelter Hashem provided us during the forty years we traveled in the desert.

tahor: pure.

talmidei chachamim: Torah scholars.

talmid: student.

tamei: impure; referring to a person or object.

Tanna: Torah Sage who lived during the times of the Mishnah and *Beraisa*.

Targum: lit., translation; also refers to the Torah commentary of Onkelos.

tefillah: prayer.

tefillin: phylacteries.

Tehillim: Psalms.

teshuvah: lit., returning; repentance.

tikkun olam: fixing the world.

Tishah B'Av: the ninth of Av; day when Jews mourn the destruction of the Holy Temples.

Torah: the Jewish Bible that Hashem gave to Moshe at Har Sinai.

Torah She'baal Peh: the explanation of the written Torah; includes Talmud, Mishnah, midrash, and other explanations.

Torah She'bichsav: the Written Torah, which consists of twenty-four books: five books of Moshe (*Chumash*), the eight books of Prophets (*Navi*), and the eleven books of Writings (*Kesuvim*).

tumah: impurity.

tzaddik: righteous person.

tzaraas: leprosy.

upsherin: (Y.) custom to give the first haircut when a boy turns three years old.

v'ahavta l'reiacha kamocha: love your friend as you would yourself.

Yam Suf: Sea of Reeds.

Yarden: Jordan River.

yeridah l'tzorech aliyah: descending in order to elevate.

Yerushalayim: Jerusalem.

yeshiva (pl.–yeshivos): study hall.

yetzer hara: evil inclination.

Yiddishkeit: (Y.) Judaism.

yirah: fear; awe.

yiras Shamayim: fear, awe of Heaven.

Yom Kippur: Day of Atonement.

Yamim Tovim: Jewish holidays.

Zaidy: (Y.) grandfather.

zemiros: songs and melodies sung praising Hashem, mostly sung on Shabbos.

zocheh: to merit.

zt"l: acronym for *zecher tzaddik li'verachah*; "May the memory of this righteous one be a blessing."

About the Author

Rabbi Boruch Oppen comes from generations of masters in *chinuch* on both sides of his family.

Rabbi Oppen attended Yeshiva Ateres Shmuel of Waterbury, where he learned under many outstanding *rebbeim*. He received his *semichah* from his Rosh Yeshiva, Rabbi Ahron Kaufman, and has a master's degree in educational leadership. Rabbi Oppen has been involved in *chinuch* for many years. He is a beloved *rebbi* and administrator, who in his creative and unique classes has inspired children, teens, and adults. Rabbi Oppen resides with his wife and four children in Cedarhurst, New York.

לזכר נשמת
איש חיל פעלים

הרה״ג ר׳ **אברהם דוד** זצק״ל
בן הר״ר **שלמה** זצק״ל **אופן**

השכים והעריב לבית המדרש
גריס באורייתא תדירא
ולא החזיק טיבותא לנפשיה
חינך והעמיד תלמידים ותלמידות
בדרך ישראל סבא במסירות נפש עשרות בשנים

נפטר ונטמן בשם טוב
בהדי פניא דמעלי יומא טבא
ערב שביעי של פסח
כ׳ ניסן תשע״ט

ת.נ.צ.ב.ה.

לזכר נשמת

בתנו היקרה והחמודה

הילדה **חנה מלכה** ע"ה
בת **גדליה ויהודית אופן**

ט"ז תשרי תשנ"ח–כ' טבת תשנ"ח
ת.נ.צ.ב.ה.

In memory of our incredible grandmothers,
who were the matriarchs of our families.
They were both extraordinary role models.
May their *neshamos* have an *aliyah*.

מרים בת יוסף יצחק ע״ה

and

brיינע בת אברהם זלמן ע״ה

.ת.נ.צ.ב.ה

In loving memory of our grandparents

לזכר נשמת

ר׳ **ישעיהו** בן **שבח מרדכי** זצק״ל

and

בלומה בת פנחס ע״ה

Their kindness and genuine *hachnasas orchim*
was felt by the many people who came to their home.
May this be a *zechus* for their *neshamos*
and grant them a big *aliyah*.

לזכר נשמת

our great-grandparents

ר׳ שבח מרדכי בן שלמה

and

פעסיל בת אשר זליג

who merited to see all of their children go in the *derech Hashem*

לזכר נשמת

our great-grandparents

פנחס בן ברוך

and

מרים בת מנחם מענדיל

A great-*zaidy* who worked hard to keep Shabbos in the time
when men were fired every Friday to keep Shabbos

לזכר נשמת

Grandma Ida

In loving memory of our grandparents

לזכר נשמת

ר׳ חיים יוסף בן נחמן ע״ה

and

חיה מינא בת אבא ע״ה

לזכר נשמת

ר׳ יעקב בן ר׳ ישעיהו ע״ה
רבקה בריינדל בת צבי שמחה ע״ה
ר׳ אליקים בן ר׳ חיים יוסף ע״ה
עטל לאה בת ר׳ חיים יוסף ע״ה
סטוי בן אברהם ע״ה

ת.נ.צ.ב.ה.

May this *sefer* be a *zechus* for their *neshamos*.

In memory of

ר׳ **ישעיהו** בן **שבח מרדכי** זצק״ל

מרת **בלומה** בת **פנחס** ע״ה

ר׳ **חיים יוסף** בן **נחמן** ע״ה

מרת **חיה מינא** בת **אבא** ע״ה

ר׳ **נתן** ב״ר **שמעון דוד** ע״ה

מרת **פייגא** בת ר׳ **אברהם** ע״ה

שמעון רפאל בן **אברהם דוד הכהן** ע״ה

ת.נ.צ.ב.ה.

From all my students, I learned…
How much more so from my teachers.
Our family was blessed with grandparents who were true teachers.
They taught us by word and example how to live a life of Torah
and *avodah*, of *ahavas Hashem* and *ahavas ha'brios*.
May we be *zocheh* to live lives that make them proud.

לזכר נשמת

ר׳ מרדכי בן אפרים ע״ה

כ״ט תמוז

ר׳ אהרן בן אלכסנדר ע״ה

י״ט אייר

חנה בריינא בת שלמה ע״ה

י״ח שבט

ר׳ יששכר בעריש בן פרומיט גליקל ע״ה

ט״ז אב

ינטא פיגא בת ראצה ע״ה

ט״ו חשון

שרה בת שאול ידידיה אלעזר ע״ה

ג׳ תמוז

ר׳ אפרים בן מרדכי ע״ה

ג׳ ניסן

ת.נ.צ.ב.ה.

אילן, אילן! במה אברכך?

In honor of our parents

Yitzchok and Rivki Schreiber
Yehuda and Linda Isaacs

Who have taught us by example what it means to be parents and how to raise children *b'derech Hashem*. We are eternally grateful to you for all that you do and all that you have given us, both the tangibles and intangibles. May you be *zocheh* to be blessed with good health and all of Hashem's bountiful *berachos* so that you may see the fruits of your labor. Together, may you receive endless and abundant *nachas* from your children and grandchildren, and *b'ezras Hashem* many more generations of offspring who are *bnei Torah* and *bnos Torah*, continuing in your ways and your parents' ways—adding more links in our family chain with your guidance, our patriarchs and matriarchs.

יהי רצון שכל נטיעות שנוטעין ממך יהיו כמותך.

With our eternal love and abundance of appreciation
BEN, DENA, JACOB, GABRIELLE,
LILLY, MAX, AND ARIELLE

This *sefer* is lovingly dedicated
in memory of

R' Aharon Shalom Krochmal, *zt"l*

ר׳ אהרן שלום בן ר׳ מאיר ז״ל

A child survivor of the Holocaust, he came to America
with his widowed mother, where he continued the family
chain of Yiddishkeit through his children, grandchildren,
and great-grandchildren. He lived with dedication to
Torah, mitzvos, and *chessed*; his holy *neshamah* surely
ascended to a very special place
in the *Olam HaEmes*.
May his legacy serve as an inspiration to his descendants,
and may he be a *meilitz yosher* for his beloved
almanah and family.

לזכר נשמת

עזריאל בן מנחם מנדל הלוי

ת.נ.צ.ב.ה.

לזכר נשמת

מרים בת בצלאל יהודה

ת.נ.צ.ב.ה.

לזכר נשמת

Our beloved brother-in-law

אלחנן משה רפאל בן יהודה לייב הכהן

MARC KATZ

DONNY AND TAMAR

Dedicated to the memory of our mothers

מרים בת יוסף יצחק ע״ה

brיינע בת אברהם זלמן ע״ה

and our granddaughter

חנה מלכה ע״ה בת הרב גדליה אפרים

May this be a *zechus* for their *neshamos*
and grant them a tremendous *aliyah*.

BINYOMIN ZEV AND LEAH MULLER

לזכר נשמת
משה יהודה בן יהודה

לע״נ
הרב דוד אברהם בן הרב שלמה זצק״ל
איש עניו תמים וישר, כל ימי חייו

הרה״ח ר׳ מרדכי בן הרב יצחק זאב זצק״ל
״אשרי נצרי עדתיו בכל לב ידרשוהו״ (תהילים קיט:ב)

ת.נ.צ.ב.ה.

Notes

_____

_____

_____

_____

_____

_____

_____

_____

_____

_____

_____

_____

_____

_____

_____

_____

MOSAICA PRESS
BOOK PUBLISHERS

Elegant, Meaningful & Bold

info@MosaicaPress.com
www.MosaicaPress.com

The Mosaica Press team of
acclaimed editors and designers
is attracting some of the most
compelling thinkers and teachers
in the Jewish community today.
Our books are available around
the world.

HARAV YAACOV HABER
RABBI DORON KORNBLUTH